Human Flourishing

Also available from Bloomsbury

A Philosophy for Future Generations, by Tiziana Andina
Humankind and Humanity in the Philosophy of the Enlightenment,
edited by Stefanie Buchenau and Ansgar Lyssy
Philosophy and the Metaphysical Achievements of Education,
by Ryan McInerney
The Moral Philosophy of Maria Montessori, by Patrick R. Frierson
The Evolution of Consciousness, by Paula Droege

Human Flourishing

A Conceptual Analysis

Eri Mountbatten-O'Malley

BLOOMSBURY ACADEMIC
LONDON • NEW YORK • OXFORD • NEW DELHI • SYDNEY

BLOOMSBURY ACADEMIC
Bloomsbury Publishing Plc, 50 Bedford Square, London, WC1B 3DP, UK
Bloomsbury Publishing Inc, 1359 Broadway, 12th Floor, New York, NY 10018, USA
Bloomsbury Publishing Ireland, 29 Earlsfort Terrace, Dublin 2, D02 AY28, Ireland

BLOOMSBURY, BLOOMSBURY ACADEMIC and the Diana logo are trademarks of Bloomsbury Publishing Plc

First published in Great Britain 2024
This paperback edition published 2026

Copyright © Eri Mountbatten-O'Malley, 2024

Eri Mountbatten-O'Malley has asserted his right under the Copyright, Designs and
Patents Act, 1988, to be identified as Author of this work.

For legal purposes the Acknowledgements on p. xiii constitute an extension of this copyright page.

Cover image © Floriana/iStock

All rights reserved. No part of this publication may be: i) reproduced or transmitted in any form, electronic or mechanical, including photocopying, recording or by means of any information storage or retrieval system without prior permission in writing from the publishers; or ii) used or reproduced in any way for the training, development or operation of artificial intelligence (AI) technologies, including generative AI technologies. The rights holders expressly reserve this publication from the text and data mining exception as per Article 4(3) of the Digital Single Market Directive (EU) 2019/790.

Bloomsbury Publishing Inc does not have any control over, or responsibility for, any third-party websites referred to or in this book. All internet addresses given in this book were correct at the time of going to press. The author and publisher regret any inconvenience caused if addresses have changed or sites have ceased to exist, but can accept no responsibility for any such changes.

A catalogue record for this book is available from the British Library.

ISBN: HB: 978-1-3504-1888-2
       PB: 978-1-3504-1892-9
       ePDF: 978-1-3504-1889-9
       eBook: 978-1-3504-1890-5

Typeset by RefineCatch Limited, Bungay, Suffolk

For product safety related questions contact productsafety@bloomsbury.com.

To find out more about our authors and books visit www.bloomsbury.com and sign up for our newsletters.

For you, Gosia.

Contents

List of Figures	viii
Preface	ix
Acknowledgements	xiii
List of Abbreviations	xvi

Introducing the Problem		1
1	Normativity, Language and Concepts	27
2	On the Analysis of Concepts	47
3	Humanness	65
4	A Sketch of Human Flourishing	83
5	'Human' Agency	109
6	Personal Growth and Development	131
7	*Summum Bonum*: Happiness and Meaning	151
Concluding Remarks		179

Notes	193
Bibliography	223
Index	241

Figures

1. Conceptual analysis. © Eri Mountbatten-O'Malley — 55
2. 'Kaninchen und Ente' ('Rabbit and Duck') a.k.a the 'Duck-Rabbit'. Credits: Public Domain via Wikimedia Commons — 61
3. Categories of 'humanness'. © Eri Mountbatten-O'Malley — 68
4. A sketch of flourishing (linguistic mode). © Eri Mountbatten-O'Malley — 87
5. A taxonomy of 'happiness' and related issues. © Eri Mountbatten-O'Malley — 155

Preface

This book is based on my PhD research by the same name. Not much has changed since the publication of my PhD, but I have updated sections where needed. The motivation for this work was the confusing nature of the literature on the concept of flourishing. I had initially intended to research using empirical methods but with all the conceptual problems evident in the literature it became apparent that I simply could not ignore the proverbial 'elephant in the room'. The choice was clear, either continue and ignore the issues regardless, picking a model off the shelf to use and apply, or else, to embark on a journey into the unknown. I chose the latter. But this meant that I had to re-train, from scratch, in the methods of philosophical practice, specifically, in the methods associated with Wittgenstein. Hence, in many ways this book is the fruit of a complex (at times, clumsy) yet wonderous personal journey of self-discovery through the methodological landscape of normative ('rule bound') concepts.

In the positive mode, this book highlights the key features and connections in the conceptual landscape of human flourishing (e.g., humanness, agency, personal growth, happiness and meaning) and considers the extent that any claim to knowledge is reliant on a putative human nature, what that nature is, and how we can better understand such notions. For example, it considers why it is important to draw a distinction between two forms of description for these kinds of concepts, namely: *normative* (taken as the linguistic, rule-oriented and categorial sense) and *axiological* (i.e., notions of value, even ultimate value). In doing so, it takes seriously the 'human' linguistic and practice-based dimensions of goodness and welfare. It considers how to nurture understanding of the *reasons* for good reasons. This amounts to an advancement of 'know-how' and conceptual mastery over allegedly 'contested' terms. It is an advocation for the importance of contextual ways of knowing, personal development, moral orienteering, and meaningful conceptions of 'happiness', all of which are seen to contribute to realizing flourishing in one's own life as well as in the lives of others. Hence, taken together this book is a comprehensive undermining of much of the literature on human flourishing. It is a redirection of attention away from generalizations that are informed by woolly, scientific, technicalized and detached conceptions of flourishing, and back to the solid ground of complex human contexts, human purposes and human uses.

The aims of this book

I am more than aware of the immaturity of my philosophizing, my failings at describing my thoughts clearly, as well as the limitations of a broad analysis of this kind. Nevertheless, my central aim in this book has been to enable and equip readers to better understand and discern for themselves the kinds of situations (including possibilities and limitations) where the concept may be meaningfully deployed in their own areas of interests and specific contexts. I certainly hope to contribute to *some* degree of elucidation, rather than noise, on this important topic. My hope for this book, then, is partly to untangle certain conceptual knots in how we conceive of human flourishing, but more so, to pass on a little bit of the kind of wisdom that has been passed down through thinkers such as Wittgenstein and Hacker; that is, I hope to be found to have been a good guide, helping the reader to 'find' their way about.[1] I aim to provide some pointers at a beneficial and beneficent way of thinking about these *kinds* of problems so that we may avoid being ensnared in these *kinds* of nets altogether. It is to provide a philosophical and academic exploration of the conceptual problems – and thereby, to nurture routes out from the proverbial 'fly-bottle' (*PI* §209) with regards to the various confusions that I identify with the concept of human flourishing.

A brief note on my approach

My methodological development has been largely influenced by Wittgenstein (2009), Hacker (2007, 2013, 2021), and Travis (2008) in terms of general key concepts and method. These were enriched through various, lengthy philosophical discussions with my director of studies, Dr Leon Culbertson, during the writing of my PhD thesis, in terms of developing an approach to philosophy which balances the right attention to general conceptual links (connective analyses) alongside explication of cases and examples (conceptual elucidation). I hope there are enough examples to bring to life some of the issues I raise. I have therefore developed practical examples of the following key concepts which have helped form the basis for the approach taken in this book:

- The distinction between empirical and conceptual investigations
- Concepts, concept formation and conceptual schemes
- General conceptual connective analysis of the logical, relational terrain
- Wittgenstein's notion of a 'grammar' of a term
- The practice of conceptual elucidation and working with particular cases
- Family resemblance concepts vs essences (linguistic and ontological)
- Forms of life
- Rules and rule-following
- Public vs private criteria
- Multiplicity of language-games vs monistic formal language
- Concept possession
- Occasion-sensitivity
- Seeing-aspects, aspect perception and aspect-blindness.

As suggested already, it is worth noting that these key concepts do not form any kind of unified theory or methodological approach to philosophy. These merely form the basis for a kind of heuristic and attitude to philosophical practice in the analysis of concepts. Although readers will not need to adopt any particular position on Wittgenstein's latter philosophy of language in order to benefit from this book, Wittgenstein's insights (as explicated and expounded upon by Hacker and others) will be useful for anyone involved in investigating the features and conditions for human flourishing, no matter their disciplinary inclination. It is informed by the central notions of the primacy of normativity when researching human affairs, language and concepts and a sensitivity for context, purpose and use.

What underpins my approach is a profound respect for the values of truth, sense, ethics, morality and human-centredness. Although this humanistic set of values is concerned with (first and foremost), the development of human agency and the moral and rational powers of individuals, it should not be confused or conflated with egoistical or individualist values. Genuine conceptions of human flourishing cannot knowingly be realized at the cost of others or the environment. Any meaningful conception of human flourishing *must*, I suggest, entail both personal and social responsibility. Just as the metaphorical flower in the field cannot ignore the conditions of its own existence, so too human beings should pay attention to the *conditions* for their own flourishing and the flourishing of others. This complex inter-relationality between moral and rational agents within a community of others and within an ecological environment, is important, and will become clearer towards the end of this book.

I would like to suggest that this book lays bare some significant issues in the literature (and related policy-practices) on the topic and is at least potentially a ground-breaking work. Although there was not space to explore these areas specifically, it is, I suggest, a useful read for anyone interested in the concept of human flourishing. This may particularly include postgraduate students and budding philosophers, but also educators, policy-makers, scientists, psychologists, coaches and others interested in how to make sense of the concept of human flourishing (and related normative concepts such as happiness or well-being) and how to meaningfully deploy such terms in their respective contexts.

I hope to contribute some insights on these issues, and to stimulate some useful discussion on the topic. Importantly, however, I hope that you, as a reader, thoroughly enjoy the process of discovery as you set your own path into the world of normative concepts with human goodness and welfare in mind.

Acknowledgements

The saying that 'no man is an island'[1] holds true for me as a person and my educational development. I would like to firstly thank my mother, Grace (RIP). You were a rare human being, an epic heroine in your own life but also someone who fought unceasingly for the rights of your children, in particular their education. I am especially grateful for your dedication and energy in helping me to understand the importance of self-expression both as an individual as well as a young person of colour and mixed heritage in 1980s London. You helped me to develop my academic confidence from an early age and transformed my experience navigating the complexities of the UK state education system that all too often favoured conformity at the expense of the intellectual engagement and agency of children.

I have also been fortunate enough to have had the ear of a range of academics within Edge Hill University and beyond. These thinkers helped me largely by providing me with alternative accounts and framing of the issues I raised with them. No doubt this contributed to my academic development and I would like to thank them all for their time and generosity. Within Edge Hill University, I would like to thank, in particular, Dr Anna Bussu, Dr Sally-Anne Ashton, Dr Marian Peacock, Dr Irene Dudley-Swarbrick, Dr Stephen Clayton (all from Faculty of Health, Social Care & Medicine); Dr Paul Bunyan and Dr Paul Reynolds (both Faculty of Arts & Social Sciences); Dr Helena Knapton and Professor Clare Woolhouse (Faculty of Education).

In terms of beyond Edge Hill University, I would like to particularly thank Dr Andrew Edgar (Cardiff University), Dr Stephen Joseph ('Centre for Research in Human Flourishing', University of Nottingham), Dr Andrew Bloodworth (Swansea University), Professor Paul Standish (University College London), and Dr Jonathan Beale (Eton College, Oxford University). Similarly, I would like to thank my PhD examiners, Professor Constantine Sandis (University of Hertfordshire), and Professor David Aldridge (Edge Hill University) for the brilliant discussions during the viva voce itself. Also, for providing me with incredibly helpful and crystal-clear feedback on the penultimate version of my PhD. It was a huge honour to be examined by such insightful philosophers who work so closely within the fields of knowledge that I love and respect so much. I would also like to thank Dr Paul Wong (Editor of the *International Journal of Existential Positive Psychology*) for his time with me and for allowing me to use edited text from the paper published with the *Journal* to assist with my final editing of Chapter 7 ('Summum bonum'). Professor Matthew Lee (Harvard Human Flourishing Programme) has also been a tremendous support, and I look forward to continuing the dialogue in the spirit of a community of inquiry.

No doubt, my PhD supervisors, Dr Leon Culbertson and Dr Damien Shortt (and formerly, Professor Fiona Hallet) have had to endure many difficult conversations with me putting up with my incessant incoherence, questioning and probing, and having to comment on (all too often) dreadful drafts. I am, and will always be, eternally grateful for driving me forward in my academic development. It would be remiss of me if I did not highlight Dr Leon Culbertson in particular; firstly, for taking me on as a PhD student, but also, for helping me to articulate my concerns with the reductive nature of much of the research on human flourishing, philosophically, in ways that helped me to find my academic voice, all the while not sparing me the 'trouble of thinking'. Finally, for providing me with the wise and steadying hand that I truly needed during the many moments of self-doubt. No tutor has had a more formative impact on me and my academic development, and it has been an incredible privilege to be supervised and directed by such a profound and astute thinker whilst a graduate student at Edge Hill University. The many hours we spent together discussing these issues were thoroughly enjoyable and have given me the confidence to tackle the philosophical problems identified in this book as well as others.

I will not, of course, forget to thank the philosopher who holds my greatest admiration, Professor P.M.S. Hacker from St Johns College, Oxford University – firstly for the sheer force of his intellect, prescient analyses on human nature, and his unparalleled exposition of Wittgenstein's works. These powerful and elucidatory texts have provided me with a guiding light through the storm of recent years. Importantly, for being exceptionally generous and helpful by allowing me advance access to the final addition of his tetralogy on human nature 'The Moral Powers: A Study of Human Nature' (Hacker, 2021); this was a profound help to me at a crucial stage of my PhD thesis. It has also been an incredible privilege to finally meet Professor Hacker in person during late 2022 in Oxford, to get to know him a bit more since where I have had the opportunity to discuss and explore many of the issues in this text. I very much felt like I met my philosophical father, a living Aristotle, for the first time. His charming sharp wit and wry humour are rare and precious qualities these days. I thoroughly enjoyed our explorations into the process of philosophical questioning and problematizing itself, and I am thrilled in the prospect of continuing the conversation.

Last but by no means least, I would like to thank my incredible wife of almost eighteen years now, Gosia, as well as my delightful children, Beatrice and Benjamin, the joys and pride of my life. Primarily for their patience in bearing with me through the seemingly endless days, evenings and weekends whilst working on my PhD and monograph, as well as the related work involved in preparing for various conferences, symposia and public talks over recent years. I couldn't have asked for more from them and this could not have been possible without their enduring love, kindness and emotional support. Words cannot quite express it, but I feel immensely blessed and grateful.

Eri Mountbatten-O'Malley (PhD)
September 2023

Abbreviations

BB   WITTGENSTEIN, L. 1991. *The Blue and Brown Books: Preliminary Studies for the 'Philosophical Investigation'*, Peter, Doherty (ed.); Oxford. Wiley-Blackwell (2nd edn)

BT   WITTGENSTEIN, L., 2005. *The Big Typescript*. TS 213. Blackwell. Oxford.

CV   WITTGENSTEIN, L. 1998. *Culture and Value* (revised edn). Oxford: Blackwell.

LFM   WITTGENSTEIN, L (1975). Wittgenstein's Lectures on the Foundations of Mathematics, Cambridge, 1939: From the Notes of R.G. Bosanquet, Norman Malcolm, Rush Rhees, and Yorick Smythies. Ithaca, N.Y.: University of Chicago Press. R. G. Bosanquet & Cora Diamond (eds.).

MS   All references to Wittgenstein's unpublished material cited in the von Wright catalogue (von Wright, G. H. (1982). 'Wittgenstein'. (First Ed.). Oxford : Blackwell), pp. 35ff.) are by MS. or TS. number followed by page number.

OC   WITTGENSTEIN, L. 1969. *On Certainty*, G. E. M. Anscombe and G. H. von Wright (Eds.), G. E. M. Anscombe and D. Paul (Trans.). Oxford: Basil Blackwell.

PI   WITTGENSTEIN, L. 2009. *Philosophical Investigations*, P. M. S. Hacker and J. Schulte (eds.). G. E. M. Anscombe, P. M. S. Hacker and J. Schulte (Trans.), Oxford: Wiley-Blackwell (4th edn).

PPF   WITTGENSTEIN, L. 2009. 'Philosophy of Psychology - A Fragment'. In: *Philosophical Investigations*, P. M. S. Hacker and J. Schulte (Eds.). G. E. M. Anscombe, P. M. S. Hacker and J. Schulte (Trans.), Oxford: Wiley-Blackwell (4th edn).

RC   WITTGENSTEIN, L. 1979. *Remarks on colour*. Oxford: Blackwell.

RPPI   WITTGENSTEIN, L. 1980. *Remarks on the Philosophy of Psychology* (Vol. I) ed. G.E.M. Anscombe and G.H. von Wright, tr. G.E.M. Anscombe, Oxford: Blackwell.

TLP   WITTGENSTEIN, L. 1974. *Tractatus Logico-Philosophicus*. D. F. Pears and B. F. McGuinness (Trans.). Revised edn. London: Routledge & Kegan Paul.
Z   WITTGENSTEIN, L. *Zettel* [1945–1948]. (1967). Ed. G.E.M. Anscombe and G.H. von Wright. Trans. G.E.M. Anscombe. Oxford: Blackwell. [German–English parallel text.] References are to numbered sections. Zettel. (1984). Edited in Werkausgabe (Vol. 8). Frankfurt: Suhrkamp. References are to numbered sections.

Introducing the Problem

'Human flourishing' is a rich, nuanced and somewhat complex concept. It is notably associated with the concept of *eudaemonia* which until recently had been translated as 'happiness', somewhat of a misleading reduction.[1] It has also been used interchangeably with other related notions such as = virtue (Jubilee Centre, 2017), well-being (Seligman, 2011)[2], self-actualization (Maslow, 2013 and Rogers, 1961), life-satisfaction, meaning and purpose (VanderWeele, 2017, 2019) positive function and resilience (Ryff & Singer, 2003). In an effort to create a more eclectic and holistic model, Larson et al., (2020)[3] and Harvard (2021) have aimed to incorporate many of these diverse criteria in one way or another and then to measure them via self-report. Almost all of these models focus on the concept of well-being or happiness with satellite concepts supporting that focal criterion. Unsurprisingly, then, there is a range of theories, models and approaches to 'measuring' flourishing including use of qualitative, quantitative, with some positing the usefulness of mathematical scales and formulas (infamously, Fredrickson & Losada, 2005). Indeed, the trend in the literature is towards developing various measurements of flourishing. Certainly, within the literature in positive psychology and well-being, researchers often place flourishing as the high point on a scale of subjective well-being, with mental disorder at one end and mental flourishing at the other (cf., Huppert & So 2013).

A difficulty arises, however, because flourishing has been used interchangeably, for example, with the related concept of well-being, and as a result flourishing has become somewhat of a 'catch-all' concept losing any sense of clarity; thus, it is a sense of mess and conceptual confusion that is what most notably characterizes study of the concept of human flourishing. It can seem to mean almost anything (and thereby nothing simultaneously). What is a common happenstance in such research, particularly research that aims to ascribe scientific causes to psychological phenomena, is that new technical jargons are developed (or reduced to a central criterion such as well-being) and perfectly ordinary words that are otherwise used in rich contexts are applied in narrow, technicalized senses as part of a theory or model.[4]

The Task

What seems clear to me, however, is that inventing new uses of words for which there are already ordinary everyday uses does not result in new discoveries or insights, but rather obfuscates our understanding. Words are ambiguous outside of a context, and the needless 'woolly' nature of such research, or indeed, related policies, can often obscure these differences, and importantly, can mask the underlying conceptual confusions. In turn, this can support a problematic research environment that perpetuates incoherence, bewilderment and poor-quality research more widely (cf. Bennett & Hacker, 2003: 2). The current research environment on the concept of human flourishing seems to offer up an ever-expanding range of competing models, each with their own strengths, weaknesses and applications, each vying for an authoritative place in the somewhat chaotic market of ideas, and each being enveloped with their own conceptual problems. Meanwhile, the truly *transformative power* of the concept of human flourishing is stifled and obscured.

This might understandably lead one to aver that the concept of human flourishing is a typical case of a 'contested' concept such as 'democracy', 'happiness', 'meaning', 'justice', or whatever. Indeed, one could suggest that are competing technicalized conceptions, no doubt. However, as Garver (1978: 168) has pointed out, viewing competing models of concepts (or conceptions) in this way creates its own problems. Garver suggested that in so doing it can lead to forms of 'skepticism' (doubt as to the very possibility of knowledge or understanding for what a concept is or means), 'dogmatism' (making claims at the exclusion of all others) or 'eclecticism' (opaque romanticization for all models having equal value and so incorporate elements of them all). Garver's analysis is just one way to critique this issue, and though not exhaustive, seems somewhat helpful. For example, in the case of the eclecticist, they are given over to excessive openness, thereby precluding the very possibility for meaningfulness of a given term. Whereas the sceptic, because of the apparent indeterminability of what a word might mean s/he tends towards a form of epistemic abandon which also results in a dearth of meaningfulness in the deployment of words. In the case of a rigid dogmatist, the risk of setting hard lines or parameters for meaning leads them to overlook the fluid nature of our words in practice. Words are used in contexts and human beings, as rational and creative linguistic agents, apply terms in diverse ways, for variegated purposes and in a plethora of cases and contexts. If we care about good thinking (i.e. deploying the skills of the human mind to tackle abstract and real-life problems) and communication (i.e. addressing gaps in knowledge within a community of thinkers) regarding philosophical issues, there is no avoiding the importance of understanding language and developing conceptual insight.

By using an analogy of sharp and blurry pictures in the context of two people recalling events and experiences, Wittgenstein (2009)[5] cautioned us about the risks of aiming to measure the unmeasurable through the simile of attempting to copy an original that is already blurry. If the original picture is indeed blurry (as normative concepts are outside of a specific context of use)[6] then there is no independent authority on which to duplicate. Subsequent copies or adaptations of blurry concepts are, then, rather arbitrary: 'Here I might just as well draw a circle as a rectangle or a heart, for all the colours merge. Anything and nothing is right.' (*PI* §77). Drawing a sharp boundary around a shape in this context is seen by Wittgenstein as somewhat of a 'hopeless task'. I'd like to suggest that much of what goes on in the study and research into the concept of human flourishing is rather like that. We draw artificial boundaries around woolly conceptions of flourishing, and we try to sharpen something that is woolly or blurry outside of a context; in so doing, we lose the richness, salience, normativity and the true power of its use in ways that leads to obfuscation rather than clarification. Fresh research builds on former research conducted in this way and hence we end up with an entirely confusing 'mess' in the literature that becomes increasingly difficult for all manner of stakeholders (academic or otherwise) to navigate.

This is why the philosophical approach I advocate for in this book is first and foremost grounded in an appreciation for sense-making and conceptual navigation. It is practical in nature, and should, therefore, help many diverse areas of pragmatic research interests on the topic of human flourishing. Hence, the problem is not unmitigable. There is a range of methodological concepts developed and used by Wittgenstein (and others), that can aid our thinking when considering these kinds of problems, terms such as 'aspects', 'language-games', 'rules', 'grammar' etc. I will aim to explore these further in the subsequent two chapters.[7] In this introductory chapter I aim to highlight some of the key issues in the literature on human flourishing, as an introductory sketch. I aim to contribute to human understanding (as opposed to knowledge)[8] with regards to the concept of human flourishing in ways that nurtures our mastery of the concept, builds our understanding of the salient conceptual networks, addresses some of the key issues raised, and nourishes our abilities to be sensitive to contexts of *use* so that we may know 'how to go on' (cf. *PI* §151) in the deployment of the term in meaningful ways and within our respective areas of inquiry and interest.

In this book, I therefore set out to draw attention to some of the conceptual problems in the literature. Such problems are wide-reaching and include:

a) ontological essentialism (e.g. in terms of the metaphysical conceptions of human nature);
b) reductionism (e.g. in terms of reducing flourishing to various forms of well-being or happiness);
c) scientism (e.g. in terms of the conflation of categories, the misapplication of reductive empirical methods to normative questions and the over-extension of the sciences); and finally,
d) subjectivism (e.g. in terms of the over reliance on self-reporting as a method and the reification of personal interpretation).

The *central questions* that drive the development of this book are therefore:

1. What are the conceptual confusions in the *use* of the concept of human flourishing? (i.e. conceptual elucidation);
2. What are the key features and connections in the conceptual *landscape* of human flourishing? (i.e. connective analysis);
3. How can we *know* that a person is flourishing (or not)? (i.e. criterial implications).

New knowledge?

It may be worth highlighting that in addressing the meaning of terms such as 'human nature', 'personhood' or 'happiness' and how these relate to human flourishing, there could appear to be a form of epistemic discovery of hidden meaning or truths.[9] Whilst on the one hand it is certainly true that discoveries in our understanding are made, this is not confirmable through empirical study. As Hacker (2013a: 449) has stated:

> As mature language users, we are masters of the techniques of using these expressions. We no more need to conduct social surveys of the ways in which 'know', 'believe', 'perceive', 'think', 'imagine' are used than a chess-master needs to conduct social surveys of the moves of chess-pieces.

Hence, when designing research, if we were to try and untangle conceptual presuppositions of some empirical research, we could not do so by enlisting the methods of further empirical or theoretical investigations, because these would bring their own conceptual presuppositions which would generate further conceptual entanglement requiring endless investigations ad infinitum (Hacker, 2001: 71). An infinite regress. In this way, the work of conceptual elucidations is logically prior to empirical research and empirical problems. Flourishing is not the categorial *kind* of thing that is located somewhere 'out there' like gravity. There are no scientific laws governing happiness, well-being or flourishing, at least not any that we cannot already know through conceptual work (such as the truism that, *ceteris paribus*, pain causes suffering etc.). The concept of flourishing is *normative* as opposed to nomological, and so, the methods of resolving or dissolving problems about such concepts are, therefore, conceptual. Solutions, resolutions or indeed dissolutions to the problems that befall us are accessible to most competent language users (cf. *PI* §89, Baker, 2004, Hacker, 2007a) through an analysis of the context-sensitive, conceptual 'grammar' (*PI* §122) of a term, and by surveying the 'logical geography' (Ryle, 2009; Hacker, 2013a: 448) or logical 'terrain' in the English language (Hacker, 2007a: 248). This is quite outside of a specialized empirical research paradigm: '[w]e do not analyse a phenomenon (for example, thinking) but a concept (for example, that of thinking), and hence the application of a word' (*PI* §383). Hence, in addressing the issues on the concept of 'human flourishing', this also helps to provide pointers for addressing related problems in the wider field of normative and axiological concepts.

What follows, therefore, is a pithy set of vignettes or sketches summarizing *some* of the key issues identified. These are for *illustrative* purposes only, and not intended to be any kind of exhaustive critique. They do not do justice to the complex nuances of the approaches targeted here, neither could they in the space available, but they should do a 'good enough' job of highlighting the central *kinds* of issues that help to bring light on the purpose of this research project, and importantly, the potential wider benefits and impact on various research agendas on the concept (or term) of 'human flourishing'. A more nuanced analysis will be explored throughout the chapters in this book, including further use and analysis of contemporary philosophical (and empirical) works where relevant. These should help to illuminate and address some of the central conceptual issues raised, and to provide pertinent insights that are useful to the aims of this book.

I will therefore briefly explore some of the dominant conceptions of flourishing, happiness, and well-being below – as seen through the respective and interrelated lenses of Utilitarianism, Aristotelianism (and neo-Aristotelianism), positive psychology, positive education, moral education and humanistic psychology.

A sketch of key conceptualizations of 'human flourishing'

Utilitarianism, happiness and well-being

Conceptual presuppositions on the nature of what it means to be human are deeply influential in the debate in what is 'good' for society. The modern development of the concept of the common 'good' in the West is often seen to be tied to the Utilitarianism of Mill and Bentham (cf. Hacker, 2021). As has been suggested already, the notion of flourishing has been intricately tied to the surrogate term of 'well-being'. The development of this concept within political philosophy and public mental health contexts has been gradual. Following on from the Epicureans it was Mill who said:

> ... Utility, or the Greatest Happiness Principle, holds that actions are right in proportion as they tend to promote happiness, wrong as they tend to produce the reverse of happiness.
>
> Mill, 1863: 10

On the role of governance in society, Bentham defined the 'fundamental axiom' of his philosophy as the principle 'the greatest happiness of the greatest number' is the 'measure of right and wrong' (Bentham, 1776: *Preface*). This notion of the greatest pleasure for the greatest number has had a profound influence on public policy in Western capitalist states ever since. However, the notion of well-being as a means to flourish nationally took on a new sense of importance during the Neoliberal era. For example, in 1971 an economist named Simon Kuznets was awarded a Nobel Prize for his significant contribution to economics for developing the concept of Gross National Product (or Gross Domestic Product) (Wahid, 2002: 38). However, this concept was later supplemented by what is now known as the 'Human Development Index', the 'Happy Planet Index', and other such measures of well-being worldwide, including more recently, the Office of National Statistics collation of data regarding our national 'well-being' index (cf. ONS, 2021). There is now a plethora of well-being and public mental health initiatives. For example, 'Five ways to mental health' uses the concept of 'mental capital' (Foresight, 2008) to explore well-being on populations in the UK; The Happiness Index supports employee and customer well-being for corporations

(The Happiness Index, 2021); and not least in higher education, the University of Buckingham (2016) has launched Europe's first 'Positive University' scheme.

These programmes are just a few available which aim to support populations or targeted groups with their well-being, mental health and resilience. However, as Davies (2015: 5–6) suggests, this trend supports an underlying neoliberal, market-first oriented policy framework agenda, which obscures some of the root causes of 'misery' and social injustice in modern life:

> As positive psychology and happiness measurement have permeated our political and economic culture since the 1990s, there has been a growing unease with the way in which notions of happiness and well-being have been adopted by policy-makers and managers. The risk is that this science ends up blaming ... individuals for their own misery, and ignores the context that has contributed to it.

What is consistent with well-being policy agendas is the tendency to lean towards hedonic notions of happiness (rather than more holistic and meaningful conceptions of well-being and flourishing).[10] It is not at all clear how simply feeling better supports either student, workers' or populations' resilience or indeed whether these measures help them make meaning of their lives; in fact, possibly quite the converse.

For example, I recently heard of one school manager instituting 'resilience' training for burnout, stressed and overworked teachers, hence obscuring the underlying problematic conditions of work. Further, in one major empirical study of healthcare students, there was 'little or no evidence of any effect' on well-being or quality of life of this training, conversely, there were also 'adverse' effects reported (Kunzler et al., 2020). The concept of 'moral distress' may also be useful in understanding why burnout occurs, although it is better to consider this in light of 'work-home imbalance' (cf., Kok et al., 2023). Although grasping meaning in life is not sufficient of itself, some have argued suffering seems to help give people a more holistic sense of personal 'narrative' with which to tell one's story to oneself in order to endure the pains and pangs that life throws at us all (Edgar & Pattison, 2016, Frankl, 2006).

The Utilitarian vision of human flourishing supports a materialist and instrumental agenda, one that is somewhat devoid of agency, narrative and meaning; it tells someone else's story. It works to detach oneself from one's own capacity for sense-making. I would suggest that it offers us a simplistic, even dehumanizing, conception of well-being, flourishing and meaning in life, primarily because of its tendency to overinflate the importance of empirical science, certainly in terms of scientific measures that reduce the complexities of human nature to mechanistic, biological, behavioural or sensory phenomena oriented around hedonic values and forms of happiness. In short, it works to reduce the complex sense of Self that we all have, into an object of pleasure, instrumentality and superficiality.

One modern manifestation of Utilitarianism is in the form of Transhumanism. Transhumanism is quasi-religious in nature. As is clear from the *Transhumanist Declaration*, Transhumanism may be described as a utopian-technological movement that aims to transform the human condition by developing and making widely available sophisticated technologies to greatly enhance human intellect and physiology (cf. More & Vita-More, 2013). Transhumanist conceptions of flourishing are tied to notions of autonomy as a primary force for good, couched in various forms of Cartesian dualism. This should be no surprise, for a great deal of modern scientific thinking is premised on categories that Descartes himself developed. These have had a profound influence on modern conceptions of human nature, the mind, and indirectly, public policy. As Hacker (2007a: 25) has noted:

> Cartesian dualism provided the framework of thought about the nature of mankind for the modern era, not merely in the sense that the dominant trend was some form or other of dualism (which is true as far as both popular and scientific thought was concerned until the middle of the twentieth century), but in the much deeper sense that it set the categories in terms of which reflection took place.

More (2013: 7), nevertheless, defends against any criticisms of dualist presuppositions by retorting that such critics are 'confusing dualism with functionalism'. As he avers, a 'functionalist holds that a particular mental state or cognitive system (i.e. consciousness) is independent of any specific physical instantiation, but must always be physically instantiated at any time in some physical form' (my text in parentheses). This seems to be a case of 'having your cake and eating it'. Working with More's assumptions, it remains logically impossible for consciousness (or indeed the mind) to be simultaneously independent from the brain and yet still require to be 'instantiated' by it or some other physical form.[11] You may as well argue for purgatory as a metaphysical location for souls waiting for heaven (or hell), it is just as esoteric and nonsensical. Whilst a premise could have a justifiable space within a particular system of reference, i.e. a belief system, it is logically incoherent. The veneer is scientific, but the substance is religious or allegorical in orientation. Importantly, it does not do the job of alleviating the flaws with dualism. There is no such relation of instantiated dependence (mind on brain), and we need not to be committed to a spooky metaphysics in order to explain human consciousness. Although ascriptions for mental concepts are indeed 'biologically rooted', they are only attributable to the 'whole' human being. (cf. Hacker, 2007a: 243; also, Hacker, 2013a: 317). Consequently, utilitarian approaches to well-being policy are prone to an excess of reductionism and conceptual confusion; in practice, they cause more harm than good. On its own terms, Utilitarianism should therefore be avoided.

The Aristotelian conception of flourishing or happiness: 'eudaemonia'

A review of the different conceptions of happiness in ancient times, Michalos & Robinson (2012) identified a dozen distinct conceptions of happiness in the period from the eighth to the third century BCE. Aristotle's *eudaemonia* (based on an already vibrant Greek tradition) was used as the term for the highest 'human good', and as such, was seen to exemplify the aim of practical philosophy itself. The term has commonly been translated (at least until recently) as well-being, happiness or welfare; however, more recently, the term 'flourishing' has been considered as a more accurate interpretation of the Greek concept of *eudaemonia* (Robinson, 1999: 91).[12] Although *eudaemonia* is arguably a specific term of significance (being historically and contextually located) and thus distinct from how we use flourishing today, it is nonetheless arguably the most important exemplar for the concept of flourishing in modern discourse, not least because it forms another basis for modern conceptions of well-being, happiness and flourishing – notably within modern discourse on ethics, virtue theory, political theory, philosophy of education (especially regarding educational 'aims'), and loosely, positive psychology. This suggests that Aristotle is by far the most influential ancient thinker of modern times.

Aristotle suggested that the 'good life' is objectively caused and evidenced by goods or benefits which lead to happiness or flourishing. This is not particularly problematic. Indeed, he later suggested that this remains an inadequate 'platitude', which leads Aristotle to conclude that happiness (insofar as it is lived virtuously) must be 'the most desirable of all good things' (Aristotle, 2014: 1097, b7). This is a teleological perspective of human flourishing because he positions human flourishing not so much in experience of the present but rather in a life well lived over the expanse of one's life as seen retrospectively (Aristotle, 2014: 1098a,

17–19). This conception of flourishing places virtue, character and civic engagement at the centre of what it is to flourish. Thus, health, wealth and other such goods are to be sought because they are seen to promote *eudaemonia* (flourishing). His conception of *eudaemonia* is derived from his biological 'essentialist' understanding of the nature of all things, in this case human nature. This is the view that the human ability to reason is the essential characteristic that is unique to human beings (as a rational animal). So, from this the logic follows, apparently, that the ideal function of a human being (being the practice of what is unique to itself) is seen as the fullest or most perfect exercise of reason. It is this which, Aristotle argues, leads to human excellence (i.e. *arête*) which in turn is seen in teleological terms as the natural end for humans who attain *eudaemonia*.

Using Aristotle's account of flourishing or *eudaimonia* in modern life is not without its problems, however, certainly when thinkers attempt to transpose the ancient Greek concept into modern life and contexts. For example, Aristotle's teleological view of flourishing is not the only way in which we use the word 'flourishing' in modern daily life (though it may be used in the past tense to speak of a life well lived). For example, Wolbert et al. (2015: 121) has said:

> It is not awkward to speak of 'flourishing children' or to call someone a flourishing human being who is not dead yet (or on her deathbed). Therefore, we think that it is helpful to distinguish between 'a flourishing life' (being the ideal) and the verb 'to flourish' (representing an actual evaluation).

Of course, though we may infer flourishing as a rough interpretation for *eudaimonia* – it cannot work the other way around. Due to the specific historicity of *eudaimonia* as a concept, Aristotle had somewhat parochial notions of flourishing. This suggests that we could not apply this notion *simplicter* into the current political climate which is much more focused on issues of social justice, inclusivity and ethics. For example, for Aristotle, only some people could study politics (as essential requirement for flourishing for him). He believed that women can never benefit from the study of politics, nor should they be allowed to participate in politics. As he said: '[T]he relation of male to female is by nature a relation of superior to inferior and ruler to ruled' (Aristotle, 2014: 1245b, 12). He had similar view of slaves and even young men (1095a, 2). Further, because of Aristotle's theory of self-sufficiency, he believed that flourishing was 'good for its own sake' (cf. 1094a, 15). But it is by no means clear that flourishing should be sought for its own sake. There are plenty of other considerations in life to do with love, self-sacrifice, care, or transcendence, for example. These kinds of issues mean that translations of *eudaimonia* into modern life are, prima facie, conceptually, ethically and politically problematic.

Newer forms of Aristotelian notions of flourishing (neo-Aristotelianism) do not differ substantially from ancient conceptions. In fact, much of Aristotle's project on virtue through engagement with political and social action is reaffirmed. Notably, MacIntyre's account of human flourishing consists of people becoming independent 'practical reasoners', who are able to use their rational powers for the pursuit of a meaningful and virtuous life. Engagement with politics (at least at local level) enables us to 'protect ourselves and others against neglect, defective sympathies, stupidity, acquisitiveness, and malice' (MacIntyre, 1999: 98). Thus, MacIntyre posits a rationalist, communitarian vision of flourishing not too distant from Aristotle's notion of rationality, virtue and engagement in the city-state (*polis*). Nevertheless, whether political engagement and a stable community are needed for people to flourish is also doubtful. One can picture a man travelling freely across the globe and doing well meeting lots of smaller communities (albeit in a transitory sense) without any commitment at all and yet he may still be deemed to be flourishing. This might be through an inner sense of peace, basic security, and fulfilment in life's varied activities. By comparison, a 9 to 5 worker in a city with limited agency, a mortgage, and an unhappy and precarious existence cannot be said to be flourishing per se. No matter how much wealth is concentrated in the city, the share of wealth and political power is not very well distributed for most citizens under current political and economic conditions across the West. Even for those that have wealth and considerable degrees of political and other forms of agency, flourishing is often stifled by the fierce and competitive conditions of modern life.

Whilst there is an emphasis on virtuous practices that develop character, Aristotelian (and neo-Aristotelian) notions of *eudaimonia* offer a rather conservative, idealistic, even perfectionist picture of flourishing which, though exemplary, may only be suited to specific circumstances and cultures where those values support such a conception within idealized political conditions. In other words, they may lack explanatory power or authority due to the inherent complexity of human life, particularly in cultures where individualism matters above communitarian ethics (such as our own). With this difficulty in mind, it is valuable to consider how Aristotelian conceptions of *eudaimonia* have influenced the thinking in arguably some of the most influential spheres of neo-Aristotelianism: positive psychology and positive education.[13]

Positive psychology and education: well-being is the new flourishing

Historically there are two central schools of thought in positive psychology to approaching the topic of flourishing, both having been influenced by Greek philosophical and theoretical accounts from millennia ago. The first is the 'hedonic' tradition, which is arguably the most prominent conception in the literature, and which covers issues such as subjective sense of well-being, happiness, positive emotions, positive affect and overall life satisfaction. These include thinkers such as Bradburn (1969), Harding (1982); Diener (1984), Lyubomirsky & Lepper (1999) and Fredrickson & Losada (2005). Most notable scholars within the eudaemonic end of the spectrum are the conceptualizations, models, and theories of Ryan & Deci (2000), Keyes (2002), Seligman (2011) and Huppert & So (2013). However, due to the heavy focus on subjective-well-being from *both* hedonic and eudaimonic schools of thought, to a large degree this distinction is superficial.

Modern context matters. Many thinkers in positive psychology position themselves in opposition to pathological approaches to psychology which focused on the *treatment* of mental illness (such as psychoanalysis and psychotherapy). Rather, positive psychologists often aim to focus on *strengths*, and to decipher the factors that contribute to happier, healthier, and more meaningful lives, whilst situating the methodological approaches of the project within the realm of 'measurable' science. As Peterson & Seligman, (2004: 89) have said,

> ...we can describe our classification as the social science equivalent of virtue ethics, using the scientific method to inform philosophical pronouncements about the traits of a good person.

In other words, positive psychology purports to be a strengths-based approach aimed to offer a 'science of positive subjective experience, positive traits, and positive institutions' (Rich, 2001: 1). As such, positive psychologists see their ultimate aim as supporting individuals to understand and foster the factors that allow individuals, communities, and societies to flourish.[14] Thus, flourishing, as a more dynamic concept, is often cited as the 'ultimate end-state' of positive psychology itself (Schotanus-Dijkstra, Pieterse, et al. 2016: 1).

One recent review of flourishing in the psychology and health literature (Agenor et al. 2017) systematically looked at available conceptualizations of flourishing, as well as the scales and combined measures of the two major eudaemonic and hedonic scales. Four emergent models were identified with six overlapping attributes of these models being identified including: meaning-making, positive relationships, engagement with life (i.e. flow), competence (socially and otherwise), positive emotion, and self-esteem (Agenor et al. 2017: 6). All of the models within positive psychology shared a common conceptualization of human flourishing centred on psychological well-being and function in one guise or another. What seems clear is that within positive psychology, the notion of well-being (specifically, psychological, and social well-being) has evolved to become synonymous with the concept of 'flourishing'. Hence, from the perspective of many positive psychologists, flourishing individuals are those who experience high levels of both 'hedonic' well-being, oriented around pleasure activities and emotions, as well as 'eudaemonic' well-being, relating to the search for purpose in life (cf. Keyes 2002, Huppert 2009).

Linked to the idea of 'challenge' is the related idea that each individual develops everyday skills, resources and efficacy exactly through (not despite) the trials and tribulations they face. This is central to what another key thinker in positive psychology, the late Mihaly Csikszentmihályi has termed as 'flow'; namely, 'the result of pure involvement' (Csikszentmihályi, 2014: 141) and the idea of a state of mind in which people are so absolutely immersed in an activity that 'nothing else seems to matter' (Csikszentmihályi, 1990: 4). Csikszentmihályi and Hunter later argue that flow is the result of feeling good about the self, excited, proud, sociable etc., as well as being constituent contributors towards flow experiences; taken together these are seen as 'the strongest predictors of trait happiness' (Csikszentmihályi & Hunter, 2003: 85). Hence, achieving mental states of 'flow' is also seen as the single most powerful contributor to 'daily flourishing', especially during crises (Cf. Liu et al., 2023).

Similarly, in their 2005 paper, Fredrickson and Losada suggest that to flourish means: '... to live within an optimal range of human functioning, one that connotes goodness, generativity, growth, and resilience' (2005: 1). This definition was built from the shoulders of the work undertaken by Keyes (2002) with his mental health continuum model where languishing is seen on a spectrum at the opposite end of flourishing. In so doing, Fredrickson & Losada claimed to have discovered 'a set of general mathematical principles' which describes 'the relations between positive affect and human flourishing' outside of which is evidence or an indicator that a person is failing to flourish (Fredrickson & Losada, 2005: 678). Specifically, participants with a ratio (rounded to 2.9) of positive to negative feedback are seen to flourish. Controversially, Fredrickson & Losada claimed that the discovery of the critical 2.9 positivity ratio 'may represent a breakthrough' in a kind of 'flourishing diagnosis'. Ironically, this is a medicalizing language where human flourishing is reduced to diagnostic tools and by placing those diagnosed into the category of a biological and/or psychological 'sick role' (cf. Parsons, 1951).[15] Naturally the Fredrickson & Losada (2005) paper attracted some critics for its reductionism, though none of those critiques were philosophical or conceptual.

Further, there appear to be a number of dualist assumptions at the heart of this way of seeing flourishing. Because so-called 'functions' are seen through the prism of pathologies of the mind (i.e. mental health or illness) as instantiated through the brain, it apparently follows that the natural next methodological step is to analyse which neurons fire up in the brain at a given moment in order to issue diagnoses into human flourishing. In fact, Waterman (2013) sees the amalgamation of neuroscience and positive psychology as being in the 'more dynamic segments of the arc' of psychological research (2013: 131). Such psychologists proclaim that this kind of neurological perspective of emotions is a natural step in the evolution of the field and an innovative 'advancement'. However, by drawing psychological conclusions from neuroscientific research, there are parent risks in making a categorial error by conflating biological with psychological categories.[16]

The notions of positive well-being and flourishing have also influenced educational practices in schools where young children are measured against metrics of 'flourishing behaviours' (Stephens, 2014). For example, research has been conducted on aspects relevant to moral education such as character 'strengths' (Hodges & Clifton, 2004); 'hope' (Snyder et al., 2002); and 'resilience' (Brunwasser et al., 2009). Indeed, Brighouse (2008: 42), de Ruyter (2004), White (2011), and most recently, Kristjánsson (2021) go as far to suggest that 'flourishing' is 'the central purpose of education'. Whether flourishing can meaningfully be said to be the 'aim' of education is up for debate. I have certainly argued against it in my public talks at the Philosophy of Education Seminar series at Winchester University (Mountbatten-O'Malley, 2021) and more recently at the Philosophy of Education Conference (Mountbatten-O'Malley, 2023a). Not because educators shouldn't wish their students to flourish, of course they should, but because Kristjánsson and others often seem to conflate a 'value' with an educational 'aim'. Flourishing is not the kind of thing that teachers and educators can *aim* for on their students' behalf, it is for students to flourish under the apt conditions for flourishing (which is the responsibility of educators to a limited extent). If educators did aim for the flourishing of their students, they would fall into the same instrumental pitfalls identified earlier with the instrumentalist methods of

Utilitarianism, and as such, this would amount to a dehumanization of their students, flourishing for flourishing's sake irrespective of the needs of individuals. Educators can and should, however, contribute to the *conditions* for flourishing students. This, I suggest, is a more apt division of responsibility and labour that allows for student skills, gifts and interests to be explored.

Further, as is common in the literature on human flourishing, Kristjánsson (2021) specifically conceptualizes flourishing in terms of (student) 'well-being', thus conflating flourishing with well-being and kicking the proverbial can down the road. Hence, although intentions are no doubt well-intentioned, there are some fundamental problems with the claims made by Kristjánsson and others, conceptually and ethically, that is, in terms of what we can and should expect educators to adopt in their respective job roles.[17] Relatedly, whilst the aims of moral education are clearly noble, because of the way that positive educators lean on the reductionist research and methodological practices of positive psychologists, many of the scientistic problems are replicated. Key concepts in education such as learning, memory, teaching, curricula, etc. are clearly normative and subject to convention; they are not amenable to empirical investigation per se, at least not in a way that produces the kind of scientific generalization that is most often claimed by researchers and educators (cf. Egan, 2002).

There is *some* acknowledgement of the wider tendency and problem of conceptual variance of human flourishing and cognates. For example, Vitterrsø (2016: 2) has said, 'the number of definitions and conceptualizations is ... quite overwhelming' and Agenor et al. (2017: 1) has also commented that, 'conceptual clarification is needed to promote comprehensive understanding of the phenomenon'. Further, there has been some movement and debate from within the positive psychology field itself. In a recent discussion notice, Ryff (2020) criticized VanderWeele's (2017, 2019) and Harvard's (2021) use of 'single-item' assessments of well-being advocating for a 'multiple measures' approach. Again, all this does is miss the point. Whilst assessing a much wider variety of someone's subjective well-being responses to questions is better than a single measure (i.e. 'How do you feel today?') a technicalization of flourishing through any measure still tells us little about whether someone is actually flourishing – at least according to the everyday way we use the term – yet it will be used as such an indicator in a range of educational, policy and other contexts. In short, there is a tendency to technicalize terms for methodological purposes and this costs researchers in terms of coherence and explanatory power. It also costs citizens, employees and students because artificial policy structures are built around these misconceived measures of flourishing. This is both epistemically and ethically problematic.

There has also been some tentative acknowledgement of the problem of the scientific 'measurement' of psychological concepts such as 'well-being' within philosophy, in particular the problem of local cultural and community context. In this regard, Alexandrova (2017) has advocated that a science of well-being can be redeemed by 'contextual theorizing'. Alexandrova rejects, however, the notion that the social world is 'too complex' for meaningful generalization, or that social explanation should be 'couched in terms of reasons not causes' (Alexandrova, 2017: xxi–xiii). But as Hacker (2007a: 6) notes, 'explanations in terms of reasons and motives is *distinctive* of human behaviour' [my emphasis]. Accounts like Alexandrova's (2017) fail to acknowledge the plurality of explanations for human behaviour (cf. Sandis, 2012a), as well as the conceptual pluralism of reasons (cf. Sandis, 2019) that we have in our linguistic toolkit. In other words, she misses why normative psychological concepts are not reducible to scientific generalization – at least not in ways that are very informative and are not susceptible to significant confusion. One of the central arguments I will be making in this book is that such a reduction is not a problem because of differences of subjective interpretation (at least not solely), but rather, because of the diverse uses of our words in the various language-games that we play in the variegated contexts that we live and act in. Like the concept of 'memory', such concepts are complicated by purpose and use. Explanations of meaning for such concepts are *normative* – they are rule-based and contextual. As such, empirical studies attempting to reduce and explain them are most often, according to Hacker (2013a: 317), 'unlikely to achieve their aims'. This is primarily because we misidentify the problem.[18] This is of central importance in figuring out why we go awry in the study of psychological and other normative concepts and the important differences between empirical and conceptual investigations.

Humanistic psychology, self-actualization and flourishing

Finally, there are more coherent approaches out there, although they do not get much attention in the mainstream. These are humanistic in orientation. Humanistic psychologists have been influenced by distinct philosophical assumptions to those in positive psychology. Such assumptions have tended to have been drawn from existentialist and phenomenologist sources, whereas positive psychologists tend to have been influenced by hedonic and Utilitarian notions of well-being (Joseph, 2015). Humanistic psychologists may broadly be categorized under the eudaemonic tradition. Whilst they also reject the dominant negative paradigm of psychology, they tend to disapprove of the 'scientific method' arguing that it is inadequate for dealing with the complexity of human nature (Boniwell, 2008: 5). Examples of conceptions of flourishing amongst these thinkers includes Rogers with his concept of 'self'-actualization (Rogers, 1961) and Ryff with his concept of operationalized positive functioning (Ryff, 1989). Humanistic psychologists have argued that actually it was positive psychological functioning and realization of human potential that was most important in order to flourish. These differences in philosophical foundations seem to suggest an incommensurability between the disciplines, as has suggested by Waterman (2013: 126):

> Because of the breadth and depth of the differences in the fundamental premises underlying positive psychology and humanistic psychology, it may be impossible for proponents of the two disciplines to find much in the way of common ground.

Yet, in speaking of an 'inner' Self, we intend to contrast that with the 'outer' Self. The phrase reflects the nature of the internal psychological or indeed phenomenal world, that is, the world of personal thoughts, ideas, beliefs, motivations and experiences. Whilst the 'outer' refers to the *external* world i.e. the domain of facts, objects, things, matter, including the body and everything else *outside* of the mind. We often say that our 'inner world' can be torn apart from confusion, pain or heart-ache; or we say that on the outside someone can seem fine but on the 'inside' (their mind, or even their heart) they are *really* in torment or turmoil. Thus, in speaking so, we often suggest that the *real* person, the true subject of our experiences and our internal drama, is the essential human 'Self' inside, as opposed to the outer person that is evident to others (e.g. through speech and behaviour). The Self then is seen as something *within* the human mind, something *essential* to it – the 'real' essence of being or 'becoming' human.[19] The implication is that if you are not being yourself then you are not being fully authentic human being, thus selfhood becomes the *sine qua non* of human-ness.

However, there are a number of criterial problems related to such a conception of the Self. For example, there is an implied entity status given to the 'Self', for to speak of the Self, using the possessive pronouns (myself, yourself, himself, herself etc.), suggests that one can *have* a Self as if the Self was something that one could possess. But the Self is synonymous with the whole person not *part* of the person. Here understood, the public Self is a kind of disingenuous and *presentational Self*, versus an *authentic* inner *Self*.[20] This is not merely unjustified epistemically but it also promotes a belief in mysterious or spooky inner substances with secret knowledge and epistemic authority over inner states.[21] On that account, the language-game of knowledge (which relies on public criteria for justification) falls apart – hence Wittgenstein's rationale for highlighting the conceptual problems with any notion of a 'private language'.[22] As Hacker (2007a) highlights, a private Self that has privileged access to an inner mind is misguided. Although, we can of course have private thoughts that we (for whatever reason) *choose* not to reveal, our thoughts are for the *most part* perfectly evident through behaviour, demeanour, expression etc., and the myriad of other ways we communicate. Although there are cases of unpublished or concealed thoughts, even sinister and deceptive thoughts,[23] for the most part, there is a broad range of perfectly public criteria for the ascription of thinking. Thus, to suggest that the inner world of thought is something private is *misleading* precisely because the criteria for use of our words is public, sharable, *and* more particularly, the criteria for the practice of thinking is for the most part behavioural and subject to public scrutiny (though of course speech, confessions and declarations of intent are also behaviour). Rules only count as rules if there are *people* to observe them, for how could we even have the possibility of knowing what a rule for the use of a word was without at least the possibility of public scrutiny (cf. *PI* §293).[24]

Subsequently, because this approach is pitted against the hedonic pleasure-centred notions of well-being (as seen within most of the positive psychological literature), methods also differ, so positive psychologists tend to prefer quantitative methods whilst humanistic psychologists prefer qualitative approaches. One criticism from Seligman and Csikszentmihályi (2000: 7) is that humanistic psychologists offer vague and narcissistic support to individuals to indulge in subjectivism; further, because research is overly concerned with qualitative methods, it apparently lacks any kind of scientific generalizability or credibility, or at least sufficient enough to support the central claims of the field. Indeed, a difference over methods is, according to Joseph (2015: 434), the central divide between the two disciplines to the point that academics in both fields hardly ever cite each other within the main journals.

I'd suggest that the qualitative approach is far more useful for understanding what supports people to flourish. This is primarily because it relies on the raw material of the individual to explore important notions of meaning and fulfilment etc. Nevertheless, whilst it is justifiable to defend the point that 'humans are different than things' (Joseph, 2015: 36), and so different methods should follow from studying human beings, there may be a tendency of humanistic psychologists to overinflate the importance of personalized meaning, thus resulting in a kind of solipsistic paradigm. Further, within humanistic psychology there is perhaps an over rigorous aversion to any kind of reducibility or generalizability (Joseph, 2015: 35). I would suggest that although too much predictability is not feasible (not least because of the reality of a plethora of differing psychological and social contexts) it simply cannot be the case that there are *no* common features of human flourishing, especially *if* we accept the following set of assumptions:

a) Terms such as 'human flourishing', in order to be meaningful, must draw conceptual distinctions in accordance to our human natures; and:
b) Concepts operate within networks of related concepts in a language (and are thus describable in some sense within that conceptual scheme, according to their use and application).

The misunderstanding occurs when we rely on an empirical method for such a generalization, as opposed to a conceptual insight. Thus, conceptions of flourishing from a humanistic perspective may not be helpful because they seem to offer a prescription that is too subjective, too ill-defined and with an over-sceptical attitude towards the possibility for some level of generalization with regards to criteria for use. Some generalizations are indeed possible, but we may articulate these through conceptual work. We do not, for example, need to research *that* human beings feel pain or disgust at being hurt emotionally or physically. We can spell this out conceptually. Statistical approaches to such insights are misguided because they have a confused and scientific notion of epistemological authority; such is the trend.

Similar criticisms could be levied against the profuse use of 'self-report' in modern research which I have used many times in the past for the various organizations that I have worked for, designing, for example, surveys aimed at members of the public or professionals. It also happens to be the chosen method for the Harvard Human flourishing programme. Self-report is a really useful way to get information and opinions quickly and cheaply, but it is hugely problematic. For example, from a purely methodological perspective, issues include a lack of ability to probe, clarify, prompt respondents etc. (see Bryman, 2015) in order to identify reasoning in responses. Such research is therefore susceptible to out-of-context and ambiguous responses, and this contributes to a proliferation of poor-quality psychological research.[25] If the point of research is to advance knowledge or understanding on a particular area of dispute or difficulty, then this kind of research is somewhat pointless, and certainly misleading. It is therefore not harmless.

Despite the fact that both humanistic and positive psychological perspectives on flourishing seem fundamentally at odds with each other (as suggested by

Waterman, 2013), there have been developments with second wave positive psychology, or 'PP 2.0' (Wong, 2004). This fresh approach is the existential bridge between the disciplines which aims to broaden further the horizons of flourishing in a number of ways not least by proposing a more inclusive and ethnically sensitive system of positive psychology (Chang et al., 2016). Brown et al. (2018) have also tried to move away from the 'positive' focus of positive psychology aiming to unravel the social conditions that might contribute towards attainment of flourishing. However, whilst this is indeed a move in the right direction (primarily because it recognizes the importance of human complexity and dignity) for the purposes of this book, insofar as the conceptions of flourishing are examined there are no conceptual advances made on human flourishing as a result of these developments; namely, the fundamental problematic assumptions and methodological fallacies remain intact and in need of redress. Doing so will contribute to better research, that is ethically and epistemically authoritative.

Chapter outlines

Chapter 1: Normativity, Language and Concepts

In this chapter, I explore a range of concepts, largely introduced or influenced by Wittgenstein, all of which are closely related to the nature of our words and concepts, their use and place in our lives as human beings. The major themes of this chapter centre on the vital importance of the normativity of language and the relationship between language and concepts in the investigation of human affairs. I draw attention to the distinction between words and concepts in order to highlight some of the problems we can get into when seeking definitions and criteria for words. This includes an account of our unique rational and linguistic powers and how these inform how we develop concepts, rules, norms, judgements and conventions. I will also relate how language is driven by our human 'form of life' (Wittgenstein, 2009, *PPF* §1).[26] The implications of this rather jargonistic term are that as such language is not susceptible to essentialist conceptions of language. Rather, how we communicate is better understood in terms of the fluidity of 'family-resemblance' concepts and the multiplicity of interlocking 'language-games' (cf. Wittgenstein, 2009; *PI* §66 and §67). As I suggest, these observations provide important limitations on how we can sensibly investigate normative concepts like 'human flourishing'.

Chapter 2: On the Analysis of Concepts

Whilst Chapter 1 offers a foundational set of concepts that assist in better *understanding* complex normative terms, Chapter 2 offers a more direct 'how to' guide into doing this kind of work. Hence, building on the important notions of form of life, normativity, language-games, grammar, rules and rule-following – in this chapter I explore some practical matters exploring the basic methods associated with this particular form of conceptual analysis. I provide an explication of the notion of 'connective analysis' (Strawson, 1992: 19), and a description of the process of making connections and relations clear between concepts. Importantly, I also explicate the technique of 'conceptual elucidation' (à la Hacker 2007a: 14) used to highlight and explore conceptual confusions. I then explore more generic philosophical tools such as objects of comparison which help to bring to light, through comparison and contrast of cases, particular features of our language (*PI* §130). Finally, I explore exemplary cases in order to demonstrate the importance of context and occasion-sensitivity (Travis, 2008) in understanding utterances on given occasions, for particular reasons and purposes. By the end of these first two chapters, readers will have a solid footing on which to proceed their inquiries into some of the direct concepts most closely connected with human flourishing, including humanness, flourishing, agency, personal growth, and meaningful happiness.

Chapter 3: Humanness

In speaking about human flourishing our interest is in the flourishing of *human* beings, and relatedly, human nature. Our conceptions of human nature are mitigated by related concepts that pertain to some putative quality such as 'humanness' (so conceived). This concept can, however, be a highly problematic one. Hence, the central aim and purpose of this chapter will be to reveal some of the linguistic and conceptual confusions that often bewitch us when deploying the concept of humanness and related terms. In this chapter, I will show how reductive approaches to humanness (evident in four key targets for this research project: essentialism, subjectivism, reductionism and scientism) are conceptually problematic and at times, patently incoherent. I do not provide a comprehensive account of humanness (nor is that possible), nor do I propose a theory of humanness; rather, I remind readers of the central ways in which we use humanness in its diverse guises, the purpose of which is, to use Wittgenstein's term, to marshalling recollections (*PI* §127) thereby helping to make conceptual connections clear(er). I show how humanness cannot be reduced to that which distinguishes us from the animal kingdom e.g. 'rationality' as the essence of humankind. Neither is it some quality that can be measured, increased, decreased or lost. Hence, I will show how problems can arise as a result of misleading metaphors, or through what Hacker terms as a 'distorted apprehension of a genuine feature of grammar' (Hacker, 2013b: 15).

Chapter 4: A Sketch of Human Flourishing

The concerns raised in the introductory chapter focus on the problems with reductive approaches to understanding concepts like human flourishing. Building on those remarks, I suggest here that human flourishing *appears* to be a complex problem largely because of a dearth in awareness of the plurality of uses for the phrase 'human flourishing'. In this chapter I will explore the central uses of the concept of human flourishing to show that there is no essence of the concept (like well-being), but that it is closer to a family resemblance concept with a variety of distinct, yet interrelated applications. Here I will perform a connective analysis (Hacker, 2013a: 438) where I explore the conceptual connections between flourishing and related concepts in order to convey the logical terrain and connections between flourishing and the possibilities and limitations of use (at least standardly speaking). I will aim to elucidate the nature and normativity of the concept of human flourishing, for example through comparing human flourishing with other uses of flourishing, as well as through various objects of comparison with related but often conflated concepts such as *eudaimonia*, success, happiness, and well-being. Because of the multiplicity of uses, my aim with this chapter is to highlight that attempts to reduce the concept and retain the meaning are misguided. The nuances and challenges of some of the problems raised in the introductory chapter will therefore be explored further here, helping to contextualize subsequent chapters related to human agency, personal growth and notions of happiness and meaning.

Chapter 5: 'Human' Agency

In this chapter, I draw out salient differences between human and animal agency through an exploration of the notion of two-way powers. This, I argue, has important implications for what it means for us to flourish as human agents. Using some of Frankfurt's (1998) discussions I aim to avoid a common tendency towards what Frankfurt critically calls a 'parochial bias', in order to develop a useful but ethical conception of agency. In tying agency to human nature, I draw a crucial distinction and contrast between some of the normative dimensions of the concept of agency alongside some of the axiological and social contexts within which we operate as moral and legal beings, as 'persons'. As I suggest, this is important in order to develop accounts of agency that are ethical, human-centred, conceptually sound and authoritative. Relatedly, I also explore the relevant links between agency, rationality and community norms with the aim of highlighting implications for personal empowerment, emancipation and justice in social contexts. Finally, I briefly explore what it means to act as an agent, *for reasons* (as opposed to because of *causes*). I do so in the context of what I highlight as the problem with a biologically reductionist conception of well-being and flourishing, taking issue with developments towards a 'neurobiology of happiness and pleasure' (Kringelbach & Berridge, 2011) and a 'neuroscience of well-being' (Berridge & Kringelbach, 2013), moves which I suggest, are misleading, incoherent, and contrary to popular claims, actually weaken prospects for genuine realization of human agency and flourishing.

Chapter 6: Personal Growth and Development

In this chapter, I draw attention to the concept personal development suggesting that it is closely connected to the concepts of growth, self-knowledge, beliefs, motivations, abilities and goals. As I suggest, when considering this concept, we are concerned with highlighting some of the contributory forces that work towards producing not merely neutral growth, but goodness and betterment in a person. Thus, I propose that there is an explicit moral and ethical imperative at the heart of this concept which is closely related to what we mean when we discuss the flourishing of human beings. Building on initial critiques of subjectivism, I also identify and explore related problems with the subjectivist notion of self-knowledge. This will include an exploration of the concept of self-knowledge and the problems that misunderstandings and self-deception cause in determining the meaning in what someone says, means or intends. Further, I analyse the various uses of notions of the personal pronoun, the 'Self' and related absurdities, and will explore some subtle confusions. I make a case for developing a well-informed 'self'-concept (cf. Joplin, 2000), or perhaps better, a conception of the Self. This is important both to help demonstrate the public and sharable nature of knowledge itself (including self-knowledge), but also to provide a simple and workable framework for better understanding what it is to grow and develop as a person with flourishing in mind.

I also explore notions of 'personal identity'. This happens to be an area of philosophy with extensive attention, but my focus will be on addressing the nature of 'identity' and its common (but problematic) association with memory. My aim here is to de-mystify the concept of Self and dislodge it from its metaphysical associations. Finally, as part of this exploration into the Self, and using Ryle's (1946) and Cassam's (2014) scepticism towards intellectualist and rationalist dogmas, I explore the possibilities for knowing-*how* approaches to gaining wisdom and insight and develop their insights into what I call knowing-*how to* live the good life. I spend some time critiquing Grimm's (2015) related conception of wisdom (which he sees as being epistemically motivated towards well-being) but I finish with a suggestion that his focus on epistemic goods is excessively narrow and reductive. However, I do argue for the importance of nurturing our innate skills and abilities to make good judgements, which I suggest is a form of practical know-*how* rather than know-that knowledge, a related but distinct category.

Chapter 7: *Summum Bonum*: Happiness and Meaning

In this final chapter, my interest is in the relations between the concepts of happiness, meaning(fulness), and effective navigation beyond various forms of self-delusion that we are all prone to exhibit. These concepts are intimately connected to each other; indeed, it is hard to imagine happiness without a person having attained a sense for what is meaningful in their life. I am therefore interested not in a one-dimensional, self-centred conception of happiness, but rather, in a morally defensible conception of happiness, which I argue is the only one that could contribute towards genuine human flourishing (at least directly). I sketch out some of the key uses of 'happiness' including exploring the relations with pleasure, joy and satisfaction with one's life. This is important to highlight and contrast the *subjective* and *objective* dimensions to happiness. I also explore Tatarkiewicz' (1976) classic four-fold taxonomy of happiness (satisfaction, experiences of greatest joy, success, and the highest good) with reference to Hacker's (2021) most recent work on the central moral categories in human life. I begin to explore the variety of uses for the word 'meaning' as well, which I suggest is important in order to develop some clarification for what *kind* of questions we might be asking when we ask what *the* meaning of life is; indeed, I question whether life is even the kind of thing that can have *a* meaning. Relatedly, I tackle what I term as conceptual 'delusions' through an exploration of the concept of *telos* and teleology; as I suggest, it is likely one of the roots of confusion as to whether life has a meaning. I also explore subjective meaning and value, drawing distinctions between two central kinds of value (trivial and substantial), for example, comparing pleasurable and transient activities with (possibly unpleasant but important) altruistic activities. Moreover, I adapt a case raised by Wolf (2007) with regards to a paradigmatic meaningless life (the 'Blob'). I explore what that life might look like and compare two competing cases of the life of the Blob arguing that whilst both lives may be redeemable, one route leads to a life that is morally justified (which I argue is what meaningfulness hinges on) and the other is not. I therefore explore the importance of moral orienteering through one's epistemic, conceptual and characterological weaknesses.

Finally, I reaffirm the possibilities explored in Chapter 6 regarding the logical space for hope that ignorance provides. This is why, *ceteris paribus*, there is always scope for improvement for anyone who is leading what I suggest is a meaningless life. This chapter, in particular, is aimed to support rich grounds for thinking so that we may lose our 'aspect-blindness' about problems related to human goodness and may develop the ability to see things aright in a liberatory and transformative sense (cf. *PPF* §257, Baker, 2004: 8). Hence, I will show that although happiness is largely used in banal and narcissistic senses, through the practice of questioning (curiosity, reflection and inquiry) and being willing to seeing things differently (rational open-mindedness, conceptual insight), we can tackle the central confusions of life and develop mastery over purposeful language-games related to the practice of happiness, human flourishing, and a meaningful life. These are matters of immense substance; grasping them well has the potential to contribute to your own personal transformation, better still, to the potential of contributing to the transformation of the lives of others, especially if you are in a position of social authority. I therefore hope that you find these explorations helpful in your own personal journey towards human flourishing.

1

Normativity, Language and Concepts

In this chapter, I explore a range of concepts, largely introduced or influenced by Wittgenstein, all of which are closely related to the nature of our words and concepts, their use and place in our lives as human beings. This is important because as highlighted elsewhere, there is a temptation in research to see words as discreet entities that may be analysed for semantic essences, described for necessary and sufficient criteria and then measured accordingly to such (technicalized) criteria. But that approach is misleading. This is not least because words have multiple uses signifying various concepts. This is important in the context of seeing how words are used *in* practice and *as* a practice within a diverse range of circumstances. In short, this is to take the idea of the contextual *normativity* of ordinary concepts seriously.

Chapter sections

In section one ('Words are not equivalent with concepts') I draw attention to the distinction between words and concepts in order to highlight some of the problems we can get into when seeking definitions and criteria for words. Following on, in section two ('The "meaning" of a word'), I explore the nature of meaning itself, focusing on this notion of practices and uses, highlighting the centrality of the 'competent' language user who is able to understand the use of a word in a context and in a particular circumstance. As I suggest, this amounts to the development of certain abilities (or know *how*) regarding the understanding of words, or more specifically, the rules for their use.

Because words are in a sense arbitrary, we use the word according to a relevant conceptual (or logical) grammar. Hence, in section three ('Language-games and essences') I extend the notion of linguistic practices (games) as an insightful means to human understanding. This is precisely because understanding the game being played helps us to see the role a word, expression or utterance has in the broader plurality of language-games. Following on, in section four ('Use, sense and agreement') I explore the crucial role of *normativity* in sense-making. After all, to speak and understand is to mutually acknowledge the role of a rule, reaffirming it through our various practices (linguistic and behavioural).

In section four ('Implicit rules, explicit practice'), I explore Wittgenstein's distinctions between according with a rule and following one. This reaffirms the role of complex and intelligent human linguistic competence and abilities, i.e. in contrast to computing or animal behaviour, highlighting (in one sense) the arbitrariness of our *rules* for use, I also explore the cultural role of logical (or conceptual) grammar clarifying a common misconception with regards to the seemingly explicit nature of rules. I suggest that this may guard us against misreading rules and grammar as 'relativistic'. Then in section five ('Some distinctions on "grammar"') I further clarify some of the tensions between syntactical and logical grammar, including misconceptions of logical universalism. I advance a conception of grammar that is first and foremost local in orientation (i.e. relative to the use).

Finally, in section six ('Occasion-sensitivity and human judgement'), I extend the notion of arbitrariness even further adopting Travis' (2008) concept of occasion-sensitivity to notions of human judgement. That is to say, not only are specific uses of our words contextualized within distinct language-games (as in, 'good person', 'good hammer' etc.), indicative of the arbitrariness of words, but in fact whole sentences are ambiguous outside of a specific cultural context, interpersonal space and point in time (cf. *PPF* §7). As I suggest, taken together, insights from Wittgenstein, Hacker, Baker and Travis help to show that language is inherently playful and pluralistic with significant implications for the designing of research into the nature of normative concepts.

It may be worth being explicit about what I mean by 'normativity'. The notion of 'normativity' is notoriously ambiguous.[1] By deploying the word 'normativity', modern philosophers tend to mean something that is related to ethical agreement and norms, or axiology, viz., that which 'ought' to be the case, for *reasons*.[2] This sense of normativity can therefore be seen as some value or deontic judgement that is 'action-guiding' (cf. Peterson, 2007). This contingency contrasts with necessary or factual knowledge and what is considered the case (e.g. science) and so is easily conflated with the use that I take here. To be clear then, I take the term following Hacker (2007a) to mean that which is focused on philosophy of language and action, namely linguistic behaviour which is 'rule-governed'.[3]

Whilst my use of normativity also contrasts with scientific (nomological) endeavours, the focus and sense of the word is entirely different to the common use today, for we are here not interested in moral rules governing conduct per se, rather, we are interested in linguistic rules governing sense and meaning. The more defined methods associated with the sciences do not help us to master a concept or see its possible applications. Once the primacy of the normativity of our concepts is sufficiently understood, it becomes apparent that detaching words from their context results in a mis-match between the research and the practices of life. Nefarious or propagandistic designs aside, if the aim of a given research programme is to have application in *real life*, as if often claimed – then there is a logical problem with the kind of research that is detached from our every-day use of terms (cf. Putnam, 2002, Wittgenstein 2009, Hacker 2007a).

In order to grasp the *life* of a complex and normative concept like human flourishing, we must 'look and see' (*PI* §66) at its *use* as embedded within the normative contexts from which it has been uttered. In so doing, we nurture development of our unique human abilities for concept-possession, concept mastery as well as emotional and rational development. Language is therefore not something abstract, calculable, hidden or mystical, but rather, is a *living* and dynamic activity, seen through the background prism of our human 'form of life' (*PI* §23 and 241). That is, it is embedded within the kinds of language-games we play, the jokes and absurdities, which are formed in the context of the fundamental facts of life such as birth, relationships, rationality, suffering, joy, pain, physical illness, death etc.[4] Hence, before moving on to more nuanced matters, I will begin with the most straightforward of distinctions between words and concepts, not because this itself may be revelatory to readers, but because it is central to why confusions in research with regards to normative concepts so often occurs.

Words are not equivalent with concepts

There is an understandable urge to view words as independent entities in their own right and this assumption is built into self-report surveys, for example, of well-being or flourishing (e.g. cf. Harvard, 2021). The practice or assumption at work here certainly seems sensible not least because we conflate concepts with words, and words have a digitized and formal nature as elements of sentences. We take a word to have a specific grammatical function in a sentence (e.g. adjective, noun, verb) where sentences are seen to contain a combination of functional linguistic entities such as subjects, objects or predicates (so conceived in terms of syntactical grammar). However, concepts are not equivocal with words for a number of reasons. Firstly, a word may signify more than one concept. For example, as Wittgenstein suggested, the word 'till' may be used to express both a conjunction, i.e. 'until', or a verb, to 'till the ground' or for supporting effective ways to exchange cash e.g. 'till' can also be a 'cash register' (cf. *PPF* §8). However, the *roles* these words play (and thereby, the *uses* they have) depend on linguistic and situational contexts and of course the purpose of their use. We could use the word 'good' as an example as well; that is, 'it's good' (useful) versus 'he's good' (morally upright) or even 'they're good at' (skilled, able) etc.

Similarly, the word 'flat' could signify the concept of something horizontal or a piece of real estate. There are innumerable other examples that one could draw upon (suit, wrap, face, case, know, etc.); on each occasion either the word has multiple uses or is a derivative of some form of metaphor (viz., human 'face' versus the 'face' of the matter; equally, 'wrap' your mind around that, versus, a burrito 'wrap'). Further, it is not always the case that a linguistic context (outside of a situational context) delineates anything meaningful either, for the 'Mad Hatter' could be the name of a fictional character, an actual person, or a pub. Thus, the words used here such as 'good' as moral versus skilled or useful, or indeed 'flat' as horizontal versus a living space etc. highlight an important distinction between words and concepts. For example, Hacker (2007a:16) describes concepts as 'abstractions from the uses of words'. This helps to articulate a simple but important truism: whilst words are indeed linguistic entities (i.e. linguistic components of sentences etc.), concepts are not 'entities' at all; they are not independent of a *use* and a context. We only understand the meaning of a given term or word as uttered within a particular 'logico-grammatical' space (cf. Bennett et al., 2009: 127). It is the logical space of the use of a term that helps us to identify which concept is in fact being deployed. This insight will become increasingly prescient as I begin to sketch out the concept of 'human flourishing' in Chapter 4.

The 'meaning' of a word – knowing *how*

A further important point is one of utility. What is important is that the *way* we use words to signify concepts within our language as opposed to the signs or sounds themselves, are arbitrary in this sense. When we speak about 'meaning', we can of course refer to a dictionary or indeed to an expert for definitions. Rather, what it is we aim to understand is the logical consequences of using such a word. Wittgenstein (*PI* §43) famously remarked:

> For a large class of cases of the employment of the word "meaning" – though not for all – this word can be explained in this way: the meaning of a word is its use in the language.[5]

Wittgenstein suggests here that a word has a meaning only in the context of a practice and for a given purpose (i.e. a *use*). In order to understand the meaning of a word, we should look to how it is used. What would it be for us to hear the word blue used to suggest what we might otherwise consider as red. The word blue matters insofar as we agree that it signifies (among other things) the hues of the sky for example. In the broadest of senses, it matters not whether we use the word blue or indeed blub. However, the fact that we have a use for the word 'blue', namely for historical and cultural reasons, means that we typically understand what is being said by the term 'blue' (as opposed to using 'blub'). Knowing *how* to use the word blue instead of, say, red is important insofar as we wish to communicate meaningful sentences in the English language regarding certain primary colour ascriptions. This is a matter of one knowing *how* to use, deploy or understand a word correctly in a given context; that is, where it fits within our language. As Baker & Hacker (2005a: 145) explicate, it is a matter of utility, rather than a putative essence:

> ...by emphasizing the conceptual connection between meaning and use, Wittgenstein reduces the temptation to conceive of the meaning of a word as an entity of any kind, no matter whether concrete or abstract, particular or universal, that is correlated with the word.

So, I can use the letter 'a' to signify 'one of' – that is understood by the context (i.e. 'a' pear fell from 'a' tree). But I can also use it in another way, that is, to signify a coded relationship within a sequence of numbers of algebra (i.e. a × b = c). Alternatively, I can use it as a means to describe a note or chord in a musical scale: A, B, C, D, E, F, G ... A, B, C etc. (cf. *PI* §10). This is simply to help show that the letter 'a' is used in any number of ways which is not immediately obvious in isolation, but is understood only within a context, and being competent language speakers, we normally understand these contexts (and the meaning) in the blink of an eye without much thinking being involved. It is only when the meaning is vague that we need to consider the intended meaning in more depth. For example, if I say, 'I love you', in one context it could mean what we might expect i.e. we care for and/or have affection for that person. However, it could also easily mean something more surreptitious or manipulative, such as 'I expect you to do something for me, or else'. The meaning is thus evident and interpretable in the *context* of the utterance and the totality of semantic and situational references available in a given context (cf. *PPF* II §7). The most fundamental purpose for any utterance is to relay meaning and communicate understanding of a given topic. Without the *mutual* acknowledgement of the rules of engaging in such activities, meaning, understanding and sense break down – a fortiori when we use psychological predicates like knowing, believing or intending – or indeed when attributing moral attributes to persons, such as human flourishing, goodness, wellness.[6] Of course, this is not merely to say that we need to speak sense in the dismissive sense, but rather that we need to say something that has a *use*, within a system of refence, and hence a meaning.

Seeing as knowing our way about our language is matter of knowing *how* to understand such uses, it follows that, more specifically, we need to understand the diverse applications of language. After all, that is what it is to know the place a word has in a logico-grammatical space. This is where Wittgenstein's notion of language-games can provide additional clarity in knowing *how* to interpret the meaning of an utterance, in a context, as opposed to the idea that we can scientifically parcel off a word for analysis independent of a context.

Language-games and essences

If any word can mean anything, what then can we say about the nature of words in sentences. How can we get a grip on what we mean or indeed have any hope of understanding each other if we sometimes use the same word to signify different concepts? Of course, one might say that we simply infer or know from the context – and this would (largely) be correct. We are *able* to infer from a particular case what is meant in such a context (of 'till', or 'wrap' or 'good' etc.) and this is part of what it means to be a competent language speaker. But why is this the case? This is where the notion of a language-game is useful. It is, broadly, the idea that language-use is not separable from the things we do; it is woven into our human practices, activities and reactions to one another (cf. *PI* §7 and *PI* §23). But this remark alone does not help us to distinguish between various *kinds* of language-game. For example, are we really playing the same kind of language-game when we ask, 'what is a rock?' as when we ask, 'what is a mind?'. These seem to be different varieties of question and indeed, game – with important categorial distinctions between physical and mental attributions.[7] Hacker (1999: 34) highlights a useful example from Wittgenstein contrasting first person ascriptions with descriptions of physical objects, in order to help bring this into focus. We must beware of 'too facile' a use of the word: 'description'.

As Hacker (1999) suggests, the concepts and activities that belong with describing one's room are 'observing, scrutinizing, examining, descrying' – these are matters of 'perceptual competence', effective use of sense organs and veracity is determined by evidence, observation and so are dubitable and indeed debatable. Here, questions of good or poor eyesight and observational conditions which might affect it (e.g. day or dusk) can be raised. In contrast, first person avowals regarding one's state of mind or indeed level of pain, are not things which can be physically observed like objects; that is, pain has no physical spot we can point to see it – indeed, it is not the *kind* of thing to manifest itself observationally in a temporal space. The usefulness that Hacker (1999) draws on here is one of contrast between two kinds of game regarding description. He targets a tendency in our language to various forms of essentialism. Whereas, it can be more useful, and certainly less misleading, to draw salient distinctions between different kinds of *use* (or game).[8]

Once highlighted, we can see how we might use similar forms of language (superficially) for completely different purposes: 'What we call "descriptions" are instruments for particular uses' (*PI* §291). Saying something in a given context, is analogous then to making a move in a particular kind of language-game, it is when we mix the games up that we err, because we conflate distinct rules for use.[9] Given the often very subtle, and somewhat implicit, nature of rules in language-games, this is perfectly understandable. But it is equally important to notice it when we do. As Wittgenstein famously highlighted, language can be used in multifarious ways (*PI* §23). It could be used to ask questions, tell stories, make commands, acting, reporting, praying, guessing riddles, cracking a joke etc. If we abandon that imperative or urge for generalization and simply 'look and see' (*PI* §66), we will notice that there is not a single definable criterion for what these activities in language are; there is no definition of language that captures them all (cf. *PPF* ix, §81), but we use the concept of language as a 'description' for all of these activities, nonetheless. This generalization is useful to a point as long as we are aware of the pitfalls when we take it too seriously; the devil is in the detail.

One example of essentialism in psychology is Seligman's theory of well-being, where he posits that the '... standard for measuring well-being is flourishing' (Seligman, 2011: 18). This is a form of essentialism, which is why he continues shortly afterwards, '[w]ell-being is a construct, and happiness is a thing. A "real thing" is a directly measurable entity. Such an entity can be "operationalized"— which means that a highly specific set of measures defines it.' (Seligman, 2011: 18–19). What Seligman (2011) does here is to offer a picture of well-being as being rooted (essentialized) in flourishing. This is why we may be tempted to see words (like 'language', 'game', or indeed, 'flourishing') as having a kind of essence that we need to discover. But this is to picture the possibility of knowledge about our words along the simile of epistemic mining, digging out the 'essential' treasures. Whereas our efforts to understand our words are, on one level of analysis, more explicit and surveyable through *use*.[10] There is indeed a depth to this effort, but it is logical, conceptual and grammatical – not empirical. It entails surveying and describing the rules for our ordinary use of our words. If there is any 'essence' whatsoever, there certainly is not one that carries across the various uses of the kinds of words exemplified above. We can only see what is essential (or rather, *natural*) to their use within the framework of the language-game in which they are placed; the logico-grammatical space. The essence of a word is relative to the *grammar* of its use.[11]

We might be tempted then to think that if there are no clear definitions for the use of our words, or indeed, analytic necessary and sufficient conditions, then anything can mean anything. But a flexibility in application of our words is *not* a relativist rubber ruler for the meaning of words; they cannot mean whatever we like. After all, if that were the case then language would not function as it does as a means of communication or expression. As Glock (1996: 50) suggests, language is somewhat impinged on by human activities and our 'form of life':

> The autonomy of language does not amount to an 'anything goes' relativism. Grammar is not arbitrary in the sense of being irrelevant, discretionary, easily alterable or a matter of individual choice. Language is embedded in a form of life and is hence subject to the same restrictions as human activities in general.[12]

Rather, because of the logical relationships between words and concepts, their meaning is interconnected and interdependent. It is then, an acknowledgement that the way we use and master our words and concepts is indicative of what Hacker (2015: 12) terms as an 'open-ended series of interlocking language-games'. There is no contradiction in the acknowledgement that language-use can be both rule-governed viz., fairly stable, and yet 'elastic', for our use of words shifts with pragmatic need, cultural favour, as well as scientific and technological progress.[13]

Use, sense and agreement

Centrally then, the insight that the sense or meaning of a sentence may be gleaned from looking at the *use* is an observation of the primacy of normativity and agreement in understanding the meaning of our use of words. A good example can be seen in the builders' language-game introduced early in *PI* §2 where Wittgenstein says:

> The language is meant to serve for communication between a builder A and an assistant B. A is building with building-stones: there are blocks, pillars, slabs and beams. B has to pass the stones, in the order in which A needs them. For this purpose they use a language consisting of the words "block", "pillar" "slab", "beam". A calls them out; — B brings the stone which he has learnt to bring at such-and-such a call. Conceive this as a complete primitive language.

The notion of a game here simply means that A *knows how* to communicate a request (by calling out) and B *knows how* to respond obediently to such a request (by conducting an activity and passing the item requested to A). In other words, the *rules* of a game are understood by both parties *and* there are consequences for B if orders are disobeyed (logical and/or practical). The aim of the game of the system here functions as long as the rules for sense-making are obeyed. As simple (or 'primitive') as this language-game is, what we have here is a complex duality of systems in play simultaneously: one governing the system of conceptual logic (stones, slabs, pillars etc. are the *kinds* of things that may be passed etc.), and another governing the system of expected behaviour (what I do in response when an order is made, i.e. obey, pass, etc.).

To order, act, respond and reciprocate *is* to mutually reinforce an acknowledgement of the rules of the game and the usefulness of those primitive systems for communication. That is, the act itself is the (explicit) affirmation of the (implicit) rules of the game. We take these rules as a given in the kinds of acts we do. Hence, if one wants to play the language-game of greetings and says 'bababababa!' in response to 'Good evening!' (misunderstandings or jokes aside) the responding speaker is clearly talking non-sense. As frivolous as it sounds, this merely highlights that there are rules to speech and communication which we normally follow in order for there to be the kind of order that makes sense in our language. Contrarily, if by saying 'bababababa' I aimed to confuse and confound someone I am speaking to, it remains a non-sense, albeit a ludicrous or humorous one (cf. *PI* §498), for we cannot call a disorder (i.e. 'bababababa') an order of a disordered kind for the conceptual grammar precludes it. The exception could be if one or more persons understood 'bababababa' to mean 'I don't want to hear you' or 'that's non-sense' etc. for then it does have a grammar of sorts, albeit one that is parasitic on the grammar of '(not) *wanting*' or '*nonsense*' respectively.

Nonsense here merely means an ordering of a particular kind within a game, which has a purpose of shared understanding within a given context. It is 'what we say' that matters, not some hidden essence that requires an expression. If it is conceptually confused, then it is nonsense – not because it is false, but because nothing is said (there is no 'use' in the relevant language-games). This is logically prior to truth-conditions and is therefore to be contrasted with that which can be proven false or incorrect.[14] That is, for something to be falsifiable it must first have a sense, and no matter how long one pursues nonsense, one cannot derive sense from it: '... there is no successive approximation to truth via nonsense' (Hacker, 1986: 159). For example, in speaking of the grammar of colours, such a preclusion merely means that in the standard sense of our uses of colour concepts e.g. of 'white', we usually explicitly mean in the positive mode, 'brightest', 'luminous'; or implicitly in the negative mode, 'not blue', 'not green', 'not red', 'not black' etc. The fact that this is, in an important sense, an arbitrary (and flexible) set of grammatical rules, does not detract from the importance of having a logical grammar, for it shows the *role* of a concept within a set of broader conceptual relations and connections. The attribution of the 'sense' for an utterance is thus warranted insofar as it is a manifestation of some kind of role or purpose within a system – viz. a role within a logical space.[15]

As with any game, rules require players and so the engagement in the playing of a particular kind of language-game requires, firstly, at least some kind of community of language speakers, and secondly, agreement on the primacy of the notion of shared rules and norms (assuming that communication is the main goal). Crucially, the social practices of sharing norms of use support the very *possibility* for the attribution of sense in the use of our concepts within a given language (i.e. the development of grammars within a natural language). There is, then, a symbiotic relationship between the practices of sharing, making sense, discovering meaning and following rules. It is to this latter aspect that I shall now turn, because it is foundational to our understanding of how language (and sense) works in practice.

Implicit rules, explicit practice

Firstly, it is worth drawing attention to Wittgenstein's distinction between 'according' with a rule (*PI* §201) and 'following' a rule (*PI* §199, §202). This will reconfigure our attention on human *abilities* rather than any notion of putative nomological laws that might govern human thought and communication (implicit or explicit for that matter). For example, it's a straightforward truism that in order to play by the rules of a game, one needs to *understand* the rules, for this is part of what we mean by 'playing'. It is not enough simply to have acted in similar ways as expected (i.e. through mimicry or perhaps as an accident, though incipiently this may form part of our learning process, for example, as children). As Baker & Hacker (2009: 155) put it, if an 'infant, monkey or a robot' moves a piece on a chess-board, it would be a nonsense to ascribe such acts as somehow being 'informed' by or following the rules of the game for use of *that* piece of chess; rather, it would be a reflection of behavioural mimicry.

Following a rule and knowing when to ascribe the concept of a particular kind of move in chess, requires criterial evidence of understanding and is thereby related to other concepts such as intention, self-guidance, judgement, scrutiny and discernment. Baker & Hacker (2005a: 148[a]) specifically outline the threefold criteria for human understanding as follows:

> There are three kinds of criteria of understanding. A person satisfies the criteria for understanding a word if (i) he uses the word correctly, i.e. in accordance with the rules for its use or the received explanation of what it means; (ii) if he correctly explains what the word means; and (iii) if he responds with understanding to the use of the word in question, i.e. responds appropriately or intelligently to utterances in which it occurs.

This simply means that whilst behaviour and action appear to reinforce and reaffirm understanding of a given move, being able to explain our reasons for such a move is important for demonstrating mastery of the technique of playing the language-game of 'chess-playing' (cf. *PI* §199).

Taken together, these insights aim to demonstrate an acknowledgement of the set of assumptions that undergird rule-following practices in a given context. An error in attribution or use (i.e. either breaching the grammar of the concept or else acting out of line with the rule) would suggest a joke, a metaphor, an aberration, a nonsense or a misunderstanding etc. If I said that you'd need to 'Bishop' my King in order to win we know something has gone awry here in the language-game (unless of course we used this as some kind of code); this is why, agreement on the expected grammatical use is vital in most cases of standard communication, but the occasion and the context will *always* take precedence over the expected behaviour regarding the following of rules in a given case.

Secondly, following a rule is a practice (*PI* §202) and we learn how to understand and deploy rules through training (*PI* §206) or induction into a particular culture. These are customs and conventions which, being bound up with conventions of language-use, cannot be followed by only one individual at one time in history. As Hacker (2001: 311) suggests:

> A rule and what accords with it are internally related. The rule '+2' for forming the series of even integers would not be the rule it is if '1002' were not the correct answer to the question 'What is the result of applying the rule +2 to the integer?' 1000?'. It is this grammatical insight which rules out both the supposed 'sceptical paradox' and its putative 'sceptical solution.'

The examples shown thus far help to highlight that the rules for the playing of language-games are intricately occasion-sensitive and purpose-driven. As such, there could be no such thing as using the kinds of methodological approaches relevant to understanding formal calculi, theories or analyses (cf. Hacker, 2015: 155), which work on models of a simpler and predicative kind. Rather, as competent speakers of a language we are able to make decisions based on our judgements about context and grammar: 'It is not only agreement in definitions, but also (odd as it may sound) agreement in judgements that is required for communication by means of language' (*PI* §242.). What this remark hints at is a shift in focus from the historic and problematic conception of language as a definable set of referential symbols used to describe putative external realities, versus language as a set of highly malleable *tools* for achieving the goal of *understanding*. This latter approach evades the fallacies of essentialist and referentialist conceptions of language by pointing more directly at what we *intend* to do with the activity of language.

In this way, our agreements take a particular *form* of grammar, as contextualized by the cultural context and specific occasion. They needn't be *that* particular way, but for various reasons, including cultural-historical reasons, we agree that they are.[16] This is somewhat controversial and there has been some debate on this issue.[17] As I indicated earlier in this chapter, I adopt Baker & Hacker's (1990) position here; namely that it makes more sense to apply this implicitly (or 'internally'), thereby forgoing any need for explicit agreement.[18] It would not, and indeed could not, alter the meaning of nonsense as long as sense and nonsense mean what they do, and have the relationship to rules that they do. This is a grammatical feature built into the function of our language and is a buffer against all manner of epistemic and other forms of private language arguments, cognitivism, scepticism or indeed relativism – all of which I find to be conceptually confused.

Agreement on rules is subtle and implicit. The normative nature of a rule both prescribes appropriate use, but also proscribes nonsense. This feature is like a power, or a potentiality of the concept (as applied). As Baker & Hacker (1990: 171) suggest, what matters is that a rule 'can be shared'; nonsense has no direct logical force in aiding human understanding.[19] This does not preclude the possibility of alternative grammars but affirms that grammar is rule-oriented. When we survey the grammar of a given concept, we look at its use in a given context and for a given purpose; in so doing we draw attention to something often implicit and taken for granted, and we make it explicit. In other words, we move what was hidden nonsense, to more 'obvious' nonsense (cf. *PI* §464). It is in drawing out the effects of those habits and tendencies to overlook the obvious that we can see things more clearly. The grammar of a word becomes clearer, and our ability to perceive the relevant logical relations draws into focus, despite our tendencies towards obfuscation and complexity (intentional or otherwise).[20] It is for this very reason that we need to remind ourselves that 'following a rule' is an historically contingent rule-governed practice of thinking with clarity, that helps us to use words coherently, as well as to orient ourselves in the world under the cultural conditions of our times.[21] Our conceptual problems are particular to us, they are framed by our situatedness, and our conceptual schemes and linguistic practices. It is then, not the kind of practice that follows nomological or statistical rules; nor is it epistemically private. It relies on the power of shareability (as does measurement), the acceptance of rules and the practice of rule-following.[22]

Not that the world of science is entirely nomological either. As Hacker (2007a: 182) suggests: '[t]he universe, according to our world picture, is not governed by laws, but is *described* by laws. It is nomic (regular), but not normative (rule-governed).' [my emphasis]. We use the language of 'laws' to describe scientific kinds of 'facts' because it is useful. But that utility only works up to a certain point and concepts in science change too (or fall out of favour). After all, Einsteinian conceptions of the relativistic nature of space-time revolutionized Newton's nomic conceptions of physics. This advance in knowledge was not a discovery in the world per se, but a change in *conception*.[23] Einstein found a useful 'way of seeing' things (cf. Baker, 2004: 269). The practice of rules is not about improving communication per se in the explicit sense (though there are obvious consequences for communication when it goes wrong, because when something is said without a sense then nothing is said); rather what is important is having practices that work to ensure that we have the very *possibility* of communication, ergo, the possibility for advancement in human understanding.

Some distinctions on 'grammar'

Because of the inherent tension between the notion of logico-conceptual grammar and context, it is worth making a distinction here between how the concept of a *grammar* is used. This is because one would be forgiven for thinking that the notion of a 'grammar' suggests a universal set of rules within a language. Glock (2009: 654), for example, equates grammar with 'our conceptual scheme' implying the overall system of rules within a whole language. To some degree, this could appear to follow Wittgenstein (*PI* §122):

> A main source of our failure to understand is that we don't have an overview of the use of our words. Our grammar is deficient in surveyability. A surveyable representation produces precisely that kind of understanding which consists in 'seeing connections'. Hence the importance of finding and inventing intermediate links.

But it is important not to conflate two distinct uses here: a universal and a local use. It is a complex enough task to survey a single word in all its uses let alone the whole system of terms in our language (if indeed that were a possibility).[24] Bearing in mind the *lack* of unity of language (because there is no universal set of rules in our language, we employ words in our language as tools in our toolkit) such a universalist conception of 'surveyability' (*übersichtlich*)[25] of grammar seems an impossible and unattainable feat, and indeed, it is. Conversely, however, we may use the term 'grammar' in a universal sense as long as all we wanted to point out is the interconnectedness of our 'web of words' and the plurality of language-games (in the broadest of senses).[26] But this could not be written down in the format of an English language grammarian's textbook; the possibilities for our use of words and the (logical) grammars that govern their use, are vast, diverse, and not uniform (hence the utility of the term 'language-games'). In principle, logically-speaking, such games are infinite. In conducting an investigation into particular concepts, our interest here then is, rather, to survey a *particular* grammar. A clearer way to put this would be to conceive of a *localized* notion of grammar, that is, an exploration into the logical relations in the use of a word specific within a given language-game.[27] With a local conception of grammar in mind then, we can see how it is used to describe a particular kind of analysis of *specific* words, concepts, expressions or phrases on specific occasions for particular purposes – not entire grammars, schemes or languages for all possibilities. If there is any hint of suggestion of a universal reading of the notion of a grammar (by either Glock or Wittgenstein), it can only be to highlight, as a general remark, that the grammars interlock in complex ways according to the purpose at hand so as to produce shifting and dynamic network of conceptual connections. The fact that we do not always have access to insights into the surveyability of a given word contributes to our philosophical problems is certainly true, hence the need for conceptual analysis.

The way to manage tensions between a putative universal grammar versus a local grammar, is by accepting the *normativity* of our concepts and by analysing the complex, linguistic and conceptual networks and connections of words as we *use* them in our various activities and practices on specific occasions for particular purposes. The fact that we use the notion of a 'grammar' differently on different occasions and for different purposes merely reinforces the point, that concepts are not fixed entities but are tools in our linguistic toolkit.

Occasion-sensitivity and human judgement

Understanding of a given term or utterance is, largely, attainable because of the insight that we may develop into the purpose of use (the language-game being played) and the situational context (other relevant factors). One phrase might mean something entirely different in another context or on another occasion and in order to see what the meaning is we should avoid thinking or theorizing too hard about it and we should simply 'look!' at the use on the occasion (*PI* §66). Such a communication needn't be verbal of course but could just as easily be non-verbal (such as a wink or a nod). The specific kind of human interaction that is employed and knowing what will follow of using such a communication in a given circumstance are all key factors in possessing a concept and endowing it with sense and meaning. Indeed, arguably one of the single most important heuristic principles for the development of our understanding is the concept of 'occasion-sensitivity'. The specific term *occasion-sensitivity* is attributed to Travis (2008) but Wittgenstein often used the phrases such as *context* or *circumstance* to highlight the same point about the primacy of context of use and purpose. For example:

> Whether the word "number" is necessary in an ostensive definition of "two" depends on whether without this word the other person takes the definition otherwise than I wish. And that *will depend on the circumstances* under which it is given, *and on the person I give it to*. And how he 'takes' the explanation shows itself in how he uses the word explained.
>
> *PI* §29 [emphasis added]

In a play on Travis' 'milk in the refrigerator' case (Travis, 1989: 18–19), here is an example: if a husband comes home one day and asks his wife if she is okay … and if she replies 'Fine thanks', in one context this might mean what it appears to mean prima facie, viz., she is fine. In another context, it might be said (or read as being said) sarcastically, that is, she's not fine at all. The case might equally be made of subject-predicate statements like "the kettle is black" where this could mean any number of different things such as the kettle is black as in 'burnt' (i.e. on a camp-fire) or the kettle is actually black in colour. Thus, the meaning of our words 'is black' does not tell us which of these ways is really the right way of counting things as black or not black (Travis, 2008: 29). As highlighted earlier, the meaning of an utterance is in no way inherent in the word itself, which merely provides certain logical parameters (at least standardly speaking); so if I said 'fabulous!', it could mean 'great' or sarcastically, 'terrible' or it could also mean 'Absolutely fabulous' the TV show (i.e. if uttered as a phoneme). The references to know which-is-which, are everywhere in the context and only minimally in the sentence or the words uttered. To further illustrate the point, Wittgenstein explores various uses of the word 'blue':

> What is going on when one means the words "That is blue" at one time as a statement about the object one is pointing at a at another as an explanation of the word "blue"? Well, in the second case, one really means "That is called 'blue'". Then can one at one time mean the word "is" as "is called" and the word "blue" as "'blue'", and another time mean "is" really as "is"?
>
> PI §35

Wittgenstein's insight here is a form of what I might call 'epistemic pragmatism'. He is interested in the use (how a word is applied, in a context) as opposed to whatever form the word takes or indeed, whatever place the word has in a sentence in terms of syntax. 'Blue' can mean something closely resembling what we might infer it to standardly mean (played in a language-game of colour ascription), but equally it might mean something else entirely (played in a language-game of naming). The relation is highlighted by Wittgenstein drawing out attention to the difference between an 'is' and 'is called'. This amounts to a difference in logical consequences for each 'use', and hence, a significant difference in the language-game and grammar of the concept.[28]

Travis (2008: 9) gives one example of an utterance that syntactically makes sense but is logically meaningless; for example, 'The length of my bed has chocolate undertones' (equivalent to Chomsky's, 1957, 'Colourless green chairs sleep furiously' example). As Travis suggests, the variety of possible interpretations of sentences are not so much due to ambiguity in the English language, rather, they each express something unique and different, like a potentiality. What there 'is to be said' (i.e. meant to be understood) is not determined by the associated meanings of the words or the referents or the private intentions of the speaker (at least not in isolation); meaning is a matter of 'judgement' of what was said within the limited range of possible candidates in a given context of references for what could have been said with that utterance (cf. Travis, 2008: 32). That is, understanding is possible insofar as we grasp the holistic set of relevant reference points in which an utterance is uttered. Wittgenstein alluded to this in *PPF* §7 when he said:

> ... the expression "I was then going to say ..." refers to a *point in time and to an action*. I speak of the *essential references of the utterance* in order to separate them from other particularities of the expression we use. And the *references that are essential to the utterance* are the ones which would make us translate an otherwise unfamiliar kind of expression into this, our customary form.
>
> [emphasis added]

The reference points include the utterance itself of course, but also to the tone, personal memories and contexts of the people involved, what they feel about that history and what is meant on that particular occasion by uttering a certain sentence in that moment – and crucially, within the bounds of sense.

Accessing the full range of reference points means that we are usually then able to see what is meant by an utterance and we can grasp it 'in a flash' (*PI* §319) or a 'stroke' (*PI* §138, *PI* §197 and *PI* §318). This is why we are able to go and see a pantomime with our whole family, including our young children, where the jokes are multi-layered so that the adult humour is pitched in such a way that only adults (or older children) will most likely understand the subtle reference points of sexual innuendo. For example, in a *Jack and the Beanstalk* panto I attended a few years ago, the Dame was at the bar called Winky's bar where the barman would say to the Dame that the only way she could actually get served is by saying 'if you give me a winky I'll give you a drinky', at which point the Winky's bar sign (a winking emoji) would squirt water in her face. This appeared to be a reference to the act of fellatio, which would humour adults whilst keeping the joke hidden from children who would be none the wiser.[29] This helps to demonstrate that internal mental processes, calculations, computations or algorithms cannot possibly account for the subtleties in communication, circumstance and context within our language for the references are multitudinous. Grasping these references require skills of *judgement* that human beings possess through their unique abilities and understanding as embodied beings situated in a particular form of life; in a social, cultural and ecological moment in time and space.[30]

Our multitudinous, complex and interlocking language-games are played occasion-sensitively. Thanks to our conceptual mastery, we are familiar with *how we should go on*, and what counts as good practice or a deviation from a norm, rule or standard of the 'game' in question. Knowing and acting out these language-games, operating within their linguistic and logical bounds – even where apt, breaking them (e.g. using language humourously) are all indicators of concept-possession to varying degrees of sophistication in the deployment of concepts. 'Grasping' (cf. *PI* §138) or possessing a concept is to know *how* to use the word correctly in a variety of contexts, and what follows from doing so. This skill requires a degree of understanding of the logical consequences of using a word, and the logical connections between that word, the concept signified, and other related concepts in the apt conceptual scheme, or, within the 'cluster of related terms' (cf. Best, 1978: 13). Hence, understanding others seems reasonably straight forward, so long as we are able to understand the appropriate range of reference points *and* we possess a certain level of conceptual competence and mastery (which most of us do, *simpliciter*).

However, there remains a risk of inflating the neatness of communication between speakers; this is not what is being suggested here. Rather, when attempting to read others we are limited by our own *ways of seeing*. Wittgenstein (1949) was not averse to this kind of limitation, as he stated:

> The older I get the more I realize how terribly difficult it is for people to understand each other, and I think that what misleads one is the fact that they all look so much like each other. If some people looked like elephants and others like cats, or fish, one wouldn't expect them to understand each other and things would look much more like what they really are.

The point Wittgenstein raises here is that although we usually grasp the meaning of an utterance because of the grammar as well as the context, understanding the motivations and interests of others is not so clear cut. Although we seem to be essentially the same kind of creature (i.e. members of the human species) we are often so fundamentally different in our values, goals, dispositions and world-views so as to warrant the ascription of other kinds of creature entirely (figuratively-speaking). But it is important to remind ourselves that language is inherently playful, pluralistic and diverse. Indeed, precisely because it is so, there is plenty of scope for misunderstanding (and humour); a fortiori, there is infinitely more scope for understanding, which, as Sandis (2015: 140) has put it, comes 'in degrees'. Understood aright, our ability to use language creatively provides the space for endless possibilities and powers of human expression. In many ways, it is what makes us distinctly *human*.

Summative remarks

In terms of understanding the nature of words and concepts, and thereby, the implications for the analysis of concepts, I draw attention to several insights useful for this book as 'background' assumptions: in particular,

- Words are not equatable with concepts; language is not comparable with a calculus; neither are language speakers comparable with calculators. If that were so then there would be no possibility of doubt for the various meanings of our words. Words are not discreet, linguistic entities that are discernible or transparent outside of a context. They function as tools in a toolkit, and like a tool they can have a multiplicity of *uses* (cf. *PI* §43);
- Relatedly, the essence of a word is then relative to the logical *grammar* of its use (cf. *PI* §92). As Hacker (2015: 12) suggests, this amounts to using words in various contexts in an 'open-ended series of interlocking language-games';
- Our concepts are, as Hacker (2007a:16) terms it, 'abstractions from the uses of words'. These abstractions are normative (rule-governed). The kinds of rules of interest here are logico-grammatical. This is not merely in the sense of explicit social norms as etiquette might be considered to be, but rather is indicative of a loose background framework of conceptual rules and relations without which sense and human understanding is impossible;
- Our ability to understand a word is a part of being a human being with language abilities. Competent users of our language are able to deploy and understand particular words insofar as they accord, follow and have mastered the rules and techniques for their use (cf. Hacker, 2007a: 14). Understanding is then, a skill and an ability that is harnessed and developed through various practices of education, induction and training (cf. *PI* §206 and Hacker, 2007a: 112);
- Our use of words is not distinct from our *practices* as human beings. They are related to the contexts within which we operate, the purposes we have, and the kinds of thing we *do* as the kind of creature we *are*. The notion of language-games then helps us to better understand the various *functions* of words in contexts of practice;

- Concepts are based on the basic facts of life (*PI* §142, §230) and form part of our distinctly 'human' *form of life*. They 'reflect our life', are not separatable from our life but 'stand in the middle of it' (*RC* III §302) and they 'direct our interest[s]' (*PI* §570) as human beings.

These remarks, given synoptically, help to raise the primacy of *normativity* in the investigation of concepts, and as such, the profile for a specific kind of conceptual analysis that respects the limits of what may intelligibly be uttered, and the relevant rules for use for a given term as set in particular circumstances and contexts. As outlined, this demonstrates the importance of general conceptual mastery (which we attain from education in the broadest of senses) as well as conceptual insight (which we attain through philosophical inquiry. This amounts to the nurturing of a particular set of techniques. In the following Chapter 2 I will aim to outline some of the appropriate techniques available to us in the endeavour to resolve the kinds of philosophical problems identified in the early pages of this book, specifically, in order to know '*how to go on*' (cf. *PPF* §300) in our use of the concept (and related cognates and conceptions) of 'human flourishing'.

2

On the Analysis of Concepts

The web of concepts relevant to a study of the concept of human flourishing will be those relevant to the broad study of human beings and the particular human form of life. For example, we are interested in concepts such as language, freedom, agency, justice, well-being, happiness etc. As human beings we are able to demonstrate a host of abilities unique to us and which distinguish us from other creatures in the animal kingdom. We have unique abilities to reason and reflect about complex relationships and ideas, and to act as imaginative and creative agents in the world. We are therefore intelligent (albeit fallible) linguistic beings; we are able to develop, deploy and grasp (or indeed, misapply, misuse, or fail to grasp) words in complex and contextual ways. Hence, understanding better what it means to be human being living within the bounds of a particular human 'form of life', with all the complexity and diversity that this implies, is of central importance to the subject matters covered in this book. It is the kind of investigation that Hacker has termed, a 'philosophical anthropology', at least in part – that is, the 'investigation of concepts and forms of explanation characteristic of the study of [hu]man [beings]' (Hacker, 2007a: 4), and in particular, human welfare.

Therefore, in this chapter, I build on the key philosophical concepts and assumptions introduced in Chapter 1, many of which are associated with the works of late Wittgensteinian thought, such as: a form of life, normativity, language-games, grammar, rules and rule-following etc., in order to explore more concretely what this kind of analysis looks like in practice. This is not an exhaustive list of philosophical concepts and methods relevant here, but rather a summary of the key approaches I have adopted for this particular purpose. Due to some differences in use and application of some of these terms (such as 'grammar'), at times the application is not always straightforward so some sensitivity to context of use will be helpful. Importantly, these philosophical terms do not form anything like a unified theory of conceptual analysis; rather, they are tools for philosophers (and other inquirers) to use in their investigations into human affairs, at least sufficiently for the purposes here.[1]

Chapter sections

In section one ('The aims of conceptual analysis') , I explore the aims and motivation for a conceptual analysis. I draw attention to the key features of the approach that I take compared with the traditional approach seen in analytic philosophy. I also introduce the main methods associated with such an approach to conceptual analysis including conceptual elucidation and connective analysis, both of which are associated with the approach used by P.M.S. Hacker. I build on these points further in section three. In section two ('The therapeutic role of the philosopher'), I discuss the role of the philosopher in addressing fundamental disquiets or confusions, particularly in the context of the problems of philosophy as traditionally conceived. Thus, I suggest that many of philosophical problems arise out of a problematic grasp of our concepts which neglect the importance of context. In doing so, I draw attention to the potential liberating effects of philosophical perspicuity as a method, most notably associated with Baker's (2004) reading of the latter works of Wittgenstein but clarified through Hacker's (2007b) critique of Baker.[2]

In section three ('A multi-pronged strategy'), I offer a more detailed explanation of the methods associated with this kind of philosophy. This is important if we are to attain *surveyability* and insight over the grammar and related philosophical problems that tend to grip us through misleading 'pictures' or misapprehensions in our uses of words. In section four ('Conceptual elucidation'), I explore conceptual elucidation in more detail. I draw attention to the differences between surface and depth grammar and reiterate the concept of *rules* for use; in other words, grammatical rules that *warrant* appropriate use of a given word on a particular occasion. In section five ('Conceptual analysis: mapping the logical terrain') I explore the method of connective analysis (originally coined by Strawson, 1992) in more detail. Using Hacker's (2013a) simile of a 'map' I also elaborate on the reasoning behind such a method, including the importance of gaining a sense of *oversight* of the logical terrain in order to see where a given philosophical problem is rooted.

Finally, in section six ('Aspect-seeing and objects of comparison'), I explore the liberating potential of juxtaposition and seeing alternative pictures or ways of seeing. This is also important for the very same reasons that particular pictures can hold us 'captive' (*PI*, §115). I highlight a way out of confusion by suggesting that in order to be liberated from the grip of a misleading picture, it helps to develop the ability to 'see' things anew, under new conditions and in new contexts, side-by-side.

The aims of conceptual analysis

As suggested, the topic of human flourishing is closely related to the study of human nature; as such, it is naturally fitted to the domain of philosophy or more specifically, what Hacker (2007a:14) calls, 'philosophical anthropology', and the 'investigation of concepts and forms of explanation characteristic of the study of man' (Hacker, 2007a: 4).[3] As such, concepts may be analysed through the application of words, alongside highlighted features of the relevant conceptual grammars, insight into the language-games being played, and the logical space such terms occupy within our language.

Conceptual analysis is by no means a new method. In fact, it is a method used by most of the major philosophers including Socrates, Aristotle, Hobbes, Mill. In many ways it defines what philosophy is as an investigative practice of inquiry into knowledge, understanding and meaning. However, in this text, I am not interested in many of the traditional approaches to conceptual analysis which tended (though not always) to aim at garnering prescriptive necessary and sufficient conditions with distinctions between the essential (necessary) and inessential (contingent) features of concepts. This is an approach which places the focus on definitive features the *concept* itself as the arbiter of truth, knowledge and meaning as if a given concept is a reflection of some underlying metaphysical reality (i.e. essentialism coupled with representationalism as a form of dualism). This traditional approach to philosophy is often misguided because it ignores the complex interplay of words, context, and practice, as Wittgenstein (*BB*, 1991: 19) remarked:

> The idea that in order to get clear of the general meaning of a term one had to find the common element in all its applications has shackled philosophical investigation; for it has not only led to no result, but also made the philosopher dismiss as irrelevant the concrete cases, which alone could have helped him to understand the usage of the general term.

The problem here is that the kind of question that is in the 'What is an X?' formation, would almost always elicit prescriptive kinds of answers as if there was a universal semantic essence to our terms, on the model of scientific or empirical 'discovery'. We are confronted with similar problems when we ask: 'What are concepts?'. The implication is that they are a 'thing'. I follow Hacker with his view of concepts as 'abstractions' (cf. Hacker, 2007a: 16). In contrast with the traditional approach to understanding concepts, I suggest a more useful and insightful approach is to develop an investigation into terms insofar as they relate to other concepts within the relevant *networks* of conceptual relations. This includes exploring context first and foremost (in order to better understand the meaning of a term), the relevant logical relationships in the web of words, and developing useful insights into relevant categories of concepts or localized grammars and schema. By way of an example from Wittgenstein, in examining the concept of 'imagination', rather than asking what the essential or metaphysical nature of images is or indeed, what goes on in someone's mind when one *imagines* something, we should concern ourselves with 'how the word "imagination" is used in practice' (cf. *PI* §370; *PI* §383). This contextual, occasion-sensitive approach is always guided by the particular interest and purpose at hand. This is important if we are to gain an understanding into how we use particular words and the concepts signified by such uses (cf. *BB*, 19).

The overarching aim of a conceptual analysis, then, is to develop a sophisticated grasp of 'concept-possession' in the inquirer (Hacker, 2007a: 239n). This is only possible because of the unique ability of human beings for the mastery of logical relations and consequences of the use of words and phrases. This ability goes far beyond the simple recognitional abilities of thinking animals (cf. Hacker, 2007a: 128, 384–5; and Hacker, 2013a: 239–40). As outlined briefly in Chapter 1, what this means in practice is to develop an understanding of the logical *consequences* of using a word (e.g. through conceptual elucidation) and the logical *connections* and relations between that word, the concept it signifies, and other related concepts in the conceptual scheme (through connective analysis). Elucidations and connections explicate what is already in plain view (cf. *PI*, §89), though often these connections are not necessarily perspicuous, hence the need for this kind of ordering, conceptual analysis, and the development of surveyable representations that enlighten (cf. Glock, 1996: 280).

Such an analysis contributes to *understanding* rather than to new knowledge because I here aim to develop and nurture particular skills of thinking. Whereas knowledge may be transferred in a stricter sense of being imparted through teaching, memorized, and reiterated by a student, understanding is something that cannot be imparted; it must be developed from an intrinsic, rather than extrinsic drive for clarity of thought. This has implications for the kind of conclusions we are able to draw from such an investigation, for there will not be a final concluding account of human flourishing here (nor is that possible in the context of the complexities of the human life). Rather, the work here is to provide certain *keys* to understanding so that readers know *how to go on* in deploying the concept in different cases and on specific occasions (*PI* §154). This is an important methodological point because failing to grasp the conceptual issues adequately inevitably leads to poor-quality and misleading research.

In the case of a 'complex' or problematic concept like human flourishing, when we see it being deployed within research in a reductive sense, we may be reasonably sure that what is being researched is a different concept entirely, such as subjective-well-being (positive psychology, education), hedonic happiness (Utilitarianism, Transhumanism) or resilience (health) to name a few. A problem occurs when we design research based on a technical delineation of a word and then use *that* as a foundation for a generalized theory for how things are in the world. This seems to amount to a misconception of a fundamental kind and if a research project relies on it the risks are serious. As Wittgenstein implies, drawing a 'sharp boundary' around a concept for a particular purpose is fine so long as we realize that this will not reflect its actual usage (*BB*, 19). Further, as suggested by Bennett & Hacker, (2003: 2), this can lead to a host of concrete problems in research design, such as:

- Poor conceptualization of the central research problem which is aiming to be addressed by the research itself (wholly or partly),
- Poor research design as a result of poor questions being formed,
- Inappropriate methods being employed which fail to coherently link the task at hand with the methodology; and, subsequently,
- Failure to interpret the findings from the ensuing data correctly resulting in poor quality reporting of the findings.

When designing research, if we were to try to untangle conceptual presuppositions of some empirical research, we could not do so by enlisting the methods of further empirical or theoretical investigations because these would bring their own conceptual presuppositions which would generate further conceptual entanglement requiring endless investigations ad infinitum, an infinite regress. As Hacker (2001: 71) has stated (speaking of the social sciences):

> ...no understanding of the phenomena described by such correlations ... is achieved in the absence of further investigations [viz., conceptual work] of the beliefs, motivations, and values of the agents, which will render their behaviour intelligible.

In this way, the work of conceptual analysis is *logically prior* to empirical research. Before we embark on scientific, empirical studies, conceptual elucidation brings light to our confusions by sifting them to the surface thus improving the quality of research and limiting what makes sense to articulate and to be empirically studied. In other words, although this method (or rather, loose set of methods) helps us to break through confusions, it also helps us better understand the limits of language and knowledge itself.[4] It therefore nurtures in practitioners the academic virtues of humility, curiosity and insight to name but a few.

Whilst the logical criteria for a given concept provides a sense for the rules for application and a sense of order at a generic base level, this is neither a dogmatic nor a theoretical move: '[w]e want to establish an order in our knowledge of the use of language: an order for a particular purpose, one out of many possible orders, *not the order* (emphasis added, PI §132). For example, explicating this difference, Wittgenstein suggested an important distinction between the concepts of explanation and description:

> ...we may not advance any kind of theory. There must not be anything hypothetical in our considerations. All explanation must disappear, and description alone must take its place. And this description gets its light – that is to say, its purpose – from the philosophical problems.
>
> PI §109

What we should aim to do therefore is to bring words back from their metaphysical packaging, and towards their everyday practice or *use* (PI §116). This is both liberatory and democratic for it entails an honest, frank, but sensitive dialogue. It is apolitical in an important sense but deeply political in others. It aims to leave language as is, but it also relocates the focus of knowledge and understanding away from 'experts' and theorists, and towards independent, autonomous, thinkers situated within a given linguistic community. If we wanted to satisfy some urge for the essentializing of concepts, the only kind of essence we could admit of is the inherent semantic *flexibility* of concepts articulated within diverse and plural contexts. But this is like saying that the only thing of which we may be certain is *change*. The generalities we can infer from conceptual analysis is not of the kind that can be reduced to anything definitive, it is more of an insight than a claim to knowledge. Indeed, even with some technical concepts that may be subject to clear and neat definitions, it would be misleading to think of the essence of those concepts as the list of definitions, because, as suggested already, many of our words are mercurial and normative – as such, lists of definitions remain subject to criterial change even in highly technical research environments.

Thus, the urge to essentialize is better satisfied by realizing that the project of essentializing concepts is pointless and hopeless. We should then see clearly enough not to want to subscribe such misleading ways of thinking any longer, and to do so by our own volition: '... it makes no sense to foist the diagnosis on him against his will' (Baker, 2004: 165). This is not to deny the importance of conceptual observations in a general sense i.e. through analysis of the logical criteria for certain concepts or indeed their conceptual connections broadly speaking – but it is to put those observations within their proper framework and order, drawing attention to the vitality of context and purpose. The conceptual meaning of a given utterance is only actually known in 'concrete cases', hence the focus for genuine and meaningful understanding must be on the context: context is King.

The therapeutic role of the philosopher

Because concepts are not at all the kind of one-dimensional thing that may be understood easily outside of a context, it helps to explore them from many angles or perspectives. Achieving depth in our understanding comes when we get a grasp of the truly rich variety of concepts deployed, their interconnections, and their embeddedness within our forms of life alongside a grasp for the contextual activities, circumstances, and occasions that we find ourselves situated in. In 'philosophy, the winner is the one who can run the race most slowly' (*CV*, 34e); that is not to suggest a need for slowness per se, but rather a need to avoid haste, particularly important where there is a risk of mis-understanding or mis-conception. This is why Wittgenstein alerted us to the logical and conceptual nature of human understanding and the intellectual pull towards 'apparent' depth with powerful implications for remedying our confusions:

> The problems arising through a misinterpretation of our forms of language have the character of depth. They are deep disquietudes ... deeply rooted in us as the forms of our language, and their significance is as great as the importance of our language.
>
> *PI* §111

On this conception, the role of the philosopher is not to make theses or to add anything per se (I realize that this statement may be anathema to empirical researchers); we merely point out what is in 'plain view' – we describe how things stand, in particular situations and contexts.

This being so, as Wittgenstein has suggested: 'it would never be possible to debate' the descriptions of a philosopher, so conceived, because 'everyone would agree to them' (*PI* §128).[5] This is an important distinction between what we might call philosophical 'descriptions', alerts or highlights, as opposed to scientific discoveries. Our role is to marshal 'recollections for a particular purpose' (*PI* §127), namely, to nurture clarity of thought. Taking this approach to philosophy, the philosopher's role should be to support human understanding, to individuate concepts, dispel confusions and guide us to clarity so that we can know the right questions to ask and how to seek answers to those questions; namely, to 'show the fly the way out of the fly-bottle' (*PI* §309). The goal of this dynamic type of analysis is to 'clarify existing concepts and conceptual connections and to discern the very patterns they exhibit' (Hacker, 2007a: 12). As Wittgenstein is reported to have suggested:

> In teaching you philosophy I'm like a guide showing you how to find your way round London. I have to take you through the city from north to south, from east to west, from Euston to the embankment and from Piccadilly to the Marble Arch. After I have taken you many journeys through the city, in all sorts of directions, we shall have passed through any given street a number of times—each time traversing the street as part of a different journey. At the end of this you will know London; you will be able to find your way about like a Londoner. Of course, a good guide will take you through the more important streets more often than he takes you down side streets; a bad guide will do the opposite.
>
> Gasking & Jackson, 1967: 51[6]

The analysis of concepts, then, is most efficacious when we have a clear problem in mind, when we are able to see such problems from a variety of perspectives, and when we are able to perceive the multitudinous connections, applications and contexts of use. This is best achieved through reflective work done in isolation but then explored through communities of thinkers. This is when we may obtain a sense of 'surveyability'. In order to elucidate the nature of the philosophical questions and problems to hand, the primary concern here is the 'dissolution of misconceptions' (Hacker, 2007a: 14); or more specifically, to expose the traps of meaningless philosophical formulations so that our urge to misunderstand (*PI* §109) may be revealed to us (e.g. the urge to *essentialize* our concepts and reduce them to specific criteria and measurement). The result should be that we have better insight into effective problematizing and de-problematizing, and what was formerly thought of as a philosophical problem 'should completely disappear' (*PI* §133). Thus, the philosophical work to make things perspicuous is for the most part, a negative one; that is, its fulcrum revolves around a focus on *dissolution* rather than solution of problems. However, in the positive mode, the work involves liberation from deceptive or misleading 'pictures' or forms of thinking that often grip us in the way we see the world and undertake research activity or indeed how we philosophize. By way of an analogy with the therapeutic process, the result of good philosophy is then a shift in aspect in the patient and a liberating re-orientation in the 'way of looking at things' (*PI* §144).[7]

A multi-pronged strategy

This quest for understanding is a deep work that has the power to liberate us; deep in the sense that we can be blind to what is right in front of us (cf. *PI* §129) and be bound by misconceptions. An essential part of this clarificatory work is the development of our abilities to have an overview of the conceptual terrain – *übersicht*[8] – so that we can 'plot the multitudinous paths' of a concept (Hacker, 2007a: 438). As outlined in Chapter 1, possession of a concept requires firstly, a context and purpose-specific level of mastery over the logical consequences of the use of a term, and importantly, an understanding of the conceptual terrain viz. the logical relationships between a given concept within the overall cluster of related terms. Consequently, where there is a problematic concept like 'human flourishing', an *interdependent* (not sharply distinguishable) set of central and complimentary methods emerges for the investigation of such concepts. Figure 1 is a diagram for the two central pillars on which my method rests; further examination will follow:

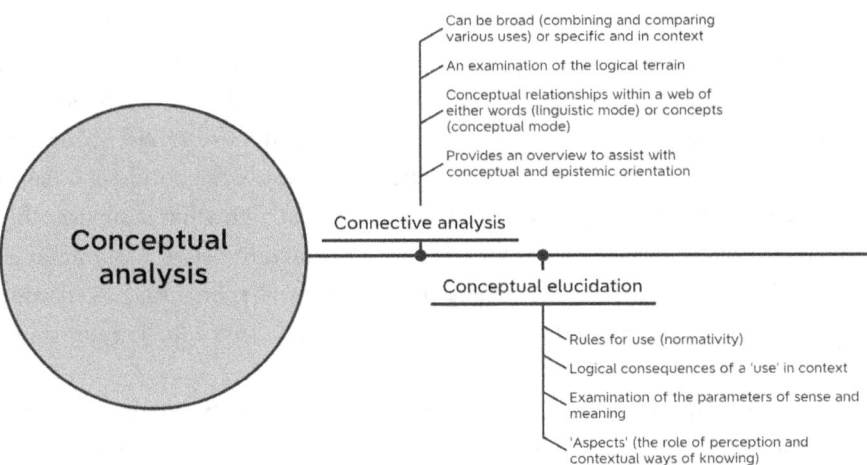

Figure 1 Conceptual analysis.

I. **conceptual elucidation,**[9] which explores the *logical consequences* of the use of a given term. This amounts to an exploration of the rules for use for given word and might typically include the use of elucidatory cases to help contextualize general remarks. It might also include objects of comparison as a temporary 'yardstick' (cf. *PI* §131–2) with which to compare and contrast features of our concepts. The result should be clarification on occasion-sensitive truths, and hence, confidence in assertability.

II. **connective analysis,**[10] which considers the *relationships* between the concept of human flourishing and related terms in the network. This requires an intermediate ordering or arrangement that should not be seen dogmatically or theoretically. Any such ordering is merely *one way* of organizing the conceptual landscape within a range of logical possibilities. It is then, at least partially, about making arrangements in order to provide a certain *way of seeing* a given problem.

This is by no means the only set of methods; philosophical problems will necessitate a different therapy (*PI* §133). Nevertheless, I will explore these two central tools because they form a helpful buttress against our tendencies to have our senses bewitched by misleading features of our grammar. And as will become clearer by the end of the book, misconceptions have a real-life, detrimental effect in real life, personally, professionally and socially.

Conceptual elucidation

Taken from the starting point that there are numerous *uses* of our words (often suggesting a different concept entirely), my approach involves an analysis of the logical consequences of our *use* of concepts, or to put it more precisely, our uses of words in *contexts*. In this sense, it may be helpful to use the notion of a 'depth grammar' (*PI* §664). This notion is aimed to contrast with what is superficially apparent to us in terms of rules for use. It is a distinction between grammar as standardly conceived (including the structural rules of syntax, classes, clauses, phrases, inflections, verb tenses etc.) as compared with conceptual grammar, or logic.[11]

It may be helpful to illustrate the utility and difference between these kinds of grammar, i.e. surface versus depth grammars, with an example of a conceptual category mistake. Chomsky (1957: 15) famously said: 'Colorless green ideas sleep furiously.' The sentence shows us that whilst the standard 'surface' grammar of the sentence seems in order (subject, predicate etc.) it seems absurd. One might be tempted to suggest that the statement is clearly false; however, it is not that the statement is necessarily false (which would require at least the possibility of being true, and there isn't such a possibility) it is simply that it makes no sense.[12] There are no language-games that can combine this set of conceptual relations together in this way. This is central because the concept of green is a category of colour; and secondly because ideas are not the *kind* of thing that have colour, and neither can they sleep. Thus, developing a sensitivity for conceptual sense here, helps to support understanding about the relative boundaries for what can be meaningfully said. This works to highlight the importance of grammar in *this* case, because in the context of the above example, the words deployed are meant in their ordinary sense. That is 'green' is here understood to signify a colour (not a proper name or something else that is not a colour), and 'ideas' is here understood as a form of thought (not an ethnic group of people or some other thing where the attribution of sleep may be warranted). This example works because of the *particular* presuppositions based on the language-games of colour ascription, mind states etc. If we were to alter the language-game in the ways suggested in the parentheses, then the rules for use would change with them, and so would what logically follows in saying them; thus, we would need another example to help bring such matters (viz., about depth grammar) to light.

Chomsky's example highlights an obvious conceptual and categorial mistake. However, our confusions are not always so obvious. If I were to wonder on the relationship between my mind and my body, I may not be aware that I have fallen victim to a *suppositio falsi* by assuming that the mind is some separate entity with a locality in the brain (i.e. attributing personhood to the brain). In making judgements about states of phenomenological or metaphysical affairs (as empirical work might) the interest is in words insofar as they help with an analysis of the logical relations between their related concepts and their use on particular occasions and contexts. This is what Wittgenstein meant when he said: 'We do not analyse a phenomenon [for example, thinking] but a concept [for example, that of thinking], and hence the application of a word' (*PI* §383, text in parentheses added).[13] Even though the line between what is empirical or conceptual is not always clear cut (cf. *PI* §85), once we have a clear question in mind, the nature of possible answers is limited and clarified because the grammars become surveyable; hence the importance of clarifying our thoughts especially when designing research. Does this mean that all our problems are 'mental' or linguistic and do not relate to the world? Not necessarily. As Winch (1990:15) has said:

> We cannot say then, ... that the problems of philosophy arise out of language rather than out of the world, because in discussing language philosophically we are in fact discussing what counts as belonging to the world. Our idea of what belongs to the realm of reality is given for us in the language that we use. The concepts we have settle for us the form of the experience we have of the world.

Our concepts form the conceptual scaffolding of our perceptions of reality from which we cannot meaningfully escape within human thought, at least as competent language-using adults, so suggesting any kind of 'objective' reality outside of a given world-view or set of presumptions makes no sense whatsoever.[14] In one sense then, 'reality' is how we conceive of it. This is not to offer a relativistic account of perception but rather to highlight the importance of concepts and conceptual understanding in relation to our *understanding* (and misunderstanding) and the variegated interests and purposes we have as human beings. The lack of such an important conceptual distinction is arguably the single strongest motivation for the attractiveness of certain kinds of foundationalist or metaphysical investigations 'urges' related to perplexing and sentimental kinds of wondering.[15]

Connective analysis: mapping the logical terrain

Whilst elucidation highlights contextual grammars, in order to further avoid the kinds of essentialist fallacies highlighted, or at least to gain a better insight into how we easily trip up around them, another useful approach is to plot a 'connective analysis'. What this looks like in practice was elaborated by Strawson (1992: 19):

> Let us imagine ... the model of an elaborate network, a system, of connected items, concepts, such that the function of each item, each concept, could, from a philosophical point of view, be properly understood only by grasping its connections with the others, its place in the system – perhaps better still, the picture of interlocking systems of such a kind.

Plotting the relationships in this network of concepts allows us to have some sense of oversight (*übersichten*)[16] on the related problems in the uses of a word. Hacker (2013a: 449) used the simile of 'a map' to explain the method:

> [What we need is] ... a map of the conceptual landscape that will show us how to find our way around. We need to call to mind the familiar uses of the words

that lie at the heart of our confusions and unclarities, to plot their complex logical relationships, and to note their position in their grammatical environment.

[my inserted text]

In so doing, we aim at 'finding and inventing intermediate links' which is of *fundamental* importance for us in developing an understanding of how we look at the world and how it is represented through our conceptual schema (*PI* §122). The way we approach this task depends on the *purpose* at hand and thereby, the specific *mode* we are in. For example, Hacker (2013a: 438) distinguishes between the 'linguistic mode', where the focus is on the linguistic terrain, that is, the 'web of words' versus the 'conceptual mode', where the focus is on the network of concepts.

In the linguistic mode, the aim is to obtain an overview of the uses for a given *word*. The distinction is made clearer by way of an example. In the case of 'good', an investigation in the linguistic mode would include all the uses of 'good' as a word, i.e. both for humans as well as for things (i.e. broadly, generally). However, in the *conceptual* mode the focus is on the web of concepts. This seeks to provide 'an overview of the structure of our conceptual scheme and of logico-grammatical relations between its elements' (Hacker, 2013a: 12). Thus, in the conceptual mode, the interest is far tighter. We would need to consider a more specific level of investigation, considering applications and uses of 'good' in the context of human beings in the web of concepts and the complex kinds of logical relations (and problems) with those other concepts. For a similar example, the concept of 'good' in the case of human beings is logically related to other concepts such as morality, agency, judgements, etc. (as opposed to useful, efficient, acceptable). This approach helps to highlight to us that there is a distinct set of logical relations when applying the concept of good to human beings versus *things* (a point I raise again in Chapter 4). A hardened psychopath could, however, use the concept of good for persons and things in equivocal ways – as if one's conception of human beings was simply as something to be used as a means to an end, as an object. This reinforces the points already made with regard to the flexibility of our words. It also further highlights the importance of context and purpose in making a judgement on the appropriate grammar for a given concept. Finally, it highlights the normative (rule-bound) and axiological dimensions of our conceptions of humanness.[17]

To be clear, in this connective analysis of a given concept, we would then need to consider the specific, occasion-sensitive nature of 'concrete cases' alluded to by Wittgenstein (*BB*, 19). This would then elicit the ability in the philosopher to make an effective judgement or clarification regarding appropriate uses and *ways of seeing* when tackling a particular kind of aporia (or philosophical perplexity). In so doing, the philosopher is freed from the grip of his or her personal 'disquietudes' (*PI* §111), assuming there are some. Thus, the focus of a philosophical aporia cannot always be ameliorated by some clear, abstract, analytical, or definitional analysis – a focus which is first and foremost intellectual. It could also aim to address people from where they are. The issues I raise in this book are widespread across our language, but an epistemic angst of this sort, that is, a philosophical sort, may only be 'person-relative' (Baker, 2004: 6); it is shaped by our personal experiences, our history, insights, biases, frames of mind and thought-processes. Taking Wittgenstein at his word that tackling philosophical problems is similar in one sense to the work of psychoanalysis (cf. Baker, 2004: 181), as far as is practicable, the therapy should therefore be tailored to the individual. This is why an analysis of this sort (i.e. this book) has important limitations. It is intended to be a provocation and a beginning to address some of the fundamental problems in our language when thinking about human flourishing, but it is not an end in itself. It is an invitation to a community of inquiry.[18]

Aspect-seeing and objects of comparison

This then brings me neatly onto the notion of *aspect-seeing*, and relatedly, the method of *objects of comparison*. I will use Freud's concept of the 'unconscious'[19] as an object of comparison. I am not, however, interested in the theoretical aspects of the unconscious which suggest hidden sexual or other biological drives or some other mystical or metaphysical phenomena. Rather, I am interested here in the shifting of perceptual perspectives and, by way of a simile with the concept of the unconscious; namely, by explorations of that which passes us by because we take it for granted as a given. As Culbertson (2015: 14) suggests:

> ...pushing aspects to the background can lead to us becoming blind to them altogether. Or, to put it another way, pulling a certain aspect to the fore can lead us to being gripped by a particular picture to the point that we seem incapable, or at least have great difficulty, in seeing things other ways.

An exploration of new conditions or settings has the effect of throwing light on a topic hereto taken for granted due to being over-familiar with a particular concept in a particular kind of setting. It was a core method of Wittgenstein's in his approach to helping readers to understand the problems he raised. For

Figure 2 'Kaninchen und Ente' ('Rabbit and Duck') a.k.a the 'Duck-Rabbit'.

example, in *PPF* §118, Wittgenstein explores Jastrow's use of the Duck-Rabbit illusion[20] and in so doing, he alludes to the fact that something can be viewed as one (a duck) or the other (a rabbit) or both (see Figure 2). Equally, one may have seen it as a duck (or rabbit) without the awareness that it could have been either. One can be blind to one aspect of the duck-rabbit.

In this context then, the concept of the unconscious is useful for a number of reasons: firstly, what is 'unconscious' by definition is *out of scope* of conscious awareness, and thus away from the scrutiny of the senses. This is somewhat of a similar concept (though by no means equivocal) to the concept of instincts in animals, for animals have little rational control of their impulses. Similarly, the kinds of problems that tend to grip researchers lead them towards particular ways of seeing. The aim of using an object of comparison in this way then, is to see things anew, not in the sense that there is any new information per se, but in the sense that new information has become *apparent to us*: '... [w]e want to understand something that is already in plain view' (*PI* §89). The alternative way of viewing a given object of comparison then becomes a new kind of 'yardstick' with which to *evaluate,* test and reconsider a problem (*PI* §131). Of course, as Baker (2004: 190) suggested, this may well lead to discovery of 'fresh problems', certainly if the new aspect is viewed dogmatically. However, the entire point of the new aspect is to highlight the problem of the former aspect, *not* to replace it with a new one. The imperative here is to evade the craving for 'generality' (*BB* 1991: 18; cf. *PI* §104) and to 'look and see' at the particular case in light of the problematic *suppositio falsi* in order to make such problems perspicuous. The usefulness of such a juxtaposition then is stated explicitly by Baker (2004: 190):

> In comparison with standard philosophical analysis, 'our method' is truly extraordinary: juxtaposing pictures with pictures, seeking to reveal no more (and no less!) than new aspects or patterns or orders.

For various reasons, researchers and philosophers tend to conflate the conceptual with the empirical, perhaps partially because we feel certainty about some basic facts of living, that is. facts like: the sun rises and sets, that we breathe oxygen, and that what goes up *must* come down (i.e. because of the laws of gravity) etc. Indeed, these are facts we can rely on, but because concepts appear to be mapped onto an objective reality (following a representationalist conception) we also feel that there *must* be an answer to questions of conceptual nature that are equally as clear cut and reliant on the empirical world reality that we have so much faith in; they *must* mean one thing, or another; they appear not to be able to be both. This is related to what Wittgenstein (*PI* §352) suggested (in speaking of such an urge for simplicity) when he said:

> ...our thinking plays us a strange trick. That is, we want to quote the law of excluded middle and say: "Either such an image floats before his mind, or it does not; there is no third possibility!".

Due to this tendency for 'fact'-based rigidity of thinking, being misled by certain analogies and pictures can lead to what Baker (2004: 268) calls 'aspect-blindness'. So, for example, in the case of the 'duck-rabbit', we may only see one because of a set of suppositions which means (for us) that we are inclined to see one, and not the other. In the case of a concept like human flourishing, perhaps partially due to the etymological nature of the concept which implies floral growth from a seed, we presuppose that there is an essential human nature and, following from that, a common trajectory for human growth, development, success and wellness which we need to empirically discover; however, As Wittgenstein remarked:

The existence of the experimental method makes us think that we have the means of getting rid of the problems which trouble us; but problem and method pass one another by.

PPF §371

Problems occur when 'language goes on holiday' (*PI* §38); that is to say, when language fails to its work. Nevertheless, the work of research and data capture and interpretation carries on regardless. Slogans like these (as well as the well-known slogan, 'the meaning of a word is its use' (*PI* §42) among others) are not ends in themselves but offer us a way of looking at things afresh by stimulating new ways of looking at things. Thus, although some general remarks may be stated confidently about how humans in general, flourish, there is a risk of facile over-simplification. The kinds of things that human beings are (in the sense of how we ascribe that concept) is incredibly diverse, and the kinds of things we *flourish in* is nuanced, particular, and dependant on the purpose and context of the question at hand (i.e. the criteria for judgements). If we do not keep the multitudinous range of language-games in mind for the diverse uses of our concepts, we are likely to be misled asking 'What is?' type questions (*PI* §24) and to seek a simple bullet list answer. That is to say, the method doesn't always fit the problem or the question aiming to be addressed. What is needed is a new way of conceptualizing the problem and thereby, possible solutions which lie before us, that are otherwise hidden in plain sight, may become clear and perspicuous. But this means we should develop a certain willingness to consider other ways of being and thinking:

> A man will be imprisoned in a room with a door that is unlocked and opens inwards; as long as it does not occur to him to pull rather than push it.
>
> *CV* 42

What I hope for is a) that readers will be willing to consider alternate ways of thinking and being, but also b) that this book will be a useful resource that will be helpful with addressing your particular set of problems or concerns, personal, or professional. As rational and responsible agents, then, before we can be liberated from the tricks and bewitchment of our language through those kinds of misleading pictures or analogies, we need to see for *ourselves* the kind of urges we tend to have for certain kinds of rigidity and generality in our modus operandi or habits of thought. Such a transformation in perspective may take place in a moment in what Wittgenstein calls, the 'liberating word' (*BT, 2005:* 302e).

Summative remarks

In summary, I have suggested here that there is no finite list of methods appropriate to tackling the range of problems identified. Rather, taking the analogy of a false picture as a form of illness in the mind, and taking the approach advocated by Wittgenstein, a multiplicity of methods is recognized, 'different therapies' as it were (*PI* §133, and cf. *PI* §255). One important way forward is by locating a word in context, and thereby in a set of conceptual relations (according to the language-game being used or applied). Further, the method of juxtaposition, comparison and contrast of certain lucid pictures, set alongside misleading pictures, may assist in order to elucidate and highlight similarities and differences between various applications of a word or indeed, ways of seeing the world. This methodological practice helps to order (or create) new language-games, connections, or intermediate links (cf. *PI* §122 and Baker, 2004: 292), and thereby contributes to sense, meaning, insight and understanding.

My core aim here is to identify where we have been led down unhelpful paths in our ways of thinking so that we may know 'how to go on' from here, not in some trivial or insignificant sense, but in a 'person-specific', (cf. McFee, 2015: 25) occasion-sensitive (cf. Travis, 2008) and thereby, a transformative sense; for the end goal here is nothing less than liberation from problems related to misunderstandings, and/or any associated anxiety of this philosophical problem. We'll know when we have arrived at that place of transformation by the end of this book, at which point this particular set of problems should no longer trouble us (cf. *PI* §133), at least not in the same ways.

3

Humanness

The term 'humanness', appears at once odd and it is not an everyday phrase by any stretch of the imagination. Yet, it does a good job at highlighting a subtle and implicit set of assumptions and understanding about an essential human nature, or quality thereof, within some of the literature on human flourishing. Therefore, the central aim and purpose of this chapter will be to reveal some of the linguistic and conceptual confusions that can mislead us when deploying the concept of humanness and related terms, rather than fully exploring a positive account of what human nature might be. This is important because a conception of human nature that relies on a notion of a discreet and hidden essence such as human dignity, rationality, biology or self-hood is bound to result in a limited, fragile and facile conception of human flourishing that is parasitic on those putative essences being instrumentally or formulaically elevated, enhanced or increased.[1] Such reductive moves amount to a neglect of the importance of normativity in the ascription of such terms as humanness or human nature. Hence, the focus of this chapter will be to highlight salient uses and features for the relevant conceptual landscape of humanness and to make these more explicit.

In this chapter, I will show how reductive approaches to humanness (evident in four key targets for this book: essentialism, subjectivism, reductionism and scientism) are conceptually problematic and incoherent. I am interested here in a philosophical exploration of the web of words in which we conceive of ourselves and our natures, with the aim of achieving a surveyable overview of the conceptual terrain on *humanness* and the problematic relationship with human flourishing. That is not to suggest that I will provide a comprehensive or exhaustible account of humanness or human nature (as if that were possible), nor will it be to propose a theory of human-ness; rather it will be to remind us of the central ways in which we use 'human-ness', human, and related terms in their diverse guises. The purpose here is one ordering among many possible orders or orderings, with the aim to marshal reminders of some of the relevant bewitchments of our language with the concept of human flourishing (cf. *PI* §127). Whilst some general conceptual connections and observations will be important here, this work can only be understood to any depth with reference to *specific* occasions of use. In this chapter therefore, I will highlight some generic observations regarding uses central to the concept of human-ness, but I will support these by elucidatory cases where apt, in order to demonstrate the primacy of normativity and occasion-sensitivity in our uses of the word or related conceptions of humanness.

Chapter sections

In section one ('Human-ness: a survey') I will begin with an exploratory connective analysis for the main *uses* of 'human' and its cognates (human-ness, dehumanize, humanity, human nature etc.) in order to support obtaining a surveyable representation of the concept (*PI* §122). That should help give us a clearer overview for the meaning of the word of 'human' and 'human-ness' in the various *contexts* of use.

In section two, ('Essences and resemblances') I will aim to answer whether reducing humanness to a human essence makes any sense in light of the normativity of the concept and what can be shown through cases of occasion-sensitivity. Whilst essentialism aims to raise the primacy of the essences of things, here I will aim to highlight the primacy of normativity and the wide array of family resemblance uses for the term 'human' and its cognates.

In section three ('Qualities, capacities and measures') I will explore the conceptual landscape of 'rationality'. I will show how, although rationality can be said to be a key feature of human-ness, this is not the same thing as an *essence* because losing some or all of our rationality can no more deprive us of our humanness than can being born without the possibility for developing rationality at all (e.g. due to some serious congenital condition). I will therefore show how humanness cannot be reduced to rationality neither can it be some *quality* which can be measured, increased, decreased or lost.

Finally, in section four, ('The "Self", the Inner and the Outer') I build on some remarks made earlier in the Introduction on options of the 'Self'. I begin with an exploration of the general uses and problems associated with a Dualist concept of the 'Self'. I also address the notions of private and privileged access to one's own thoughts and feelings as conceived within the highly misleading 'inner-outer' dyad.

Human-ness: a survey

Figure 3 highlights the numerous uses of the concept of 'human'. These abound within theoretical (usually compound) concepts where the concept of *human* in them and where the humanness is the focal concept; for example, human-capital, human-capability theory, human-migration, human-population, human-genome, human-embryology, humanitarian, human-resources etc. The central link between them and perhaps the most notable use of humanness is when we speak of human beings (and related concepts such as human organism, humankind, humanoid, hominid, mankind, *Homo sapiens*) to identify what distinguishes the human race as a *biological* living species from other living beings; namely, from the animal kingdom. The context will dictate the sense in the use or comparison and so humans may also be compared with inanimate objects like statues (e.g. 'he's built like a Greek god') or machines (e.g. 'He works all day long – he's like a machine'). However, these uses will usually be applied humourously, sardonically or metaphorically.

The scientific categories of humanness tend to focus on our biological characteristics. For example, in speaking of *hominid* we assume a particular theory of the development of mankind as a species of ape, thus in an evolutionary sense (Goodman et al., 1990). Similarly, in speaking of *Homo sapiens* we might be relying on evolutionary principles and categories with regards to particular stages in human development as a species (Nowell, 2010). We might speak of *proto-humans*, being those humans who lived around 2.5 million years ago, as compared with *modern humans*, the species of human (of which we are part) that had developed since then.

In this sense we might use the term 'humanity' for the current developmental position of modern man over time. Thus, there are numerous terms related to humanness which are linked to scientific theories and consequently will have a range of associated contingent concepts that help give them their meaning within the bounds and limits of theoretical validity (such as microevolution, natural selection or speciation etc.). So, if one of these core concepts is proven weak in terms of validity the whole theory is shaken because the grounds, or premises on which the theory rests, are disturbed. In one sense then, such terms may eventually be proven weak in their power to support particular theory-based arguments, but they are nonetheless not particularly problematic (at least insofar as their respective theoretical criteria are straightforward for measuring their validity). However, whether we can reduce humanness to a biological essence is doubtful; we are more than the sum of biological functions

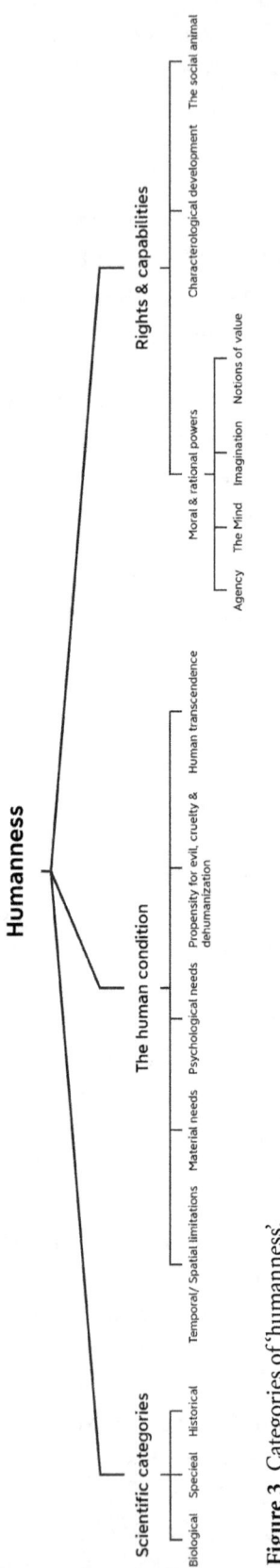

Figure 3 Categories of 'humanness'.

and processes. Admittedly we do tend to share the same likeness and basic features, capabilities etc. But that appears far too general to be worthy of comment. We must wonder which criteria we can use to ascribe human-ness then? Does having an opposable thumb make us uniquely biologically human? Is it this physical capacity that affords us the unique ability to make tools and develop societies? Arguably not, for people born disabled or with physical impairments are perfectly able to adapt with aids to use their hands in like manner.

There is also a range of terms which point to the complex predicament of humanity, or our *human condition*. For example, being subject to the concept of time, we are said to be impacted by a range of temporal concepts such as conception, birth, growth, development, physical or mental pain and anguish, healing and restoration, death and the after-life. Being human means in part having a physical body, so we have basic physical needs such as food, water and shelter, and we can suffer in terms of physical and or mental health if we lack these. Having a body made of soft flesh, and not, say, hardened scales, also means that we are susceptible to being injured and harmed. Thus, we are said to live precariously until we die.

We also talk of being *merely human*, that is, in speaking of behaviour that is *typical* of being human, such as being prone to human error or having a human nature, that is being filled with the full range of human passions and pride etc. We similarly talk about being a *flawed* human being, that is, someone who is typical of their species, i.e. fallible, imperfect, prone to err. In this use there is a hidden standard comparing humans to the alleged perfection of the 'gods' or some other normative standard above and beyond what is said to be humanly possible (most notable in the Greco-Roman and Judaic conceptions of a god or the one God).

When we speak about someone acting as humanely as possible, we mean that they are acting with as much mercy and compassion as is possible under the circumstances, which might be one where a person is pressed under some kind of moral dilemma. For example, a doctor in a war-torn hospital might have to decide who to help and who to leave alone to die. As a human being we can also be said to be *especially* human, that is, despite flaws typical of being a human, someone who loves and was loved by others and who expressed the full range of human abilities (particularly, in the sense of the application of moral powers). We can also be said to love the gentleness of the human touch (or be averse to it); and in seeing a human face we can respond emotionally to physical tenderness. Being self-aware of our predicament means that we are prone to having feelings and emotional states of mind, such as hopes and dreams, fears, likes and joys, and we are also able to be objects and subjects of affection and love.

Further, in saying that someone is being inhumane or inhuman, we mean that they are acting in ways that are cruel and unforgiving, or *less than* human. Likewise, in behaving sub-humanly, we mean someone who acts in a beastly manner, impulsively or lacks rationality, like an animal. Relatedly, in dehumanizing another, we mean treating someone *less than* human or less than a human deserves (e.g. breaching their basic dignity). In this sense, dehumanizing someone misleadingly suggests a sense of *loss* of some-thing, some feature or some essential quality of humanness (e.g. dignity). Equally, by re-humanizing someone we mean to reintegrate them back into normal human life; but these uses point to *metaphorical* uses, not metaphysical ones. These *uses* point to the fact that humans are social creatures, and as such we are said to have *social needs*, needs which nudge us towards building social relations, norms and conventions. As a consequence of the challenge to balance our particular needs (and those of our families, kindred-folk or nations), we are prone to fight for resources and leverage for power in our multitudinous forms of politics.

Relatedly, we speak of the human will, human freedom and human liberty, human agency and human autonomy; all of which are fundamental concepts related to the normative concept of *human rights*. The notion of human rights rests on our universalist views of humans being in possession of an essential feature, and a fundamental *human dignity*. As important as these concepts are, and they are *vitally* important in a literal sense, one must wonder why we would feel the need to base such significant concepts on a fragile, essentialist conception of human nature. Having human *capabilities* means that we possess the unique physical or mental human capacities to develop the full range of human abilities such as rationality, agency, imagination and complex emotions (cf. Hacker, 2007a). But these capacities are not essences; that would be a leap too far. Being an agent with the capability of making rational choices means that we have the option to make decisions on a daily basis, standardly-speaking. Consequently, we are also said to display certain human *strengths* or *flaws* of character, (virtues and vices) as well as errors and defects in our discernments and judgements. But rationality is equally problematic if we are to take this as our human essence, because we are certainly not reducible to rationality or reason (although our *ability* to reason through language is arguably our distinguishing feature). Similarly, having a *human mind* means having the capacity for complex and abstract thought. Possessing a human consciousness means in part, to have complex powers and capabilities of self-awareness, memorization, self-identity and agency. Further, having such capacities means that we strive for *human greatness*; indeed, the monumental achievements of our *human civilization* (including its tragedies) are linked with the complex fabric of our history and identity (or histories and identities).

As humans, we are prone to creating human *hierarchies* of value benefiting those humans who reach a particular status (or closer to it) and so we create legal systems to help mitigate disparities of justice generated in those systems. Primates clearly don't develop such complex systems but who's to say they don't have other systems which help maintain social equilibrium? They too develop social relationships and friendships.[2] Relatedly, is the ability to achieve human happiness and being desirous to seek meaning, pleasure and fulfilment. But is the desire for happiness unique to humans? In deploying a concept like human flourishing, we usually mean that through hardship and challenge, we are the kind of being that can succeed, grow and develop, set goals and realize our own potential. This too reflects a system of normative (rather than essential) values. Chimpanzees do not only perceive the '... surface behavior of others' but also understand intentions, goals and perceptions of other chimps too (Call & Tomasello, 2008). Why can they not also flourish? Of course they can, but *as* chimpanzees.

We also have a range of concepts that suggest a sense of *scale* of human-ness, that is, conceived of as being placed either beyond or below a standard of human-ness. For example, we speak of being super-human (that is, like a god); or transhuman (that is, going beyond normal human capacities and abilities, standardly through some form of technological or genetic enhancement). Largely these adaptations or enhancements are in the realm of science fiction. Nonetheless, if anything like them is achieved it will certainly challenge what we mean by humanness so that a new vocabulary will be created to help mitigate the lacuna.

Essences and resemblances

The normative rules for the use of these terms, related in one way or another, to the concept of human-ness, are clearly variegated. We have seen various kinds of biological, theoretical or scientific classifications; normative, cultural or civilizational uses; concepts regarding human values, needs, character, judgements, rights and responsibilities. We have also seen uses that seem to *quantify* the *essence* or unique *quality* of humanness with misleading implications for some-'thing' (called human-ness) that can be reduced, lost or amplified.

One central feature that links these uses in their multitudinous forms is that the concept of 'human' is either the subject and/or the object in every case; if the conceptual scheme of humanness were a story, then the 'human' being would be the protagonist. But is this enough to say that we have some form of defining characteristic here? Is it justifiable to attribute a form of linguistic or metaphysical essentialism to human-ness, some homogenous quality or feature? One problem with this particular line of reasoning is that it simply cannot be sufficient to suggest that because everything we have seen heretofore refers to humankind, that this then indicates or suggests a central *essence* of human-ness. That would be stretching the usefulness of generality to the extreme. Imagine for a moment if we argued that when we speak of windows, doors, hallways, pipes, roofs, walls, electrical systems, plumbing, support beams, load bearing walls, gutters, breather walls, bricks, mortar, etc. that we speak about things related to *buildings* in the sense that these are component parts of buildings. As true as that is, if we were to ask, 'what about the wiring?', could we then answer: 'of course, I'm talking about buildings' as if to suggest that in responding 'about buildings' an adequate response has been made. This just couldn't do. Something has gone wrong in the language-game here, there has been a *failing* to draw apt distinctions. The concept of an essential humanness does a similar job for what use is it to speak of humanness in these generic ways? The range of uses limits what sense can be made (or claimed) from such a conceptualization.

That said, there is a generic use that is useful in the right context. For example, if the question was on that most general of levels, it could have a use e.g. this might make sense in educating a child about what electrical wiring was. So, if a child was pointing to some exposed wiring they might say 'what about the wiring?', and one could rightly answer that it forms part of the fabric of most buildings (though not all) in order to provide access to electric power for various appliances. But past that, the question is far better answered in responding with precision to the question at hand. The question is perhaps better answered by outlining the *location* of various elements of the wiring system (e.g. 'what about the wiring, where is the X'); or perhaps in asking questions about *where* the plans for the wiring loom are (e.g. 'what about the wiring, where are the plans?'); or *whether* everything is in order (e.g. 'what about the wiring, where are the branch circuits, capacitors, transistors, transformers, panels, ducts?'). Alternatively, *performative* questions could be asked about whether certain jobs have been done (e.g. 'what about the wiring – has the job been done yet?'). In each case, the query is *problem*-driven. There was more information given than at first; the additional information is often implicit in the context and on the occasion of the utterance, rather than spelled out as I have done here. What this aims to show in a rather simple sense is that a term outside of its context is somewhat limitless in potential and possibility; it is the concrete case which helps us to provide a sense of meaning. It enables the very possibility for understanding.

The problem in the case of *humanness* is that it operates implicitly on that kind of generic level. As always, it is within a given context and on a given occasion the meaning may be garnered, and so to simply utter the words here on a page cannot possibly give us the meaning. Nevertheless, for the purpose of this exercise, it is sufficient to use an example like this to highlight the importance of occasion-sensitivity, but also to show that the concepts explored briefly earlier (human rights, *Homo sapiens*, being inhumane, merely human) are in one very *loose* sense conceptually linked with the concept of human-ness, but only in the same way that wiring is linked with a building – in the most general of ways. In fact, *so general* as to render any attempt at finding some linguistic (or metaphysical) essence or homogenous connection pointless. It just doesn't help our understanding any further to think of humanness as a quality or essence. Such a quest is precisely the kind of mistaken endeavour which Culbertson (2007: 209) suggests is a blurring of the important distinctions between, for example, humanness as *behaviour* versus humanness as 'biology'. It amounts to a failing to draw apt conceptual distinctions, which in turn can lead to categorial error.

Instead, it is the *context* and *purpose* of an utterance that matters, and it is that which helps bring meaning to a particular use; there is nothing mystical or essential about it. Any allure here to the concept of humanness can be an example of us being bewitched by our grammar: a 'substantive' misleads us into looking for a mystical 'substance' (cf., Hacker, 2007a: 14). But there is no such 'thing' as humanness any more than there is such a thing as a 'length' (cf. *BB*, p. 1[3]; Baker & Hacker, 2005a: 212). These are grammatical remarks, conventions used in our language for a given purpose, as opposed to some metaphysical entity or essence. Acknowledging this simple truism can help us to avoid category errors and related mistakes.

What *is* useful however, is the very exercise of showing that there are a multitude of uses of human-ness, humanness cognates and related compound phrases and concepts. This is so because it goes some way to demonstrate that humanness is clearly a family resemblance concept; that is, a concept that possesses a 'complicated network of similarities overlapping and criss-crossing' with other concepts (*PI* §66) where we cannot neatly define or reduce it to some *linguistic* or other *essence* or meaning. What we have seen by surveying the conceptual landscape is that humanness has a range of uses which suggest a swathe of inter-related concepts without a homogenous essence, a family of sorts, each of which are linked to the *predicament* of being human, insofar as they refer to those basic features in the family, such as humans being biological animals, kinds of thinking and reasoning creatures, and living beings caught up in the circumstances of a range of physical, psychological and social impingements, having particular strengths and weaknesses etc.[4]

Individuating concepts with 'blurry edges', does not diminish their usefulness any more than talking about plants (in a general sense) requires us to explicate the various minutiae and differentiations between plants (cf., *PI* §70–71). In such cases an indistinct concept is exactly what we need, and humanness is useful for those purposes. This ambiguity is not problematic unless it is a neat definition or essence of humanness is what we seek; however, this is a dead end for most often it is not what we need. What we need (and have) here is simply a generic term for a range of concepts related to human life and this need not be problematic if we are clear about the limits of language. The level of precision required therefore simply depends on the situation, the nature of inquiry and purpose at hand; thus, the acuity and sharpness we seek is brought to light by looking elsewhere, that is, within the *context*, not solely the term and it's signified concept/s.

Qualities, capacities and measures

So far then, we have seen that looking for some sense of essence in our uses of humanness and related cognates is somewhat a fool's errand. Even though there appears to be so much commonality, that is only on the most *general* of levels which has some sense of usefulness as long as we do not then jump ahead to impute humanness (in a strict sense) as the essence of these uses. However, it is worth asking (because many do) about what would happen if we were to try to find some essence to humanness outside of the standard uses of our terms; that is, 'metaphysically' speaking. But there is no sense in speaking about understanding humanness outside of the conceptual boundaries of the ways we conceive of human-ness; this is because the a priori nature of things is pre-determined by our conceptual grammar (*PI* §371) which is 'not a mirror of the scaffolding of the world, but the scaffolding from which we describe the world'

(Hacker, 2013b:12).⁵ Therefore, in exploring this further, I mean to tackle any objectors who might argue that dealing with the family resemblance of humanness is one thing whereas the *real* human essence (as some might claim) is quite something else. Therefore, let's have a *look and see* if we can find some sense of the real essence for humanness that has thus far eluded us in the central feature and distinction of our species, the mind and our capacity for reason.

In seeking out an essence of human-ness, it makes no sense to suggest that the mind exists as a thing outside of language, or indeed to give temporal priority to the mind. What would it be to have a mind with no language? Would that be consciousness minus rationality? Rather, what we *can* say is that because we are the kind of creature that has the capacity to develop linguistic abilities, we can also develop a mind (Hacker, 2007a: 3). In seeking out any putative essence of human-ness, it would be a distraction to look for the nature of the mind which is a composite concept describing a range of abilities in any case, not a 'thing'. Rather, what would be more fruitful is if we look at our *uses* of 'rationality'. But how are we best to understand rationality if we are to seek out some essence. The obvious candidate would be to ask a '*What is*' kind of question – i.e. 'What is rationality?'. But these kinds of questions are misleading for the precise meaning is only made perspicuous by the use within certain logical parameters, and crucially, within the *context* in which a concept is uttered.⁶

As was shown in Chapter 1 the capacity to be rational is a first order human power. Although we are born with the capacity to reason, the *ability* to reason takes time to master through induction and training over time within a community of language-speakers; thus, our rational needs (as opposed to emotional or physical ones) are said to take precedence over the course of life as we mature into adulthood, and we learn the *rules* for use of our terms in our linguistic communities (family, friends, employers, neighbours etc.). So, as children we usually learn that to behave rationally, usually means to conduct oneself in ways conducive to logic, reason and to limit negative emotions etc. (not unproblematically so). Fundamental to the entire possibility for rationality then, is the importance of learning, training, induction, respect, order and mentorship. This helps to show the primacy of convention and normativity and the related links between rationality and our capacity to articulate further refinements in our language.

The development of rationality is also linked to our developed sense of agency and autonomy. Based on what we know or what we believe, weighing knowns against unknowns, cause and effect, we can decide to act or think in certain ways for particular reasons. Doing so, we can make choices which may be deemed as immoral or just, and we can seek truth or accept falsity; we can act selflessly or in our own interest; and we can be persuaded or dissuaded from particular views. In all cases, behaving rationally suggests using one's ability to think and reason in order to come to some reasonable decision.

Conversely, we can also say that someone is lacking rationality, behaving or thinking irrationally, or relatedly, thinking emotionally in making certain judgements about people. For example, we can say that someone who is behaving irrationally is acting brainlessly, densely, half-wittedly, mindlessly, thoughtlessly, obtusely, senselessly, like a vegetable, a robot, machine, or automaton. These uses suggest some kind of judgement about intellectual competence where the contrast is usually intelligence versus stupidity (broadly speaking). Alternatively, we can also have uses which suggest a lack of reasoned grounds (where truth or objectivity is important). For example, when someone is acting or behaving irrationally, we can mean to suggest that someone is behaving unreasonably, disagreeably, or thinking emotionally, illogically, or in a way which is otherwise uncompelling or unconvincing. The comparator here could be a child (who does not yet meet the criteria for the ascription of rationality except in the most basic of senses). Let us therefore consider the following uses and comparisons:

a) In buying the house Judy made a rational (considered and justifiable) decision.
b) George has been under stress for some time and is now unable to think rationally (did not think clearly, but rashly, emotionally).
c) Whilst suffering from a fever, Peter acted irrationally, like an animal (deliriously, without thinking).
d) Jackie, the data typist goes to work every day and does her job without any need for reasoning (like a robot, without the need for thinking).

It should be clear enough that in all these cases (*a–d*) the use suggests a sense of measure. However, more specifically, in cases *a* and *b*, thinking still occurs, albeit in an impaired sense. This suggests the imperfect execution of our ability to reason and entails a sense of missing the mark (quantitatively, admitting of degrees, how much we think or reason). More troubling however, in cases *c* and *d*, these uses suggest a distinct lack or *loss* of the ability of thinking (qualitatively, the *absence* of thinking or reasoning).

The important thing to consider here is what follows of suggesting that someone has lost part or all of their rationality (whether in terms of degree of totality) – for example, by virtue of comparing them with animals or automata. If we take rationality to be the elusive essence of human-ness, then the implications are that someone can be 'de'-humanized, that is, can lose their humanness inasmuch as they lose their rationality – whether quantitatively or qualitatively. The ethical implications are obviously wide-reaching including for foetuses or infants, those with low or severely impaired IQ, some disabled, the severely mentally ill and others. Thus, although it can rightly be said that rationality is one of the central features of human distinction (in terms of complexity perhaps), pinning the essence of humanness to rationality is reductive, excessive and ethically problematic. It is far more satisfactory to say that rationality is standardly (but not always) a feature, a power, or a capability of humans, and that a person's abilities to be rational can be developed or impaired. These are conceptual truisms about normative standards and nothing to do with any metaphysical or hidden essences of human-ness. But again, any useful answer to a question will depend on the context and purpose at hand and a different answer could be given in cases where, for example, the kind of rationality which affords us the ability to develop written language systems, which is clearly unique (though still not an essence); we are more than the sum of our parts.

In the following section I will begin with an exploration of the problems associated with the essentialist and dualist concept of the 'Self' including addressing the notions of private and privileged access to one's own thoughts and feelings as conceived within the highly misleading 'inner-outer' dyad.[7] This leads to an unfortunate and misguided obsession with so-called 'Inner' truths and 'real' selves prominent within humanistic circles. I will finish with a brief analysis of the problems with scientistic accounts of human nature and show that biology is only *part* of what it is to be human. This is important to help dispel the notions that we are reducible to various parts and that these parts are amenable to scientific investigation in order to make generalizations about 'whole' human nature; thus, I will show how the scientistic accounts of humanness are excessively reductive and conceptually conflationary.

The 'Self', the Inner and the Outer

The concept of 'Self' and how it relates to 'personhood' is complex. We have a physical body and a mind which permits us to have a range of human powers, yet we are not identical with our bodies or minds. The Self is connected to a range of psychological concepts such as personhood, consciousness, identity, perception, knowledge, belief, agency etc. We are said to possess a unique personal identity with personal needs, wants, opinions, views, motivations, emotions, drives, ambitions, individual tastes, views, morals, beliefs, memories etc. Further, the Self is also tied to a range of social and legal concepts and as a person it can be said that we are an entity with a political identity with social and legal status. At least in the Western tradition, this will usually mean someone who is entitled to individual rights, liberty, agency and recognition of dignity under law.[8] Conversely, certain criminals, prisoners or terrorists are denied aspects of their personhood because they may have been deemed to have transgressed the fundamental rules of a community. Persons categorized as such can lose their citizenship (as in the recent case of Shamima Begum, the 'ISIS bride');[9] their rights to access to certain elements of the justice system (such as voting rights for prisoners); or their rights to a public fair trial (as in cases of breaches of Martial law in the United States of America).

In cases of international politics, diplomats can also be deemed as *persona non grata* (that is, someone no longer recognized as having diplomatic protections or rights). Similarly, within certain religious communities (such as Mormon, Catholic, Amish) members can be excommunicated for breaches of community rules and norms. These are examples of sanctions being used against persons who are refused access to aspects of their personhood; or more particularly, denial of a specific conception of what it is to be or what *counts as* a person within a given community.

In extreme cases, such as in Nazi Germany, certain sections of the population were treated as de-humanized enemies of the state, that is, as enemies of the public, non-persons, animals or automata (such as Jews, Slavs, disabled, political dissidents and other excluded groups). During the disintegration of Yugoslavia in the 1990s, the Bosniaks, Serbs and ethnic Albanians were ethnically cleansed in Herzegovina and Kosovo. Contemporaneously, moralizing public discourse may be deployed for political purposes, such as the pejoratives of 'conspiracy theorists', COVID-deniers, or 'COVIDIOTS' which have been used as terms of abuse, to describe those who are seen as being excessively suspicious of authority (even paranoid) or who go against public health advice amidst the coronavirus outbreak.[10] Whether any criticism is justified (or not) for what may be deemed as socially irresponsible behaviour, the very nature of these weaponized terms are Othering, demonizing, dehumanizing and polarizing – often leading to direct denials of social status for those groups. Importantly for the point here, such terms of abuse are used to create a social environment of hostility and thereby a political environment which can justify all manner of social sanction, segregation and persecution against political dissidents. In other words, toxic political language provides the conditions for populational abuse and totalitarianism. The legal aspects of the concept of personhood ascription are, therefore, real and tangible. No matter what someone may *think* or conceive of themselves, in terms of *Self* or identity, the legal concept of personhood is always a qualified right of ascription which can be gained, lost, or removed within a community context where adjudicatory powers are held, whether political or religious etc.

On the individual level, we can say that we 'love ourselves' when we look after our physical bodies, seek out positive experiences and do not accept harmful influences in our lives (or at least aim to limit them). It can also be used to signify vanity of course. This phrase is often used within interpersonal and relational contexts where someone is (or is not) deemed to be sufficiently careful with their choice of lovers or relationships. Similarly, in dangerous contexts we say that 'self-perseveration' is vital if we are to stay alive, so we seek food, shelter and other basic securities. Relatedly, we can also say that we are 'self-destructive' when we fail to look after our basic physical or security needs, such as if we act in dangerous or erratic ways, take illicit drugs or place ourselves in otherwise needlessly precarious situations.[11]

There is also another set of uses which refer more to the reflective abilities we have as individuals. For example, we speak of 'selfishness' or 'selflessness' (which imply various degrees of a scale of narcissism and altruism). Likewise, we say that someone is *self-motivated* when they are able to push themselves to undertake particular actions (usually in the context of self-improvement) despite all of the standard kinds of de-motivations that beguile most human beings from one time or another, such as laziness, apathy, depressiveness, lethargy, lack of focus or drive etc. When we talk of someone being 'self-effacing' we use the phrase in cases where someone presents themselves deprecatingly in public. When we talk of someone having 'self-mastery' we usually mean that they know something about themselves or have developed a particularly advanced skill set in controlling their emotions which suggests a certain degree of reflective and emotional intelligence. As shown already, the criteria for such ascriptions are *public* and *sharable* and not reduceable to subjective opinion or feelings regarding personal motivations, intentions or thoughts (cf. *PI* §337).

An exemplar case for normativity

In order to help to draw attention to the importance of public criteria, I would now like to present a hypothetical case for how a few people (let's call them Oliver, Erin and Dai) deal with a challenge in the workplace. For instance, let's say that Erin is in a situation at work where he might be particularly troubled by his new manager (Oliver) who is, for all intents and purposes, considered to be quite difficult to work with. The difficulty is caused by the fact that Oliver is new to the company, and he is quite keen to make an impression and an impact. He asks frequent questions and makes various requests for tasks, often causing disruption to existing work-flows without allowing sufficient time for said tasks to be completed. The behaviour seems erratic to both Erin and Dai (employees under Oliver) and it makes work challenging for both. Consequently, Dai reacts by gossiping and taking any opportunity to undermine Oliver. Dai often responds to Oliver's various requests in an abrupt and curt manner, even though Oliver is his superior. Dai gets away with this because he is a long-term employee having served for twenty-plus years at the company.

Despite the apparent inappropriate behaviour towards a superior, Dai *tells himself* and others, that he tries hard to get along with his new boss and states to other colleagues that he *feels* as though he is being extremely patient with Oliver because he could do a lot more to make his life difficult at work if he wanted, for example, make official complaints. In this case, although Dai is at liberty to make such a complaint (as there may be grounds), he does not appear to be demonstrating self-mastery. This is because, as difficult as the situations might be, he is clearly behaving in a reactive manner to whatever situations arise, thus losing some sense of rationality and objectivity. Alternatively, when Erin is questioned by Oliver, she responds with patience and etiquette, she actively listens, and reflects and paraphrases in order to show understanding and respect. Thus, although Dai *feels* like he is being patient (a key criterion for ascriptions of self-mastery and indeed, professionalism) it is clearly Erin who can more accurately be said to meet many of the public criteria for 'self-mastery'.

Similarly, at risk of labouring the point, Seamus *claims* to love Sorcha dearly. They met five years ago and Sorcha has moved away from her community and family in order to live with Seamus. They both have careers and talk of owning their own home and having children. However, Seamus continually mistreats her (physically, emotionally etc.). For example, he is often impatient, shouts at her, humiliates her by calling her names and at times is physically violent. Further, he expects her to be grateful that she is with him and manipulates her into believing that she is the cause of all of the problems in the relationship. Sorcha is understandably deeply unhappy but is afraid to leave him because he has threatened her numerous times.

The trouble with a putative *self*-ascription of love for another is that it must be tested against the criteria for one of the language-games of love. In our culture, the concept of love is interdependent on a range of other concepts and is 'embedded' in our cultures, conventions and linguistic practices. It is woven through the fabric of life. For example, the criteria for the concept of love *must* include consideration of well-being, treating someone well, caring for them, behaving tenderly and performing acts of self-sacrifice when needed etc. If it did not then it would not be the concept of love. A personality trait, skill, emotion or attitude is not epistemically authoritative because one *thinks* patiently, attentively, politely or, for example, loves in their mind secretly. Rather the evidence for such ascription is in what *they do* and *enact* (i.e. through their behaviour); an inner process is standardly in need of outward criteria for such an ascription (cf. *PI* §580).[12]

Summative remarks

We conceive of the world in far more effective ways when we pay particular *attention* to our uses for the meaning is often evidence in its use (*PI* §43). What I have aimed to achieve with this chapter is to provide a surveyable representation of the concept of humanness (*PI* §122) in order to see how essentialist notions of human flourishing based on such notions make no sense. This is helpful for the entire book in order to expose the traps of meaningless philosophical formulations so that what was formerly thought of as a philosophical problem may disappear (*PI* §133). The quest to raise the primacy of the essences of things has been shown to be misguided. Rather, because of the range of uses with criss-crossing similarities with other uses on the most general of levels, humanness is arguably a family resemblance concept without any such homogenous focal point. We are biological, yes, but importantly, we are *social* beings with sophisticated rational and moral powers. This isn't an essence, it's an innate potential for all human beings. Crucially, it is an ability that may be nurtured or inhibited dependent on the beneficence of the social structures and systems we are fortunate enough to have been mentored into. Hence, in the search for a resolution to our essentialist confusions, we should therefore not only be interested in man as *Homo sapiens* (man as a self-knowing, biological being) but in man as *Homo loquens* (man as a concept-deploying creature within a community of language-speakers).

The *recognition* of innate human potential, then, has significant ethical implications for our understanding of human flourishing, for it is in the responsible nurturing of the right *conditions* for flourishing (i.e. recognizing human agents as social beings with complex rational and moral powers) that we then are enabled to create opportunities for others to engage with life well, and to enact their unique sets of skills and abilities. A basic recognition of human *dignity* is at the heart of any serious concern for human welfare. The development of human rights also happens to be one of the cornerstones of Western civilization. It is when human dignity is (socially, politically, economically) recognized that flourishing can meaningfully occur. It is to the central concept of interest then, that of 'human flourishing', that I now turn.

4

A Sketch of Human Flourishing

The concerns raised in the introductory chapter focus on the problems with reductive approaches to understanding terms like human flourishing. I suggest here that human flourishing *appears* to be a complex problem largely because of a dearth in awareness of the plurality of uses for the phrase 'human flourishing'. There is a failing to acknowledge that our problems are largely conceptual. Hence, we tend to resolve apparent confusions with inadequate tools to begin with seeking instead to resolve such problems through empirical or theoretical means.

The phrase of human flourishing is, however, a concept that is related to a cluster of concepts centred around what it is to be the specific *kind* of being that we are, as well as what it is for this kind of being to 'do well' in life, that is, to succeed in life. These simple truisms are not independent facts in the world; nor are they subjective feelings in our minds. Hence, they cannot be researched outside of their particular context of use. These truisms (often platitudinous or humdrum) are 'landmarks' in the logical terrain of the concept of human flourishing (cf. Hacker, 2007a: xi). More specifically, they tell a relational story for what it means for humans to flourish within our conceptual schema, for example:

- That we are a unique sentient being on this planet with advanced *two-way powers* of commission and omission; that is, powers to decide to perform a given action, as well as not to perform it;
- That we have unequalled abilities for *learning and development*, which in the natural course of life, we tend to do;
- That we have a need for the *exercise* of those abilities which we have to various degrees according to the application of our will in the midst of the vicissitudes of fortune (under socio-economic and cultural circumstances that are largely out of our control);
- Finally, because we are the developmental kind of being that we are, our chances for success in life are often complicated by our *emotional responses*

to life, our stage of life, our feelings and perception of the world, the ideals and values that drive us through such difficulties.

Because words have various conceptual connections according to context of *use*, they also carry with them a range of potentialities (or at least it can *seem* so when uttered out of a clear context). Thus, within a given context, a word which might typically signify one focal point for a concept, could instead suggest another focus of the same concept, or else a different concept entirely. For example, the use of the word of 'flourish' as a term to suggest a final *burst* of activity in a rugby match, on paper, in a musical score, or with a gesture of the hands in a theatrical play, has an almost completely different set of logical relations when compared with, say, flourishing as a journey of recovery from illness or misfortune. That said, these distinctions need not be so stark and so need not necessarily suggest another concept entirely as the former examples suggest; indeed, there are also differences with uses of flourishing which are more closely related. For example, flourishing as an indicator of character development has a different but closely related set of conceptual relations to the use of flourishing which relates to being happy and doing well; the distinction is slight and reflects more a difference of *emphasis* than concept.

This suggests that whilst a survey of *uses* will be helpful, it is only the beginning. What we really need is a 'surveyable representation' of the concept (cf. *PI* §122) as embedded within a 'web of words', so that complex linguistic connections may become more perspicuous (Hacker, 2007a:11). The benefit of this oversight is that we can better know where we go awry, for example, by gaining insight to where we might conflate the relations between the various uses, or indeed, fail to notice important subtleties and differences. In discussing the conceptual nuances and difficulties related to the concept of flourishing, my aim is therefore is to develop certain kinds of understanding, oversight, or surveyability of the concept and its logical role and space in our language (cf. *PI* §127). This should help us to go beyond *mere* possession of a concept, but further, to gain *philosophical insight* into where we often go wrong when we think about our human nature, what flourishing might be, and indeed, what it is to flourish. In this sense, we aim at grasping the 'salient features' of a concept and the variegated relations between *use* and other 'problematic terms' (cf. Baker & Hacker, 2005a: 284).

At least in part, by making the various forms of flourishing apparent, my aim here will be to show that there is an important intersection between the various *uses* of the concept and the various conceptual relations and points of focus relevant to those uses. That is, each variation might indicate quite stark logical differences. Of course, we could clarify that in any case there is no such thing as *the* concept of human flourishing, but rather, different applications of loosely connected conceptions.[1] We need not fetishize the concept by seeking something that is essential to it. Echoing the importance of occasion-sensitivity and individual cases (à la Wittgenstein & Travis), Hacker (2013a: 232) has stated that there is 'no substitute for attention to the particular'.

All that said, as I will explore further shortly, the connections that I draw on are oriented around the (metaphorical) concept of 'growth'. When speaking about what flourishing might mean in the context of human beings, this is no easy thing to consider. As I will suggest, in the general use of the term, flourishing for human beings amounts to something like a *maturation of character* above and beyond other domains of life with which it is standardly associated – i.e. whether mental or biological health, success, or well-being etc. Of course, there will be practical import to character development; such progress should be evident in the quality of decisions in one's life, and *how well* life is going for one generally. Ultimately, for a human being to flourish means, at least partly, that someone with adequate human powers and abilities, has developed the necessary skill-set for life in a given context. In important senses this amounts to a form of *knowing-how* to live the good life.[2] This will certainly be my focus. That said, due to the vicissitudes of life (largely out of our control) and our variegated responses to the experiences of our lives, this is by no means a settled matter. Nevertheless, I suggest that if we can equip ourselves with the apt *skills for life* then we will be best placed to flourish, and this is what matters because this *is* in our control.

These are not theoretical, dogmatic or doctrinal statements, nor are they essences, they are conceptual and logical truths of the sort that nurture clarity of thought by allowing us space to conceptualize our concern properly in the appropriate categorial domain. This is important to help us to recognize the conceptual relationship between notions of the generalizable (human beings with moral and rational powers) alongside notions of the specific, including insights into the particular set of life-skills and personality traits that helps to shape who we are as agents in the world. The particular relation between these ways of seeing or knowing are specific to a given context where differing emphases are set against the broader criteria subject to the occasion. I suggest that this is how we can navigate the concept of human flourishing effectively, meaningfully, and ethically.

Chapter sections

In terms of how to address these hopes and concerns in this chapter, I will broadly adhere to the following structure.

In section one ('"Flourishing" – a survey of *uses*'), I will begin with a brief survey of the diverse *uses* of the word 'flourishing'. This is important in order to understand the complex range of concepts implied by the uses of the word 'flourishing' that relate often to vastly divergent conceptual relationships e.g. performative, indications of success, and development of 'things' (as opposed to humans) and finally, the flourishing of human beings as a species versus 'persons'.

In section two ('Objects of comparison'), extending some of the work undertaken in the former section, I will then explore some of the central concepts connected to the particular kinds of 'flourishing' that we are most interested in this book. In particular, I will compare human flourishing with happiness and well-being in the context of both ancient (Aristotelian) and modern research approaches to *eudaimonia*, success, happiness and well-being. This section is crucial in order to demonstrate how we err when we conflate flourishing with other related concepts which have substantially differing criteria for use with important distinctions between, for example, misleading dichotomies between notions of subjectivity and objectivity.

In section three ('What flourishing is *not*'), I will then finish with some comments on other important criterial matters, such as what flourishing is *not*. I will do this with reference to Austin's (1962) 'trouser leg' concept in order to analyse how we often have an antonym in mind as the dominant feature of a particular *use*. This will help to elucidate some of the conceptual tensions that are not always apparent or explicit in the various uses of flourishing; this should help us to better grasp what kinds of cases can lead researchers, policy-makers and others into confusion (no doubt helpful if we are to avoid falling into those traps ourselves, as inquirers).

'Flourishing' – a survey of *uses*

Figure 4 is a sketch for the central uses of flourishing (in the linguistic mode) that I will explore further (in the conceptual mode) through the subsequent section and sub-sections. It is crude and non-exhaustive but offers us an indicative map for what I suggest are the central issues at stake, including problems with the conflation of related concepts. One observation, however, is

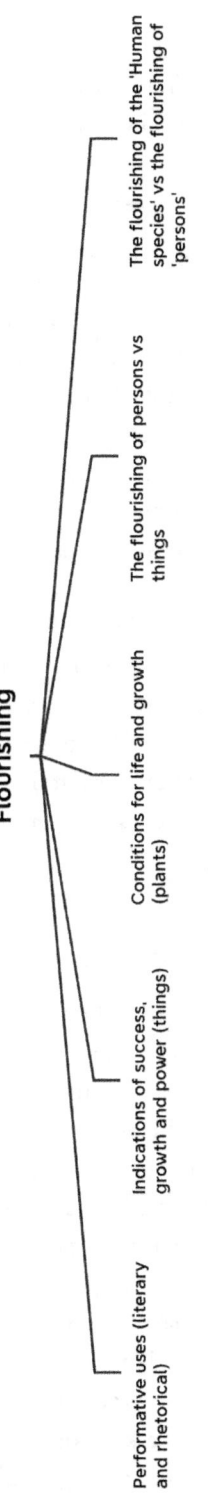

Figure 4 A sketch of flourishing (linguistic mode).

that these uses have some common features relating to 'growth'. What will hopefully become apparent is the *moral* dimension of flourishing when speaking about it in the personal, psychological, human context (i.e. *good* growth). This is important.

Performative uses (literary and rhetorical)

One of the immediate senses of 'flourish' is as a noun, as opposed to a verb, used to describe a stylistic form of expression. This use suggests a sudden burst of intense gestural or oral activity, usually within a literary or thespian context e.g. 'Grace finished with a flourish' or 'George spoke with a flourish'. In such contexts a flourish need not suggest anything good, happy, or positive whatsoever. The form of 'flourish' here (as in, for example, the case of the ending of the book of Shelley's *Frankenstein*) suggests a sense of final, dramatic force, decorative or dramatic finish. Although this can be verbal, written or enacted, this use is only loosely related to the uses we are centrally interested in here, insofar as it relates to the same etymological roots suggesting *active growth*. Nevertheless, such uses are worth a brief mention because of their complex metaphorical and conceptual connections with other more widely known uses (implying vigour, energy, growth etc).[3] This will help to draw the relevant distinctions between those and the cases we *are* interested in, namely, those relating to active, healthy, beneficent, personal growth for human beings.

Indications of success, growth and *power* (things)

Uses of flourishing in the context of *things* (not persons) suggest growth, influence – and in particular – 'power' of political or social units. For example, we say that under certain conditions, various kinds of *communities* (political, cultural, religious) can flourish. But this is not necessarily related to the concept of 'goodness'. Further, a particular kind of Christian culture flourished at Freising and Salzburg just prior to the rise of Charlemagne's power and influence over the interrelated flourishing culture of the Rhine valley (McKitterick, 2008: 120). No doubt, the growth of Charlemagne's Europe was however at the expense of ancient Germanic pagan nations, particularly of northern Europe; thus, any sense of goodness or morality is muted. In any case, such uses cannot simply be reduced to what was 'good' or beneficial for Charlemagne either (in *his* subjective sense). This is not a use that suggests a kind of *personal* or *human* flourishing; rather, this use is meant to indicate that the religiosity of the period contributed to the flourishing of political *culture* of a particular sort; that is, theocracies within an emergent Frankish empire during the period.

In more contemporary times, Whitfield (2004) suggests that for the pre-Second World War progressives in the United States of America (USA), there were social problems in America with the 'inefficiency of institutions that allowed sin to flourish' (2004: 12). Similarly, during the prohibition period in the USA (1920–33), *crime* flourished as mobsters like Al Capone capitalized on public demand for alcohol. This again suggests no morally evaluative mechanism to judge whether one kind of flourishing is either good or bad. With the opportunities that scientific and technological advancements in the future will bring, it is likely that the nations of Asia will flourish at the expense of the West, and in particular, the USA, although this remains a disputed topic (cf. Heinze et al., 2019). In some senses this is a zero-sum game: there is an expense to one nation's flourishing as a result of another's (though as suggested, we must remember that the use of flourishing exemplified here is, ordinarily, *neutral* in terms of moral judgements).[4] *Ideas* can also flourish too. For example, after the explosion of the internet in the 1990s, *conspiracy theories* flourished (communication of ideas in general did). But there is no necessary link between flourishing *ideas* and morality or rationality. It matters not whether flourishing ideas are good, ethical or rational, all that is required is that they grow in popularity, use and influence; indeed, they may flourish *irrespective* of the empirical evidence in support of them or indeed their logical warrant. This can apply equally to religious, political or scientific theories as it can to folk theories, or indeed, some conspiracy theories.[5]

Conditions for *life* and growth (plants)

There is an understandable association, because of the etymological root of 'flower', 'growth', 'bloom' etc., with flourishing, to associate the concept with that which is *conducive* to life. This is nowhere more pronounced than in the uses that relate to *plants*. For example, we say that fruit trees 'flourish *in*' sheltered, moist and sunny climates; whereas geranium can even 'flourish on' high, windy ground. Relatedly, we can also say conditionally that quality cottons do not normally flourish when introduced into non-native countries. The conceptual links to life then, suggest something which is of *benefit* (i.e. 'good') for the plant itself, where matters relating to contributing factors like acidity or mineral levels in the soil, levels of heat, water and oxygen etc. are all important.[6]

Of course, plants don't have the possibility for possession of concepts or conceptions of 'good'. However, the work that the concept of 'good' is doing here effectively amounts to 'healthy for' (i.e. not 'good' in the conventional sense). In the case of plants, there is a sense of what is 'good' for *it* and this is according to our criteria that we set for the good of the plant itself, or perhaps plants around it, e.g. within a garden setting where there is a balanced ecosystem. But this is not a conception of good with a moral dimension. A plant may flourish (like a human culture) at the expense of living organisms around it, such as other varieties of plants in the environment (as is the case of weeds and hence, the need to manage them). The tension between flourishing plants and surrounding varieties then is a matter of human *intervention*, control and management through the various skills, crafts, traditions and knowledge (both tacit and cognitive) as developed within disciplines such as horticulture, agriculture and science. Thus, the focus of what 'good' or 'beneficial' or 'conducive to life' means in these contexts, suggests matters related to the *health* of particular plant varieties, for plants do not have a moral dimension. As such, this is one conception of flourishing that we can share with *all* living beings, including plants and animals. This is because the conditions for the welfare, health and flourishing of human beings, like plants and animals, is fundamentally 'biologically rooted' (cf., Hacker, 2007a: 175).

As we have seen, flourishing (as a metaphor for growth, success, goodness etc.) is a flexible concept in the sense that it can be used to apply to almost anything that lives in some form or another, or at least has the *character* of dynamic change and interaction with its environment. For example, flourishing can be used to express the growth, success or development of an idea, (e.g. global capitalism *flourished* after the Industrial Revolution); a business, (e.g. Monsanto flourished after securing 23 per cent of the global seed market); an economy (e.g. the American economy flourished after the Second World War); a culture (e.g. Viking culture flourished after 790 CE); a person (e.g. Frank flourished as an academic during his PhD); a species (e.g. humans flourished after they discovered fire); a plant (e.g. Silphium was one of the important plants that flourished during the Greek and Egyptian dynasties); or even a disease (e.g. Ebola flourished due to the international and accessible nature of modern tourism and cheap flights). What we notice here is that in *almost* all cases (this is an important qualifier) it does not matter whether a living thing, or phenomenon, that is said to flourish is either good or bad in a moral sense; in other words, there appears to be an absence of a requirement for moral judgement. Thus, the flourishing that takes place is, for all intents and purposes, ethically *neutral* (as is the development of technology). Indeed, in such contexts evil can be seen to flourish just as much as can good be seen to flourish, without any logical or ethical problems whatsoever. Here, the meaning is not *standardly* seen in some moral evaluation of good, but rather in the neutral goods of success and development within an environment that is conducive to growth.

The flourishing of *persons* vs things

From a neo-Aristotelian perspective, the kind of 'good' that is intended here is in fact the same concept for human beings as it is for other phenomena; perhaps it is just applied in different senses according to a naturalist framework. Accordingly, in *that* sense, flourishing could be seen as both generally the same (implying growth, development, and benefit to the 'flourishee' or phenomena) *and* yet also unique and specific in the sense of how it applies to the individual *thing* that is flourishing. For example, MacIntyre (1999: 64) suggests that:

> [w]hat it is to flourish is not of course the same for dolphins as it is for gorillas or for humans but it is one and the same concept of flourishing that finds application to members of different animal-and plant species ... And what it needs to flourish is to develop the distinctive powers that it possesses qua member of that species.

According to this model, for Monsanto to flourish it means that something good is happening *to* Monsanto as a company, quite irrespective of the costs to others, such as small organic farmers. Similarly, in the case of the Viking raids on Britain and Ireland in the eighth century, and the related spread of Viking culture, something good is happening to Viking culture. Like the example with the expansion of the Holy Roman Empire during the Dark Ages, we are perfectly happy to say that the Vikings flourished in the UK during this period irrespective of the negative impact on the Celtic-Christian monasteries of Britain and Ireland etc. As intuitive as this seems, I would like to challenge this neo-Aristotelian model of flourishing and instead suggest that because of the moral dimension, the criteria for what 'good' means in a general sense for *things*, is not the same thing as it is for *human beings*. Fundamentally, this is because different *uses* (applications) of a word signify different *logical consequences*, which then amounts to a different concept entirely (cf. Baker, 2004).

We may be able to speak of a flourishing murderer or a flourishing thief – but that is in their 'role' not as a human being, even if they may be good ('skilled', 'efficient') at it, or if they *think* or *believe* that what they are doing is morally justified, or it is good for them. If someone subjectively *enjoyed* self-harming, they cannot be said to be flourishing. Nor indeed do we have a use for flourishing for cases where abusive individuals believe that the harms they inflict on others contributes to their own flourishing or the flourishing of others (as is often the case with abusive partners, psychopathic killers, some cult leaders, or religious, political leaders etc.). Although these latter points have a bearing on the important issues with the subjectivity of flourishing, they also help to show that one cannot simply have a reductive formula (as is suggested by MacIntyre) such as: *flourishing* = good of the thing. The logical warrant for each use has particular limits in such a way that highlight illuminating differences for what logically follows of the use of the word 'flourishing'. If we blur the important distinctions and begin to assume that the word equates to *the* concept (as I believe MacIntyre seems to do) then we are bound to get confused about what the apparent 'essence' of flourishing might be – such as a putative 'good'. Thus, there are a number of things we could mean by uttering the word 'flourishing', but when applying it to the *person* as a whole, we are somewhat restricted, i.e. by the relevant criteria for the development of moral and rational human powers. Unlike the former cases discussed about *things* such as cultures, diseases etc, in the case of a *person* there must be a sensitivity for the interpersonal, social, and even ecological environment – the harmonious and common good – not merely a subjective or individual good (so conceived or perceived). For human beings, flourishing suggests that s/he is a developed, socially conscious agent, who is able to operate effectively and in relative balance with the world around him or her. This is also why, it may be helpful to see both the individual and political dimensions of the role that civic responsibility has with human flourishing. Flourishing occurs when both dimensions work well together in balance.[7]

In contrast, the moral dimensions of corporations or companies relate to the social or ecological or economic *impact* of the actions of the management of a given firm. This is why there is an amoral use when applying to companies too, even though companies are run by humans. Like a human person, corporations have 'legal personhood' as a prerequisite to legal capacity in the forming of contracts and obligations (cf. Martin, 2003); thus, in one sense, they have similar (but not the same) rights and responsibilities as *human* legal persons. However, there are distinguishing logical consequences for corporate legal persons when compared with human legal persons. A corporation cannot be 'hurt' like a biological, emotional, human being can; it is not a sentient being, it cannot feel emotional pain either (though we do say that the company can 'suffer' through bankruptcy, restructuring, take-over etc.) – although the financial well-being of the company can be impacted and there can be a general malaise within a company made up of the sum mood of its workers. The moral dimension of corporations, for example, a concern for the 'well-being' of its stakeholders is often criticized as being instrumental to its other goals for either profit, expansion, or 'control'.[8] Polemics aside, amorality happens to be a logical feature of the kind of entity that a corporation is, i.e. profit-driven and insentient, which is why we should not be surprised when we see amoral behaviour from such structures. Similar observations can be made about political entities like States. This is not to demonize the corporation or the State per se, although they can indeed behave in reprehensible ways just as human beings can, but it is to assert the internal logical features of the corporation, or the State are distinguished from that of a human person.[9] This is why they require *more* (not less) regulation than individuals do, because they are conceptually conflicted between their unethical instrumental ends and the sentient human beings whom they are supposed to serve.[10]

The flourishing of 'Human' species vs the 'flourishing of' persons

As we have seen, flourishing is used in a number of contexts: for humans, diseases, companies, economies etc. But when we apply the word for human beings there is a further distinction to be made between the *general* (species) versus the *specific* (person). If we take the context of the flourishing of the human species, namely, that which applies across humanity, then we are clearly making very broad claims indeed – claims usually based in some notion of what is 'natural'. But these are difficult kinds of claims to make, at least in a positive sense, for as we have seen, claims to an essential human nature are fragile; although can make some general remarks, useful for policy-makers, educators etc., what *counts* as human nature is always both contextual and occasion-sensitive. Yet, taking human nature in an essentialist direction *is* the basis for most theories of human flourishing and human well-being, including those espoused by thinkers as diverse as Marx (cf. Struhl, 2016), Seligman (2011), Nussbaum (1986), and MacIntyre (1999) and so on.

Taking discussion of flourishing in the direction of a more specific claim such as: 'Jack (the person) is flourishing', our interest can be put more specifically in its more logical form: 'The flourishing of Jack', or the more ordinary form 'Jack is flourishing'. In that case, we would not misunderstand that we are interested in the flourishing of *all* human beings, but merely the flourishing of Jack.[11] However, seeing that Jack is (for our purposes) a human being, our interest in Jack does carry, by implication, a sense for what is at least relevant in a general 'specieal'[12] sense for humans. Hence, the phrase 'human flourishing' is more aptly applied to the *species* of human beings – whereas the 'flourishing of N' or 'N is flourishing' forms are applied in specific cases of persons with the general assumption of 'human flourishing' as the backdrop to the particular. The distinction between the two uses: 'human flourishing' and 'flourishing of' is useful, not least because we use the term 'human flourishing' in both the specieal sense as well as by implication, in the individual, personal sense. Of course, it is not always the case that when we use 'human flourishing' we mean it in a specieal sense. It can also be used to differentiate human flourishing as a concept in general – as has been explored already – from the flourishing *of* specific human beings. The title of this book is a case in point ('Human Flourishing: A Conceptual Analysis'); there is a degree of ambiguity (unless a context is given) in using the phrase 'human flourishing', for, it could just as easily apply as a phrase denoting the common good as it could the personal.

Now that we have surveyed the central *uses* of the concept of flourishing, it is important to consider some of the central conceptual *connections* in those uses. Broadly speaking, then, some of the central conceptual connections for human flourishing include: the 'good' for 'human beings'; human agency, abilities, and powers; personal growth, development, and transformation. There are more, including success, meaningful happiness, and meaning in life. I will explore the most important cluster of relevant concepts in subsequent chapters. For now, it will be useful to explore further, by way of comparison and contrast, some of the key distinctions between flourishing and the related but often *conflated* concepts of *eudaimonia*, happiness and well-being.

Objects of comparison

'Eudaimonia'

In the consideration of what is 'good' for humans, an important comparison for flourishing is the Aristotelian conception of *eudaimonia*,[13] not least because, as was suggested in the introductory chapter, *eudaimonia* has become equated with what we might mean by flourishing in modern literature too. This should be no surprise because as Hacker has suggested, Aristotle developed eudaimonism with great sophistication, and his theory has become 'a prototype of a naturalist account of a good human life' (Hacker, 2021: 274). However, Aristotle's conception of *eudaimonia* (also known as happiness, well-being or flourishing), whilst having some close similarities with our modern conception of 'human flourishing', also has some important differences. Before we look at this more closely, it is important to highlight that Aristotle's conception of *eudaimonia* is of course couched within the context and culture of his time. This was a culture which was foremost patriarchal, highly competitive, and perfectionist in orientation.[14] It is important to note that Greek society was vastly different to our own and so that words which Aristotle might have used do not necessarily carry the same connotations as they do for us. After all, the historical-cultural and thereby linguistic contexts were significantly different to ours. This implies, as Sandis (2021: 1) notes as a general comment, that 'there may well then exist ethical questions that seem open to us but not to Aristotle'. As discussed in the introductory chapter, among these differences is a contrasting modern sensibility and concern for women, slaves, the young etc. so that Aristotle's conception of human nature (and thereby eudaimonic happiness) is somewhat limited by the prejudices of his time. Indeed, as Crisp (Aristotle, 2004: xiv) also notes, as a logical consequence of the emphasis on virtue during that specific ancient Greek period in Athens: 'a vicious or immoral person literally has nothing to live for, and indeed that they might be best advised to commit suicide'.

Nonetheless, from what can be known from Aristotle's explicit interpretations and philosophizing there certainly appears to be some common elements between Aristotle's *eudaimonia* and the more modern concept of flourishing. These dominant cultural features help to contextualize Aristotle's own conception of *eudaimonia* as the 'good life'. For example, Aristotle's approach to dealing with some of the complexities and problems of interest to us here, such as the nature of 'good' for a human being, was to pin the good to the 'characteristic activity' of the thing in question; this is known in the evolving literature as the 'function' argument (Korsgaard, 2008: 129). Aristotle summarizes for us his functional approach to eudaimonian 'good' for human beings as 'doing well':

> For just as the good – the doing well – of a flute-player, a sculptor or any practitioner of a skill, or generally whatever has some characteristic activity or action, is thought to lie in its characteristic activity, so the same would seem to be true of a human being.
>
> NE, 1097b[15]

Indeed, he dedicates the entirety of the *Nicomachean Ethics* to explore this notion of what is 'good' for human beings. He arrives at the conclusion that the one thing that we do most distinctively is exercising rationality well, which for Aristotle, amounts to doing so in accordance with the virtues. *Eudaimonia* then amounts to the complex interaction between rational expression of the soul, in accordance with the virtues (of the time):

> ... if we take this kind of life to be activity of the soul and actions in accordance with reason, and the characteristic activity of the good person to be to carry this out well and nobly, and a characteristic activity to be accomplished well when it is accomplished in accordance with the appropriate virtue ... the human good turns out to be **activity of the soul in accordance with virtue**.
>
> NE, 1198a [emphasis added][16]

'Practical wisdom' (*phronesis*) viz., the ability to make right choices under the right circumstances, is seen as the cardinal intellectual virtue for it most closely evidences the exercise of rationality in human beings (cf. NE, 1142b). Like flourishing, *eudaimonia* is concerned with the things we do, not merely the things we think. *Eudaimonia* is not seen by Aristotle as a state of mind, for if it were, we could achieve *eudaimonia* in our sleep (NE, 1176a). Similarly, one cannot flourish in one's mind (at least alone), nor in one's dreams or once one is dead. Flourishing, like *eudaimonia* (NE, 1169b), requires engagement with life and activity of various sorts. This is an important feature because as will become increasingly clear, unlike some uses of happiness, it makes no sense to discuss flourishing as a subjective state of mind, for flourishing necessitates engagement with and growth in life. Neither is *eudaimonia* a fleeting mental experience; you cannot feel *eudaimonia* any more than you can feel flourishing. Rather, *eudaimonia* is something 'complete' (NE, 1177b), that is, descriptive of an overall objective state of affairs in one's life. Further, although a flourishing life in many senses requires some basic goods of social engagement of sorts, food, shelter etc, similarly *eudaimonia* is not primarily concerned with material goods or social power. As Aristotle (applying his concept of 'self-sufficiency') suggests, these are means to other ends i.e. eudaimonic happiness (cf. NE, 1096b).

However, Aristotle's *eudaimonia* goes further than is perhaps suggested by the concept of flourishing when he suggests that major negative events might ruin an otherwise eudaimonic existence. For Aristotle, using the example of King Priam of Troy who lost his kingdom to the Greeks as a result of allowing in the famous Trojan horse, it makes no sense to say that someone had a eudaimonic life if they come to such an impoverished end: '... [n]o one calls someone happy who meets with misfortunes like these and comes to a wretched end.' (NE, 1100a). One key difference, then, notwithstanding minor misfortunes, is in terms of how Aristotle seems to provide some limitation for *eudaimonia* in terms of the requirement of a 'complete' eudaimonic life. This notion of 'complete' appears to at once mean something like 'holistic', in terms of covering all facets of a human life (which is applicable to flourishing in some senses), but also 'complete' in terms of over the course of a complete life-span. Naturally, that requires a (largely) unblemished life, at least one without any major catastrophes. A form of perfectionism.

In contrast, someone might well flourish for a period of their lives and then falter at the last hurdle, and this would not detract from their flourishing during those former periods (e.g. where someone flourishes during a period of a happy marriage but then flounders post-divorce). Hence, in terms of flourishing, the misadventures or misfortunes of life would not ruin such an ascription in a similar case, provided perhaps that we use a qualifier, such as that someone might have lived an *otherwise* flourishing life or might have had an *otherwise* flourishing career etc. The difference here is slight but important because it highlights the difference in qualifying ascriptions for *eudaimonia* during ancient Greek times appears to have been concerned more with third party ascriptions of *eudaimonia* (historically and culturally specific, and normative in the axiological sense) than we might suggest with our modern uses of flourishing.

Of course, some certain *conceptions* of flourishing remain misleading (such as those too closely reliant on success). There remain, then, important similarities in terms of the *goal*-oriented nature of *eudaimonia* (as something at 'which everything aims') because the network of concepts connected with flourishing suggests a tendency towards desiring and *aiming* at the 'good' in similar senses. However, for the reasons outlined, it is problematic to conflate the historically specific Aristotelian notions of *eudaimonia* with the modern concept of flourishing. With this in mind, I will now turn to the connections of flourishing with 'success'.[17]

Flourishing, prospering and 'success'

The concept of success is another central concept. Indeed, when using flourishing within a teleological context, we might often mean that we intend to *succeed* at doing something. As such, flourishing becomes somewhat of a cognate for the concept of 'success'. For example, we say: 'I intend to flourish as a philosopher' ... or, 'She wants to flourish as an athlete' etc. Such uses are relatively trouble-free, notwithstanding the risks with conflation of the two concepts which have some important distinctions. For example, success is a value-laden term which is context dependant, so one's value-system might take preference for wealth over intellectual development etc. though these need not be mutually exclusive. 'Success at what'? or 'For what?'... someone might ask.

However, if we mean that we intend to succeed in the broadest of senses – i.e. 'at life', then we should ask ourselves, in what context might this make any sense? In order for it to make sense we would have to assume that the other option would be to do badly at life and fail at everything. Although *doing* the work of success is clearly a matter of *intention* and choice, we can only assume that if flourishing were to be used in that context, i.e. as an intended aim, then *that* person must be somewhat languishing, depressed etc. for who normally, *ceteris paribus*, would in their right mind *choose* to fail at life.[18] In this context, this could mean that someone has given up on engaging with life, or are depressed (sleeping all day, fails to clean themselves or eat etc.). However, attributing failure to someone with clear mental health problems seems excessive, judgemental and unjust – notwithstanding that many of us will experience mental ill-health at some point in our lives.[19] Exceptions aside then, because we do not tend to aim at flourishing per se (though we may aim for the good life); rather, flourishing seems to comprise of a life well-engaged with, a practice and an activity. Hence, it is somewhat problematic to use flourishing teleologically except where we mean it to act as a conceptual cognate for something else like 'success' (as in we aim at succeeding at V'ing etc).

That said, judgements are not always so simple. In terms of reviewing the problematic cases of a person willingly trying to fail, we could still imagine some kinds of context where failure at one thing could mean success at something else. For example, if a school child did not want to go to a private/elite school, they could *intentionally* fail an entrance test (i.e. resulting in the success of not going to that particular school). Similarly, we could imagine that someone had lost their will to live, or lost hope in living due to some kind of trauma (bereavement, divorce, loss of career etc.), and therefore committed suicide. But this is not the same thing as *aiming at* or *intending* towards failure, for the loss of will to live merely suggests that there is no energy for dealing with the everyday struggles of life. For that kind of use, as indicated, we would expect mental ill-health to be present (or in some cases, malevolence).

Conversely, we could imagine that someone could aim at flourishing as a result of refusing to give up on life. This simply suggests that they wish to overcome the forces (psychological, relational or practical) that pull them back into despair. This then expresses, for example, the specific conceptual focus (or emphasis) of 'character development'. Thus, although goals and intentions are seemingly central to the Greek concept of *eudaimonia*, they are somewhat muted in relation to the concept of flourishing per se and come into prominence when flourishing is used as a cognate for a related concept such as 'success'. The kinds of goals that we may accept, however, as more relevant here, relate to specific roles, actions, or activities (notably in the 'flourishing as' uses) – that is, activities within life, as opposed to the whole of life – where, all things considered, it is standardly taken as a given that we want to flourish in the sense that we want to engage with life and to live well. After all, our daily activities and behaviour engaging with life, which in a fundamental sense includes getting up, washing, speaking etc. is evidence of the motivation to live and to flourish. This includes having goals (such as career, spiritual or character developmental goals) and attaining them at times, and of course, failing to attain them on occasion and so revising or pursuing them, according to one's level of practical wisdom. Whilst at other times one might not attain them, as long as one continues to pursue new goals then it is perfectly sufficient to warrant flourishing. In other words, although doing extremely well is naturally within scope of some uses of flourishing, the bar need not be so high as to suggest (as some have, cf. Keyes 2002), that in order to flourish one needs some maximal sense of subjective well-being. Rather, we need to nurture an *attitude* to life that is conducive to flourishing, despite circumstances; that is often enough.

As unexciting as it sounds, we do not need a 'Hollywood' version of flourishing for it to do its work; one merely needs to engage with the everyday requirements of life (such as taking basic care of oneself); responding to the challenges that arise as they occur (e.g. being on average, resilient); pursuing goals as appropriate to your particular circumstances (e.g. as is needed in order to live, pay bills, develop personally etc) with a reasonable degree of success. This is not an empirical claim but a conceptual truism. Of course, in justifying ascriptions of flourishing, it's not that states of mind and the emotional realm do not matter, they do; one cannot, at least standardly, flourish whilst miserable or unhappy. Hence, I will now aim to introduce some of the key relations between 'happiness' and flourishing as these are important to justified ascriptions of a flourishing life.[20]

Flourishing and 'happiness'

The concept of happiness has a range of uses. However, let us here consider the behavioural use which we tend to associate with happy facial expressions. This is important because we might be tempted to assume that one needs to have a particular kind of 'positive' disposition to life in order to flourish. It sounds odd to imagine a flourishing person who is visibly unhappy or indifferent. However, is this really necessary for such an ascription? In one sense yes, and in another no. What range of criteria is important here? Let us consider Jakub, a retired Polish builder with a range of health-related problems. He has a stoic countenance, and you don't know him very well. If for all intents and purposes he is 'getting-on' with daily of life as best he can i.e. he walks to the shops, albeit with a walking stick, he has friends and hobbies, he takes care of himself etc. who is to say that he is not flourishing? He smiles on occasion but in general has a stoic countenance. He does not seem to be happy. But is it fair to suggest so because he has a stoic countenance and does not appear to be happy? Is it not more important that he is engaging in positive activity, which, for example, might include basic engagement with life's challenges as they arise? ... or having a close and loving family etc.?

The difficulty is that a happy countenance and/or a positive attitude, although might often be mistaken for flourishing, at least as conventionally conceived, or expressed, cannot be sufficient for ascriptions of flourishing. This is not to detract from the utility and virtues of positive habits and mindsets. But it is to suggest that someone can appear happy and successful and not be flourishing seems excessive. Indeed, they might be in a terrible state of suffering and yet be full of smiles. Equally, someone might appear to be indifferent (as Jakub) and not at all happy but may merely be inclined or predisposed *not* to express their happiness in ways that we might, in the West, be accustomed. After all, energetic smiling is an often-misleading cultural marker, perhaps prominent in some aspects of modern Western societies, as a signifier to conceptions of both happiness and flourishing. Equally, someone, like Jakub, might even disclose that they were not particularly happy (perhaps because in their culture happiness is not really a topic of interest). Yet, the fact that he is engaging with life is itself an affirmation of life's worthiness, import and meaning to him.

Conversely, let's say that there is a local young man who had a severe mental disability and merely mimicked other people's smiles as he saw them. As long as we knew this, we would then know that this is not sufficient to infer any meaning to an ascription of either happiness or flourishing for that person. This is important partly because expressions of happiness require more than mere mimicry (we do not ascribe happiness to either babies or animals who either have not developed or else cannot develop the concept of happiness).[21] The de-coupling of flourishing from 'apparent' happiness then, also helps to highlight that there is an important relationship between flourishing, adversity, and attitude to life so that it makes perfect sense to say that one flourishes *through* adversity, or that they are flourishing *despite* their circumstances. If this is correct, as Edgar & Pattison (2016: 102) have suggested, flourishing then is in fact a feature of life that is in fact *activated* through the very circumstances of difficulty, not apart from them:

> [If] ... flourishing can be understood more as a quality of positive resistance and resilience that comes into its own when the going gets difficult, then there is no more apposite idea to explore in health care today (my insertion).

If someone we know normally smiles energetically when they are happy then we might correctly infer that they are not doing so well when their countenance is sunken. Even if someone claims to be happy, they are not necessarily so; and if they claim otherwise, they are not necessarily floundering. The point simply reinforces the need for occasion-sensitivity because in order to make judgements about a given case (whether someone is flourishing) we need as many of the relevant reference points as possible (cf. *PPF*, §7). This all seems to further suggest that self-report as a method for researchers, whilst having a place and a purpose, is hugely limited. In fact, we need a great deal more information about a person in order to make a judgement about what is sufficient evidence for an ascription of flourishing. We need to have access to, among other things, their motivations, reasons, and other relevant reference points in their life. Insight into those behavioural and circumstantial reference points, such as: physical appearance, health, insight into their level of resilience, success, intimate knowledge about their personality, drives, achievements, relationships, ways of thinking and behaving etc. is what gives us the necessary information about that person in order to make such an ascription reliable. Judgements of happiness are more than mere self-report and superficial inference, they rely on particular insights into a life of a person. That said, as Sandis (2015: 140) points out, this is not to suggest that certain generalizations cannot be made or inferred, they can. We can draw certain conclusions as a matter of generalization and understanding can come 'in degrees'. Much depends on what is at stake. For example, if we wish to draw an epistemic claim regarding happiness or indeed flourishing authoritatively, the bar is set higher than everyday 'folk' generalizations; epistemic authority also seems to come in degrees.

Although eudaimonic conceptions of flourishing focus on the highly problematic Aristotelian notion of 'function' in life, the insight of active engagement in life at least in part helps to dispel the traditional conceptions of flourishing in health, as well as the most prominent models of flourishing in the field of positive psychology. As outlined already, among the errors that some thinkers in both health and positive psychology make is too often to place an excess of focus on subjective well-being and mental states in their conceptions of flourishing, often simply due to the desire to generalize under conditions that are inhibited by pragmatic constraints or inconvenience. I will now explore these concerns a little further.

'Well-Being' as an object of comparison

With some minor provisos, the concept of well-being is largely hedonic in nature and is associated with positive mental states, subjective well-being, happiness, positive emotions, positive affect and overall life satisfaction (Bradburn, 1969; Harding, 1982; Diener, 1984; Lyubomirsky & Lepper, 1999; and Fredrickson & Losada, 2005). The exceptions include scholars who focus on the more complex eudaemonic conceptualizations of well-being, including 'purpose' and meaning in life. This conceptualization includes mental and physical health (WHO, 2020), but also encompasses related concepts such as 'happiness and life satisfaction, meaning and purpose, character and virtue', as well as healthy 'social relationships' (VanderWeele, 2017). However, due to the heavy focus on subjective-well-being from either perspective to a large degree the salient distinction between hedonic and eudaimonic conceptions of well-being is artificial. As was discussed in the opening Introduction chapter, 'Introducing the Problem', over recent years, flourishing is seen as a scalable measure of almost anything related to overall health and/ or well-being. On the one hand, we can see why it might be tempting to equate flourishing with 'total' well-being where flourishing means wellness in every aspect or domain of life (mental, social etc.). But there are important differences. Well-being – after all – is transitory.

For example, one can feel well one minute, and awful the next. Once's well-being can dip and rise as a result of either biological factors, immediate stresses, or long-term stresses. Perhaps I haven't had my coffee yet . . . or perhaps I didn't win the lottery . . . or perhaps I had a serious row with my partner last night. We can talk about mental well-being, social well-being, financial well-being etc. but each facet of well-being fluctuates. This is important because it exposes what might otherwise be masked connections with what can broadly be termed as the 'mental'. Although well-being can suggest a mental state, does it make sense to suggest that flourishing can be equated with or described as either a mental state, or a feeling? Does flourishing ebb and flow like feelings do with the various affective stimuli and responses of daily existence including mood swings, anger, hatred, disgust, lust, various cravings, desires, likings, urges, romance, loving or feeling loved, positive, or negative attitudes etc? I can feel well as a result of cuddling up on the sofa with my partner, watching my favourite programme on television, and/or eating my favourite meal … but can I flourish as a direct result of cuddling up? Thus, precisely because of their fickle nature, the kinds of situations and contexts where we think and speak of well-ness or well-being are transfixed on our sensations, often associated with biology, feelings and emotions as transient or 'occurrent' states (cf. Hacker, 2007a: 115). Flourishing, on the other hand, though impacted by feelings and states, certainly chronic states, is not a state of mind at all, and certainly not the kind of state that is reliant on the whims of feelings or emotions, not least due to the aforementioned exclusions from transitional periods of time (although it is impossible to experience life fully without such experiences).

Further, whilst it is nonsense to feel *both* well and terrible simultaneously – for the one logically excludes the other – you could in fact be flourishing and yet be feeling absolutely terrible in a given moment. For example, if Janice, a supermarket worker, was *otherwise* flourishing it would make no difference if she felt sad or disappointed one day as a result of failing to get a promotion (though it could be a trigger to a series of bad states or decisions which ultimately leads to her languishing or demise etc.). Equally, had she had in fact secured the promotion, her feelings of elation and excitement associated with those positive events would not tip her flourishing in any particular direction (not least because flourishing is not the kind of thing that can be tipped in any particular direction in the immediate sense). However, either of the cases could as a potentiality, transform her life, making it either more or less likely to flourish. The emerging point here is that one could be feeling unwell, bad, or even depressed for a *short* while, and still be flourishing overall (a failed promotion does not *necessarily* impede Janice's flourishing – it depends on the attitude she adopts over time to the event). Equally, one could feel perfectly well as a result of some good news (such as a lottery win), and yet not be flourishing e.g. a sudden flurry of cash does not detract Janice from her own inner sense of lack of self-worth and so leads to a pattern of hedonic self-destruction. All this discussion may make readers feel like flourishing is complex and unwieldy. But it's only complex if we see it as an *essential* thing, for we then seek out complex theories to explain the inconsistencies. However, flourishing is in an accumulative sense, a potentiality. It is within the agential powers of human beings to flourish and to create the conditions for flourishing lives.

It is this obsession with a science of happiness and well-being that drives the problematic method of self-report in the research literature. Indeed, it is far easier to ascribe flourishing to others – in the third-person – than it is to oneself. I can tell you very easily if a child is flourishing (especially my child) or my wife or a friend etc. *I know them* well enough to know how to use it in a given context and someone hearing me will perfectly well understand what I mean as long as I have been clear about the context. This also works vice versa, so I can understand others perfectly well when they use the concept in a given context insofar as that context is clear with all the points of reference to hand (verbal, non-verbal, intentional, historical etc.) – at least as many as is needed contextually.

However, upon being asked 'are you flourishing?', we are faced with greater difficulty. How can one answer such a question? It can easily send one into some kind of anxious 'mental cramp' or a 'philosophical disquiet' (cf. Baker, 2004: 184). One is tempted to ask: 'in what sense?' Consequently, as a philosophical inquiry we could ask ourselves misleading or nonsense questions like 'how do *I* know *I* am flourishing?' . . . or, 'What is a question?'. These amount to a failure to draw distinctions between diverse language-games (*PI* §24). Once we know the game being played, the rules, we are better able to play, and any competent user of the English language can manage this with a little thought.

The reason for many of the difficulties seem to be at least in part due to the criteria for flourishing being subject to a greater degree of public criteria than its commonly used cognate terms. In contrast with how the criteria for well-being operates with a first-person lead, with flourishing an objective qualifier (or at least a greater weight on objectivity) is required. Thus, an immediate kind of response could be: 'in what sense am I flourishing?' . . ., i.e. in my career? . . . as a student? . . . as a person? etc. Would others agree? These are all evaluable objectively. Like other claims to authority, what is important is that we need to fix our concern in order to fix the criteria; we need a specific purpose. Hence the usefulness of the notion of 'flourishing as'; it helps to pin the purpose of the inquiry more tightly, certainly in terms of self-report.[22]

Thus far, I have been interested in exploring what flourishing is (in terms of use and by comparison with similar terms). To help provide a counterbalance to this endeavour, in this final section I will explore, briefly, what flourishing is *not*. This should help to enrich the picture we have so far into ever sharper focus, laying a solid foundation for pressing on with subsequent chapters on more nuanced issues and concerns in the cluster of concepts related to human flourishing.

What flourishing is *not*

It's worth asking here what is supposed to be contrasted when we speak of the flourishing of human beings? Firstly, we can understand rather straightforwardly that conceptual distinctions are intended to lay before us some kind of discrimination in the use of a concept. If we were to espouse the notion that everything is everything, then we would be caught within a tautology and will have said nothing at all. Everything in this sense is in fact, *nothing* at all (cf. *PI* §15). Rather, in drawing a conceptual distinction, we should be aware of what conceptual presuppositions we intend to rely on.

With this in mind I am reminded of Austin's conception of the dominant 'trouser word' according to which, part of knowing what a given concept is, is knowing 'what it is not' (Austin, 1962: 70). Austin uses the case of a 'real' duck to exemplify a typical trouser-word. By using the qualifier 'real', Austin suggests that we not only limit and exclude possibilities for confusion, that is, by contrasting the real with 'not real', 'synthetic' etc. But further, that we actually mean to affirm a 'negative'. In this way, concepts such as 'hard' have no meaning in a world where everything is hard; rather, it only has meaning insofar as it is useful to signify its opposite i.e. 'not soft'. This notion of the antithetical is bound up implicitly in the grammar of the concept. Similarly, 'white' means, at least in part, 'not black' (or any other colour, tone or shade in the spectrum); and 'good' means in part, 'not bad'. So can we consider what exactly is intended to be distinguished when we use the concept of flourishing? Two subsequent questions emerge:

a) What kinds of negative, oppositional, antithetical pairing are we implicitly taking as a *given* of what flourishing is, when we grasp the concept of flourishing at a stroke? And,

b) Which leg is dominant in the trouser-word relationship? The affirmative, to flourish (being well, doing well, growing, developing etc.), or the negative, its opposite? (i.e. X is not languishing, not suffering, not floundering etc).

Well, in the general affirmative sense, we know rather intuitively what flourishing is not:

I. It is *not* languishing or being in a state of suffering or self-loathing (though you may suffer and still flourish);

II. It is *not* regularly failing at the enterprises that you take on for yourself (though you can still flourish through failure *if* you overcome those failures; in fact, success requires lessons to be learnt through failure);

III. It is *not* being in a state of disease (although you can flourish *in spite of* a life-threatening illness);
IV. It is *not* having a debased or immoral character (though you can flourish as a result of lessons learned through the experience of bad decision-making); it is not having a bad reputation (though reputation must always be qualified against the evidence against the person);
V. It is *not* having a bad reputation (though reputation must always be qualified against the evidence against the person);
VI. It is *not* being mad or senseless (though, similarly, to suffering through illness, you can be in a state of bliss and growth despite your circumstances).

Hence, in the negative trouser sense, to flourish means something like: 'Jack is not failing' (e.g. at life).[23] Here, then, we have a sketch for what flourishing is by surveying their respective and often interchangeable conceptual *antonyms* which, I suggest, is helpful when considering the meaning of words in contexts for a distinct oppositional contrast may be applicable in one context and not in another. Further still, in some cases the affirmative will be dominant (i.e. what flourishing *is*), and in others, it will be the negative (what it is *not*).[24]

Summative remarks

To conclude then, I have shown that in order to better understand the concept of human flourishing (and related conceptions) we need to gain a sensibility for the grammar of the concept, in context. This includes an awareness for the methods of analysis applied in this chapter; namely, an exploration of uses, conceptual connections, subtleties and emphases or varieties of meaning. Further, I mapped out the central conceptual connections (e.g. growth, success) as well as some salient comparisons (such as *eudaimonia*, happiness and well-being) with a view to gain better insights into some of the conceptual problems that often befall research projects on the topic of flourishing.

I finished then with an exploration of some of the central criterial issues that can arise including reductionism and subjectivism. In order to better understand how to use flourishing, we need to develop a sensitivity for where we might use the word but mean something else entirely. We also need to understand the kinds of conceptual focus between the subtleties in uses of flourishing (positive or negative 'trouser leg') because each focus will have its own logical consequences and emphases. As highlighted, such important subtleties are often overlooked, not in everyday parlance, but particularly in research or policy projects which use the term for their own ends in order to be able to drive an agenda of generalization. We can be 'tempted to ask and answer questions in the way science does' (*BB* 18), and hence, in the process, we often mask internal conceptual incoherence and important conceptual differences between the uses of our terms.

These illustrations of growth and goodness direct us towards a conception of flourishing that is both conceptually and categorially sound, as well as agent-specific. We are now, however, faced with a series of related problems with regards to the importance of somewhat philosophical terms such as 'agency' and related ordinary terms such as autonomy or self-direction; in particular, what these related terms might mean for a sophisticated, social and developmental being like us. Hence it is to the related concept of 'Human agency' that I turn to next.

5

'Human' Agency

The concept of agency is somewhat of a technical concept, not used ordinarily outside of academic discourse. Focusing on the social and normative aspects of agency, it has been described in critical cultural studies as 'the socially constructed capacity to act' (Barker, 2002: 14); in welfare economics as the 'freedom to achieve well-being' (Sen, 1999: 3). In certain forms of philosophy, it is used to contrast human intentional action versus that of the causal processes or happenings seen in natural phenomena (e.g. McFee, 2000; Hacker, 2021). Most recently the notion of having a 'sense of agency' has been used to highlight the complex dynamic between self and others (Houlders et al., 2021). Alvarez's (2010) framework for understanding the criteria for practical reasoning is also framed in agential terms. For Alvarez, what makes practical reasoning 'practical' is not merely that there are 'reasons for acting' or 'expressions of intention' but that these are aimed at goals that have a 'goodness' about them, that is, a moral purpose.[1] These conceptions of agency draw out aspects of agency that pertain to a specific line of inquiry and within a given discipline. For example, Barker's (2002) and Sen's (1999) relate to social norms and justice, whereas McFee (2000) and Hacker (2021) focus on the conceptual relations as part of a broader interest in the project of 'philosophical anthropology' aimed at tackling, among other problems, scientism. Houlders et al. (2021) relate their work to epistemic issues that have a bearing within specifically 'therapeutic' contexts for the young where there is risk of undermining their conceptions of self-efficacy. Nevertheless, in these cases, there is a common sensitivity to issues of social justice, the potential for the abuse of power, intended or otherwise, and the importance of morality. In other words, conceptions of agency have a practical and moral bearing on human relationships, specifically regarding relations of power. Further, although other beings like amoeba, insects and animals have teleological and worthy lives (in a limited sense), they are not meaningful per se, apart from the meaning that we attribute to them. This is because the capacity for reasons are features of what it is to have moral agency, meaning, and purpose in life. A fortiori, sunlight-beams or super-novae are excluded from living what we might consider to be a meaningful life for they are not sentient life-forms, have no ability to reason, no emotional life, and no ability to develop goals. These humdrum remarks are intended to highlight the importance of *qualitative* difference in ascriptions of agency to various forms of life.

Hence, because to act is not merely a power that human beings possess but is also socially afforded (and limited in important senses) my aim in this chapter to draw these somewhat distinct but closely related conceptions together and to flesh out the central logical conceptual connections for the concept of agency, insofar as these relate to concepts within the broad cluster of concepts around flourishing, such as: abilities, powers, reasons, actions, intentions and personhood. By the end of this chapter, we should have a clearer understanding for the importance of agency and its relationship with the concept of flourishing. This is useful in order to make perspicuous the landscape of conceptual relations between these concepts, but importantly, to shed light on some of the confusions and problems in discussing the concept of flourishing within, for example, reductionist accounts of human nature, well-being and flourishing. As I will suggest, these can have a pernicious, rather than liberatory, impact in the affairs and relations of human beings.

Chapter sections

In section one, 'Human vs animal agency' – I raise the spectre of a problematic conception of agency that divides human beings vs animals too sharply. Using some discussion of Frankfurt's (1998) discussions of agency, I wish to introduce an ethical conception of agency that draws distinctions between human beings and animals in specific and elucidatory ways but evades the parochial bias or speciesism that Frankfurt is concerned about. In section two, '"Acting" vs mere doing', I explore this line of thought a bit further, drawing distinctions between sentient beings that act versus those that seem to merely do. This distinction is useful to help draw out some initial discussion about the levels of our automaticity and agency, what is unique and powerful about human agency, and our unique ability to control our environment and change course.

In section three, 'The distinction between one- and two-way powers', I explore a distinction that Hacker highlights between acts and doings (or happenings). As I will suggest, agency as a power is logically prior to agency as an ability. Where possible, we can use our agency in ways that helps us to express ourselves as authentic persons and creative beings. This has both social and moral implications for flourishing. Then in section four 'Two normative aspects of agency: biological and social', I explore a further distinction between agency as powers or abilities in the context of social life. Particularly, I suggest that social and political context places significant demands, restrictions and possibilities on the agent. Agency can in this sense be seen as a similar notion to autonomy or a *freedom to act*.

In section five 'Agency, emotion and emancipation', I explore the role of emotion in human affairs to shape our lives. This will include, for example, an initial taxonomy of the concept of pleasure. I will suggest that our sophisticated abilities to feel emotion is a source of both power and strength but also dehumanization. What is important is our *practice* or *performance* of agency. I also briefly discuss Sen's (1999) critique of modern economic theory for having too 'narrow' a conception of human beings. My focus, however, is on the relation between the personal and the political, highlighting the relevance of Wittgenstein's method, and the importance of moral courage in achieving liberation philosophically, politically and personally.

Finally, in section six 'The problem with biologically reductionist conceptions of well-being', I address a trend in the literature towards biological reductionism and (by implication) determinism. The central point of tension is the contrast between causes and reasons for our well-being. Exploring some of the most recent literature in the 'positive neuroscience' of well-being and flourishing. Using Bermúdez's (2016) critique of 'bottom up' explanations, I highlight that crucial distinctions are missed between different *ways* of explaining (*explananda*) human action highlighting the incongruence between the conceptual schemes of neural and human behaviour.

Human vs animal agency

Drawing distinctions between human beings and non-human animals can be problematic. We can see animals as mechanisms or automata (as Descartes did),[2] resulting in a wholly different set of ethics and attitudes towards the lives of non-human animals. Frankfurt (1998: 78–79) famously warned us of imbuing our conceptions of agency with a 'parochial' species bias. His conception of agency is of the kind that is common to *all* living creatures.[3] Whilst this could lead one to have the thought that there is a 'scale' of agency metered out to animals on a scale of intelligence or such like, perhaps a better way to understand Frankfurt would be to understand that sentient creatures have diverse *forms* of agency that are particular to the kind of creature that they are. If we wanted to split hairs, we could suggest that this amounted to a different concept entirely because distinct logical consequences are said to follow from such discussions. Nevertheless, I believe that Frankfurt's point is one of ethical emphasis. It is useful to highlight the commonality between human animals and non-human animals (hereafter, simply animals), despite the sharp differences in rational powers and linguistic abilities. I wish to emphasize this difference, though not in ways that support extensions into speciesism.

Though we share much with the animal kingdom (i.e. relevant in matters of ethics) there is no doubt that we are unique and distinct in our abilities for conceptualization, expression, and creativity. Our ability to reason for our actions, to explain and justify such reasons renders us uniquely capable and responsible 'moral agents' in ways not accessible to animals (cf. Hacker, 2021). This is why the distinction between human beings and animals is important because it lays out the clearest contrast and set of examples we might have for a comparator of sorts. As such, we are able to work towards creating a life that is tolerable, worthwhile and filled with possibilities for self-expression, mutual support, loving support, helping others and supporting personal growth and development. We take care of ourselves, our health and our fitness e.g. by going to the gym, or running, walking or whatever; we nurture our community and social relations, primarily through family and friends but also through work and engaging with the wider community (e.g. through volunteering); we develop our careers through training; we engage with other professionals in our particular field by attending relevant meetings or gatherings; we support our spiritual development by engaging with rituals of various kinds in order to support a sense of meaning in the world. These are actions and activities performed by moral agents with complex linguistic powers and who have advanced or high order powers to do (act), or *not* to do (omit to act) in the course of a life filled with successes, failings and opportunities and expression of our unique form of agency (cf. Hacker, 2007a).

Acts of commission and omission are not 'mere' acts *simpliciter*; we don't only choose, rather, we choose *how* to choose; we decide the frameworks for choosing within our purview of conceivable actions. This is something like what Frankfurt (2006: 18) calls our 'reflexive capacity', that is, an ability to reason and form desires about what we want and what we *want to want* (or not as the case may be). This discussion is, broadly construed, relevant to the field of 'practical reason' and wisdom.[4] Hence, our unique form of 'human' agency is fundamental to our capacity for creating and contributing towards conditions for civilizational flourishing (or languishing). Crucially, without the possibility for agency in human affairs, purpose and meaningfulness are logically excluded. Meaningfulness only has a place in a conceptual landscape where agents have *options* for making judgements (and acting) in ways that are purposive, teleological, and subject to evaluation and action. Thus, the concepts of reason, decision, belief and perception all matter here, for opportunities to flourish in life may be missed by agents who are blind or blinded to such opportunities.[5]

'Acting' versus mere doing

Frankfurt's implications that agency admits to degrees on a scale of complexity between sentient beings may, therefore, be partially defended. If that is the case, then a fortiori, agency can admit of degrees in the context within human affairs. For example, a simple act might be to pick up or nudge an object, whereas a more complex act (or series of actions) might include premeditated activities like building a house or perhaps writing a book, both of which require a significant and sophisticated degree of planning, designing, structuring, editing, refinement, and complex expressions of intelligence. These more complex acts are a possibility in societies or communities that have a developed language, though not necessarily the same kind of language that we possess. One could imagine, for example, ancient cultures using fingers, hands and elbows as means of measurement without the need to have any grasp of complex mathematics or geometry. Similarly, grasping the concept of weight is typically a rudimentary tactile skill in a form of life where gravity has a bearing, like our own. It's also worth noting that though we live in times of advanced inculturation of a particular kind, it is by no means the default position of human experience. Our present epoch could be seen as somewhat of an accident of our socio-cultural history.[6] The global society we live in didn't need to evolve into this particular form, though evidently it did.

Here lies an important distinction between two distinct kinds of agent. Although we use the same word there are vastly distinct logical consequences. On the one hand, agents of a self-conscious and sentient kind e.g. human beings, perhaps including some intelligent animals; and on the other, agents that seem to follow some kind of natural process e.g. unintelligent animals, microbiological phenomena, plants etc. Although biological entities 'do' things (they move, affect their environment, seem to have a purpose of sorts, in a responsive, intuitive sense), they cannot be said either to act or to take action for this would require *conscious* reasoning; to take action is to decide, to reason, to weigh things in the balance etc. Thus, even though we have other uses for the notion of an 'act',[7] for our purposes here, we can draw a distinction between what I'd like to term as 'nomological *doings*' versus 'agential *actings*'; that is, ways of acting that suggest automaticity as opposed to conscious, purposive behaviour or decision-making. Hacker (2007a: 131) discusses a related distinction in the context of plant life:

> ... a plant itself cannot be said to have purposes of its own or to pursue goals. Nevertheless, what a plant does is explained teleologically – that is, as being done for the sake of a goal (to obtain more light or water) or for a certain purpose (e.g. to facilitate pollination).

The uses of terms such as 'act', 'purpose' or even 'behaviour' in the context of plants are therefore not like human acts, purposes or behaviours. We ascribe to plants and other beings or phenomena, the qualities of acts and purposes as a consequence of their 'behaviour' because we find the simile useful. The distinction is important to avoid becoming misled by apparently similar uses we have for the word 'agency' (cf. *PI* §109).

That said, as human agents are biological beings, we are still subject to some kind of automatic processes *like* we see in plants and other biological phenomena, though these may be subject to a degree of conscious interference. For example, standardly speaking, our heart *beats* involuntarily in order to pump blood around our bodies; our lungs *expel* and *inhale* air, so that we may breathe in order to ingest oxygen and expel carbon dioxide (among other gases); and our stomachs *digest* food for nutrition etc. Although it is our various bodily organs that *do* all the doing here, they are part of our unified personal, biological system. It is just as well that these automatic processes are indeed 'automatic' for otherwise, though we would have great skill at doing them, we would have no time for meaningful agential activities typical of a worthwhile human existence. Indeed, one of the main reasons that we have the time to create art, write literature, listen to music, engage in politics, make bows and arrows, play backgammon, chase birds, enjoy the fruits of our labour, have goals, aims or achievements etc. is that, subject to effective maintenance, bodily processes (for healthy human beings at least) effectively run themselves. We are freed then, in a significant sense, to pursue our agential ends by virtue of our biological automaticity.[8]

I will now draw on Hacker's (2007a) distinction between one and two-way powers. This will further help to draw out the particularly 'human' conceptual connections in the context of our unique powers and potential which will be useful to ground my ethical reasoning and concern for flourishing and what is to count as the *good* for human beings.

The distinction between one- and two-way powers

Hacker (2007a) draws attention to a distinction between one- and two-way powers, that is, between *agential* and *procedural* powers.[9] For example, he contrasts 'one-way volitional powers' (typical for most simple animals and all biological or chemical processes) with 'two-way volitional powers' (the powers virtually unique to human beings or perhaps some intelligent animals). These are, 'powers to do things that we can do or refrain from doing at will'. In one sense, we are more or less unique in possessing these kinds of complex, 'two-way' powers; unique in the sense that what it means to be an agent with such powers means something entirely different for us; viz., we can do so much more with them. For example, we have potentiality for choice, to make decisions which are reasoned or impulsive, good or bad.[10] Such powers are therefore subject to standards of evaluation (e.g. ethical, rational or indeed, conceptual). In many ways they mark out one of our most distinctive features *qua* human beings: the ability to be spontaneous, amusing, exciting etc. As Hacker (2007a: 135) states:

> To do something simply because one wants to is the opposite of constraint. Indeed, doing something simply because one wants to, defines liberty of spontaneity.

This agential power is therefore, among other things, a power to decide (using a range of options) on what kind of person we'd like to be, or what kind of future we'd prefer to direct ourselves towards, or what kind of activity we'd like to engage in. To flourish or, to languish; to do well, or to fail; to act based on well-reasoned decisions, or to act impulsively, or exercise poor judgement. In this way, agency as a *power* potentiality is logically prior to notions of agency as an *ability* for such abilities flow out from our human potential; if we do not have the potential (e.g. through some injury, impairment or disability), a whole range of abilities are logically precluded. However, by virtue of being what we are, in the right environments, we are standardly able to display a wide array of advanced abilities.

An implication of the notion of 'two-way powers' is to raise the connection between 'personhood' and agency, for the power to do or not to do affords us both moral rights and responsibilities. For an agent to be an agent, it must be a person who has 'self-consciousness' of a kind so that it has potential for direction and choice (not mere movement, but rationality and decision-making powers too). Following Kant, in his analysis of the concept of personhood, Hacker (2007a: 313) suggests:

> To be a person is not to be a certain kind of animal, but rather to be an animal of one kind or another with certain kinds of abilities.

Here Hacker seems to be suggesting that animality, by implication *qua* a living being alone, is not sufficient for the attribution of personhood, even where we might consider other criteria such as the fact that animals seem clearly to have inner lives, personalities and characters. The salient distinction that Hacker draws here is that although the category of a human being (i.e. *Homo sapiens*) is a 'biological' one, the concept of a *person* is a 'moral, legal and social one' (Hacker, 2007a: 4) subject to 'moral laws and responsibility' (2007a: 285). Being a person means to be an agent of a particular kind, one that has the potential to develop certain abilities and is *afforded* such a place within a moral community. In this sense, and building on the notion of two-way powers, only human beings may be attributed with personhood. As Hacker (2007a: 14) has suggested, other than in the context of circus or related performance, we tend to speak more readily of animal 'behaviour' rather than of 'the acts animals perform' so whatever notion of agency we might attribute to animals it is not of the kind that we attribute to human beings.

This point is not uncontroversial for we know that animals do have communities, as well as emotions, even codes and expectations of each other, and that we share much in terms of social cultures with chimpanzees for example.[11] As Wild & Brandt (2012) has also said, 'separating man and animal betrays the obvious fact that animals behave in very similar ways to human beings and that human beings are animals too'.[12] We have much more in common with animals (certainly the higher animals) than we have distinguishing us. However useful certain distinctions are drawn e.g. for the purposes of a conceptual analysis, making *too* strong a distinction between human beings and animals is bound to lead to vast over-generalizations, speciesism or, as Glock has more particularly argued, a form of 'lingualism'.[13]

Following Lockean criteria based on the primacy of 'experience' and the possibility of animals having a 'unified mental life', Rowlands (2016) has, however, made a recent case that animals may be ascribed personhood. In support of such an experientialist view, it would not make any sense if we were to ask whether a robot, or even an algorithm could possess agency (other than metaphorically speaking). This is partly because robots and algorithms (even AI) cannot (at least yet) act per se; they follow functional and procedural rules that human beings program them with. They may be said to succeed, not for their own sake, but rather for *our* purposes – for they cannot have purposes of their own; only self-aware, conscious *persons* can have purposes in that sense. Hence, in these kinds of cases, although we share an increasing vocabulary with AI and other technological forms of life, this is largely figurative. What it is to be an agent *is* to have a mental life in which decisions can be made *for reasons*, towards goals, and formed, partially at least, by emotional attitudes etc. These are central features in the range of an interlaced cluster concepts related to human agency and personhood.

Two normative aspects of agency: biological and social

Although we may at first conceive of agency as something which the 'individual' possesses, it is significantly mitigated, shaped and impinged upon by cultural and social environments that *reward* some forms of agency and *limit* others according to the dominant norms prevalent at the time. Norms and sub-cultural forms of life impinge on what kinds of agency are valued in. A form of life has many variances: such as the ancient Greek form of life, the English form of life, or even group identity sub-cultures such as punk, emo, goth etc. The utility of this distinction is made clear in the context of a range of epistemological reference points that impinge on how the world is 'seen'.

Consequently, social context will place demands on the agent, who will for example, find that their agency is both limited and encouraged in diverse ways according to a given culture, their particular dispositions and abilities, and their place in a given social order. Just as the Renaissance period produced some of the finest artists and painters in the history of human civilization (according to common standards in terms of complexity and refinement), other periods will have produced diverse kinds of human expression. So, for example, the environment of the Industrial Revolution produced rapid and exponential expansion of technology and mechanical innovation which favoured a particular kind of skill set (entrepreneurial, mechanical etc.).

This is where agency becomes synonymous with *freedom to act* (as qualified in the code), for example, in being codified through laws, customs and rights (such as the freedom of expression or of conscious religious belief as seen in the Human Rights Act 1998).[14] Of course, there are also a range of unspoken customs which act as behavioural inhibitors too, for example, 'don't jump the queue'; 'don't bump into people'; and most recently (due to the outbreak of COVID-19), 'don't shake hands or hug!'. Those rules have an impact on how we live out our lives, the degree to which we may enjoy it, how much power we have over the central choices in life, and indeed, how we may nurture environments conducive to our flourishing *qua* human being and as an individual. As Hacker (2007a: 133) suggests:

> What is deemed a necessity today may have been unnecessary in the past, or a luxury rather than a necessity, or altogether unimaginable. Neither absolute nor minimal needs are simply statistical notions, but rather partly normative ones, the former being dependent upon the axiological conception of health, the latter upon the conception of the requirements of a tolerable human life.

'Partly' is the operative word here. Whilst in one sense, norms of use for given concepts change with the fluctuations of politics and culture, such changes must map onto existing conceptual frameworks. These inhibitors are framed by various historical, social and political factors which have an important bearing on how we may *act* (and relatedly, where we might want or choose to live).

In a similar way to how the concept of normativity may be distinguished,[15] on the one hand we may distinguish then between agency *qua* human being (criterial), and on the other, the *exercise* of agency is limited in important senses by contextual and contemporaneous social norms. The latter admits of degrees relative to cultural appraisals and allowances, whereas the former generally does not, notwithstanding issues of capacity. We are not born with the ability to walk, to speak, to lift heavy objects etc. In the usual course of affairs, these are developmental features of human life (of both a practical as well as conceptual nature) that we gain over time as we mature in social environments, standardly-speaking.[16]

Normativity (A) and Normativity (B)

In this sense, one use of agency is 'normative' in the sense that it is contingent on categorial criteria about our human nature as biological beings with complex linguistic powers, desires, wishes, wills etc.[17] I'd like to call this normative (A) because it is foundational. On the other hand, there is a use of agency that pertains to our social nature as moral and legal beings, as persons, which I'd like to call normative (B). Hence, in terms of normative (B) senses of agency, it is limited in important ways:

I. The degree to which I have been *allowed* or encouraged to develop it (within a social context of power relations), and

II. The degree to which I have an *interest* or aptitude to express it (as a matter of personal values, virtues and vices, abilities, experience, and level of personal development etc.).[18]

As such, how we see, conceive and recognize human agency e.g. in our political or educational systems and other cultural practices, matters hugely. It has a *direct* and cogent bearing on the flourishing of human beings. That is, as members of the species, as moral and legal persons, and of course, as individuals with unique interests, goals, aptitudes and dispositions. Arendt (1976: 479) has stated, rather poignantly, that '[b]eginning, before it becomes a historical event, is the supreme capacity of man; politically, it is identical with man's freedom'. This suggests to me that Arendt implicitly proposes the following, in the context of agency (and related, everyday terms):

- On a personal level, we should work to adopt and nurture an *attitude of hope* for new beginnings even in the direst of circumstances; and
- On the political or social level, if we want to provide human beings from diverse backgrounds with the best chances to flourish in life, that we should pay close attention to the importance of creating the meaningful *conditions* for flourishing. Namely, by creating *possibilities* for new beginnings, without which human flourishing is both logically and practically precluded. Flourishing requires growth and growth requires space for action and innovation.

Doing so could act as a buffer against some of the worst effects of harmful elements of political and cultural life (including tendencies towards forms of authoritarianism and totalitarianism). Equally, failing to do so seems to suggest an inevitable cycle of re-learning the same lessons and warning about the pernicious effects of dogmatism from history.[19]

I will now explore the relation between emotion and agency. I suggest that it helps with our understanding of how humans think about themselves, about how we care for our loved ones, and how interdependent we are with each other in ways that is unique to the human species. My view is that the implications are that any conception of flourishing *must* recognize the conceptual connections and role of positive emotions like love, care and compassion.

Agency, emotion and emancipation

All sentient living beings, both human and animal, that can shape their lives according to their desires (whether for good or for ill) have hopes and fears.

Animals may be attributed with some form of intentional and instinctive set of non-linguistic conceptions useful for their survival, and arguably, emotions too. This of course implies the capacity for a mind. We see in the behaviour of animals that they respond to love, to care, to touch, to mistreatment etc. They also care for each other in communities. There are, however, some important distinctions to be made between human beings and animals. The emotional repertoire of an animal is distinct from the kinds of hopes and emotions of human beings. Not least because human beings have the linguistic (and conceptual) ability for the reordering of the world around them. We can choose to see things in a particular light. Animals seem rather limited in that sense, although they can adapt their attitude to another animal through experience.[20]

Due to the complexity of our concepts and schemes, each emotion may be somewhat networked across a wide array of criss-crossing and interconnected concepts that, unlike animals, appear to follow diverse and complex pathways from both a psychological as well as behavioural perspective. This is not to suggest that animals are mechanical, as already outlined, they clearly are not. It would be dogmatic and cruel to suggest that a sentient being that can express and feel emotion, pain, joy and love as mechanical (as Descartes is often accused of doing). Rather, it is to say that – being somewhat simpler in nature, *and* more immediate in terms of their awareness or consciousness – they are subject to a greater degree of *immediacy* and *automaticity*. For human beings, due to our rational, reflective and imaginative powers, pleasure can take innumerable forms. We can enjoy living in a world of pleasurable sensations. We may also take active steps to enjoy our capacity for feeling and sensation. Having the power of sight, we may enjoy the sunset or sunrise; being able to smell, we can savour the aroma of a good meal or flower; having a body, we may enjoy the sensations of sex or chocolate; being an emotional being, we may become elated with spirituality, religiosity or indeed love from another person we hold dear; being a rational being (or one capable of rationality) we may hold a theory, belief or an ideology in high esteem. These faculties of pleasure may therefore be deemed either active and teleological (things we seek out) or passive (things we simply enjoy as a sentient being).

In like manner, as sentient agents we tend to avoid pain, displeasure or discomfort. Such aversions can also be active and goal-oriented (avoidance) or else passive experience (e.g. forbearance). However, as self-conscious human beings, with abilities to develop language, we have a 'complicated form of life' (*PPF* §1). For example, although dogs can communicate with simple barks, whines, yelps and other like sounds, they do not possess linguistic abilities and are precluded from an inner dialogue per se, which is why Wittgenstein remarks that we 'do not say that possibly a dog talks to itself' (*PI* §357), the possibility of language and concepts are excluded. Similarly, although a dog does not need to possess the concept of fear in order to be afraid that his master will beat him (simple fear can be instinctive, reactive etc.), we do not say that 'he is afraid his master will beat him tomorrow' or that his master will come back tomorrow (*PI* §650, *PPF* §1). Though we may attribute the concept of fear and hope respectively, we may not attribute understanding of the concept of *time* to a dog. The more complex (in terms of powers and abilities) the kind of being, the more 'potential' for agency, and thereby, the more potential for complexity in emotional states of both pleasure, pain and the various sensations and experiences.[21]

The notions of pleasure described here, then, suggest a range of *uses* and concepts and we may see that an initial ordering of the concept of 'pleasure' emerging:

- emotional, aesthetic, transcendental (imaginative)
- intellectual (rational)
- axiological, preferential (dispositional)
- sensual, somatic (physical).

As such, whilst animals may like the stroke for its own sake (as we can too), they do not have the capacity to think about why they like the stroke or in what manner they like it. That is afforded to beings with linguistic powers. Unlike animals, we can look forward with hope for certain pleasures or else fear their loss (or fear pain). Our capacity for complexity in our inner life (as founded upon a rich *form* of life), magnifies the potential for sensation and expression of our emotions e.g. fear, anxiety, loathing, or exhilaration and ecstasy. Indeed, the possibility of a complex inner life is largely why dehumanization is possible because we can be treated like insentient or primitive sentient beings; we can be treated like we are mechanical. Indeed, by behaving instinctively, a person may inhibit their moral agency by feeding unhealthy habits, appetites, cravings, urges, addictions and compulsions, e.g. to drugs, alcohol or other substances (thus leading to a form of self-dehumanization).[22]

In this way, our notion of humanity is closely tied to the degree to which we *perform* (act out, practice) our agential responsibilities well and thereby provide space and opportunity in our lives (freedom) for our individual expression of emotion and relations. This is both a personal as much a political concern. Adopting an interest in conceptual work and insight, moving from 'unobvious nonsense to obvious nonsense' (cf. *PI* §464), is liberatory on a personal level, and the problems between the personal and the political are not unrelated. If you have a misconception in one area, it is bound to lead to a problem in the real world.[23]

The implications of my exploration of agency and flourishing, then, are twofold: firstly, we must recognize agency is partly attributable to human beings *qua* human beings irrespective of individual cognitive or physical ability (as outlined, normative [A]).[24] This is a categorial remark regarding what it is to be a distinctly human kind of being. Secondly, because of the normatively established moral status afforded to all human beings, normative (B), I suggest that we have an ethical duty to uphold systems of thought that contribute to the right kinds of conditions for the exercise of all manner of exercise or *expressions* of agency, because it is this exercise that creates the kinds of conditions where flourishing can occur. This is a matter of personal character, choice, judgement and moral courage (as it was for the German families hiding Jews during the persecution of Jews in Nazi Germany). It is during times of persecution of minorities (ethnic, racial, disabled etc.) that ordinary citizens, politicians, artists, etc. must decide to be complicit, or not, in the marginalization of victimized groups. These are issues that often press on each and every generation in one form or another, and this provides the historical backdrop to the development of human and civil rights, indeed the values that we cherish (at least explicitly) in the West.

Although highlighting this moral duty has implications in the political realm – I do not make an empirical claim. I merely point to the complex nature of human beings, being both biological as much as social creatures who possess unique powers and abilities, *qua* human beings, and who require the apt social and political conditions for the possibility of their exercise. Of course, there are numerous expressions of agency that need not take the particular form we tend to have in the West i.e. one largely based on libertarian principles.[25] There is, however, practical import in drawing attention to these features of agency.

For example, distinguishing ways of seeing a person's 'interests' and their fulfilment, Sen (1999) criticizes modern economic theory for having too 'narrow' a conception of human beings, seeing them as 'rational fools' incapable of making good decisions about their own lives; i.e. lacking rational agency. This leads him to advocate his concept of the 'freedom to achieve well-being' (Sen, 1999: 4). I do not intend to defend Sen's philosophy of economics, but I do think that his assumptions with regards to human nature are helpful to highlight the ways in which problematic assumptions and world-views (viz., reductionism with regards to human nature, and paternalism with regards to political philosophy) inevitably lead to conditions of injustice and a frustration of human potential. A misleading supposition is not innocent in its ability to cause harm, it can and often does lead to an injustice. As Read (2020: 331) has suggested, there is ... 'already a politics implicit, in the very method of our figuring out where we will allow or (if you will) will the limits of any concept – starting with the concept of language itself'. This is one of the reasons why a clearer conception of human nature can support the kind of conceptual landscape that is *emancipatory* in orientation. Hence, on the one hand, seeing humans aright (i.e. having a beneficent, broad, ethical, pluralistic conception of human nature) can lead to emancipatory politics and policies; conversely, having a 'narrow', reductionist or distorted conception (as exemplified by Sen's analysis of reductionism in economics) can lead to forms of injustice and frustrated conditions for living where flourishing is substantially inhibited. The recognition of the implications of seeing agency aright then has significant import to conditions for flourishing socio-politically.

Having covered some of the key conceptual issues with regards to agency in the context of human powers, I will now turn to a brief discussion of some of the pernicious effects of determinist ways of thinking about human nature, well-being and flourishing. This is important because any such a view would nullify, or at least limit what McFee (2000: vii) calls the 'possibility of genuine agency' in human life.

The problem with biologically reductionist conceptions of well-being

The impulse to search for etiological sources of well-being and flourishing is the latest manifestation of an old urge to demystify the nature of reality. As Sandis (2012b: 13) has stated, '[s]earches for causal determinants have been advertised as searches for the true or real reasons behind our actions'. One example within the behavioural sciences is for researchers to be concerned with psychological or behavioural development problems in children. They may be interested in figuring out what the *causes* of these problems are so that they may address those *causes* and possibly even 'cure' them or 'prevent' similar problems in the future. An example in the emerging field of 'positive neuroscience', Greene et al. (2016) aim to resolve the problem of insensitive parenting, that is, parenting that is associated with abuse or neglect. In particular, the authors are interested in the role of the father in rearing children and the neural correlates to sensitive parenting for *both* parents and children. In doing so they use a range of empirical, neural and behavioural data, including studies based on invasive techniques from experiments on rat brain chemistry and neurology, as well as less invasive techniques on human subjects (such as neural imaging equipment and hormonal testing). Their interest is in developing a 'neurobiology' of 'paternal' care as they feel that they have enough data on the neural links between mother and child (Greene et al. 2016: 26). This work is alleged to begin to garner information regarding the paternal relations with their children.[26]

Further, Kuo et al. (2012) posit that 'genuine' biological fathers had 'stronger' neural responses to their infant cries, specifically in the insula and amygdala regions of the brain, thus suggesting closer bonds and emotional ties. The inference is that a genuine biological father would be more likely to bond, and less likely to physically abuse their children. Thus conceived, the explicit interest for such a project is to construct an 'understanding of the *biological bases* of paternal care' (Kuo et al., 2012: 30) (author's emphasis). In this pursuit, metaphors and phrases such as biological and neural 'bases', 'mechanisms' and 'neural machinery' are deployed (Kuo et al., 2012: 2) in order to explain psychological behaviour and action. This follows what Bermúdez (2016: 17) terms as a 'bottom up' approach, where human action and behaviour is seen to progress in various levels of explanation from 'molecular action potentials', through to the behaviour of neurons, through corresponding mechanisms in the body resulting in human behaviour. The *picture* given here for human action then, is one of stimulus and response; cause and effect; stimulus, mechanism and output.

Admittedly, the relationship between the brain and the mind is, as Bennett et al. (2009) suggest, puzzling and 'difficult to bring into sharp focus'. It may be that such an explanation is itself a confusion about the nature of the mind. However, a significant part of the problem here is that we have a great deal of ambiguity in the application of our words and in some contexts, it's not at all clear what might count as *behaviour*, *action* or a *cause*. These terms are often used ambiguously by some neuroscientific researchers, so for example, neural behaviour is conceived as essentially being the same concept as human behaviour but at a different level of operation. In other words, neurons are attributed with agency. But it's not at all clear how this could be so. The behaviour of neurons (such as action potentials, spikes, or movement within circuits)[27] follows procedural, chemical and neuro-electrical paths, which in turn are seen to impact on human behaviour in mystical ways. But what would it be for human action or motivation to be explainable in terms of agency? What counts as behaviour for a neuron could not possibly amount to the same thing as the behaviour of human agents, operating with various psychological and dispositional considerations in complex social contexts. For example, Crick (1995: 7) had said that 'a complex system' like the brain can be 'explained' by 'the behaviour of its parts'; that is:

> ... to understand the brain we may need to know the many interactions of nerve cells with each other; in addition, the behaviour of each nerve cell may need explanation in terms of the ions and molecules of which it is composed.

Whilst understanding the brain in reductive senses is not in and of itself problematic, conceptual concerns emerge when the mind (a psychological concept) is conflated with the brain (a biological concept). In the current era where science dominates the major research enterprises (not least in psychology, health and education) it should be no great surprise that there is an increasing interest in the development of ways of knowing more about complex concepts like happiness, well-being and flourishing. Such approaches may broadly be termed as reductionist in the sense that they tend to seek ever reductive explanations for what might ordinarily be considered to be psychological phenomena. Thus, in making this conceptual leap, there has been a recent development within well-being research where empirical researchers have sought the biological causes of psychological phenomena.

Notably, for example, Kringelbach & Berridge have developed a growing set of research papers and book chapters with related topics and headings. For example, the 'neuroscience of happiness and pleasure' (Kringelbach & Berridge, 2010), the 'neurobiology of pleasure and happiness' (Kringelbach & Berridge, 2011) and the 'neuroscience of well-being' (Berridge & Kringelbach, 2013). In Kringelbach & Berridge (2010), the authors intentionally avoided the complex discussion on eudemonic measures of well-being (viz., those related to meaning in life) and they focused instead on what they consider to be achievable causal links between the pleasure aspects of brain activity and the felt emotions of happiness and pleasure (viz., assuming that hedonic measures of happiness and well-being are related to a 'liking' scalable measures). Hence, by looking for responses in the brain to particular stimuli, the hope has been to gain insight 'into how brains work to produce' happiness (Kringelbach & Berridge, 2010: 659), as if happiness were some kind of chemical released by the brain. As Bennett & Hacker (2003: 365) aver, neural explanation cannot 'displace or undermine the explanatory force of the *good reasons* we sincerely give for our behaviour or invalidate the justifications we give for rational behaviour' (original emphasis). What is it to be happy? Is it to feel tingly? To have a rush of blood to the head? To feel butterflies? All of these sensations may well *accompany* our emotional responses to a given situation, or even to a thought or flight of fancy, but they could not explain it. We could not, for example, say that our neurons made us feel good, content, satisfied, or irritable etc. Our explanation for emotion is most often based on reasons (though not exclusively).[28]

In another recent study which combined data from genetic sources as well as self-report questionnaires, the authors claimed to have discovered important genetic markers in the aetiology of well-being. Baselmans & Bartels (2018) suggested that there is a similar genetic causal link for both *eudaimonic* well-being – which is linked to notions of meaning – and *hedonic* well-being – which is linked to sensations of pleasure. This appears to be a move which conflates the concept of physiological phenotypes (observable features such as height, eye colour, blood type etc. of a given genotype or organism) with an implied notion of psychological phenotypes (e.g. psychological expression of a given genotype or organism). Thus, it is tempting for such researchers to think that when we use words like 'happiness', 'well-being' or 'flourishing', that we refer either to some discreet biological process or mental state consisting in such processes. As Kringelbach & Berridge (2010: 18) have said:

> Affective neuroscience research on sensory pleasure has revealed many networks of brain regions and neurotransmitters activated by pleasant events and states.

Whilst it is perfectly plausible to formulate explanations with regards to pleasure sensations and aspects of neurological activity, to suggest that this can explain human behaviour is a leap. In using brain-imaging techniques, there is no doubt that these scans can be of *correlational* interest, i.e. to explain which parts of the brain light up during pleasure activation – it is important to remember that just because we have a name or a concept for a phenomenon – it does not follow that it is a 'thing' at all, or indeed that it can be measured. Kringelbach & Berridge (2010) appear to erroneously infer causal links between biological concepts (e.g. nucleus accumbens, ventral pallidum, brainstem) and psychological concepts (like well-being, happiness, pleasure) that in fact require public criteria rather than biological criteria.

For example, if Joseph was in a coma it would not follow that he liked his feet being tickled purely because his brain-imaging scans were to show activity in particular parts of the brain during those moments. This is because the criteria for 'liking' are public and shareable. The criteria for what is to count as 'liking' is a normative matter. It is 'agreement in judgements' (*PI* §242) that qualifies what counts as a particular concept, subject to the various conditions of our cultural practice (liking may not always be clearly expressed). Thus, although it is difficult to see the sense in ascribing 'liking' to someone like Joseph who is unconscious, ordinarily, if we wanted to infer 'liking', we would need to see public and shareable behavioural evidence such as changes in facial expression, smiles, or perhaps verbal praise or laughter etc. Still further, even if we had this set of data (that is behavioural plus neurological data) we could not then infer biological *causes* to such 'liking'. The most we could do is infer correlation.

But then we should ask ourselves, if we take a preference for the behavioural evidence, what value does the neurological data hold for us? (viz., outside of the biological, as opposed to the psychological). As Wittgenstein (*PPF* §371) had commented: 'The existence of the experimental method makes us think that we have the means of getting rid of the problems which trouble us; but problem and method pass one another by'. I suggested earlier, it is understandable that we struggle to grasp these links (largely due to false pictures about human nature) but this does not mean that we should simply make the leap regardless.

Empirical researchers that seek out the biological 'causes' of psychological phenomena make a number of errors; notably, with regard to the conflation of distinct conceptual schemes and the fallacious attempt to find 'causes' for psychological and other behaviour. Bennett & Hacker (2003: 364) use a related phrase: (lack of) 'bridging principles'; and Bermúdez (2016: 35) uses the phrase 'interface problem'. Bennett & Hacker focus on the incompatibility of attributions of psychological predicates to parts of humans such as brains or neural processes (i.e. a mereological fallacy); whereas Bermúdez focuses on the incompatibility of what he terms as four main *pictures* of mind (autonomous, functional, representational, neurocomputational). Both Hacker and Bermúdez describe the problem of incompatible conceptual schemes between neuroscientific and psychological *forms of (reductive) explanation* for human behaviour. All this is to suggest that the self-confessed 'quest' for the neurobiology of well-being, happiness, pleasure or indeed flourishing is in fact to misunderstand what those concepts are – tools and abstractions for particular context and occasion-sensitive purposes – as opposed to discreet biological phenomena or causes of psychological states. It is to run against the limits of language. In order to gain understanding into psychological states, predicates and behaviour, we need to look at our use of concepts rather than to the imaging techniques used to outline neurological, genetic or other reductive data. Such approaches amount to various forms of reductionism, and in particular, differences in forms of explanation between, for example, 'causes' and 'reasons'; that is, conflations between two central *ways* of explaining human action and behaviour.[29]

When researchers declare their interest to reveal 'a better understanding of the pleasures of the brain which may offer a more general insight into happiness, into *how brains work to produce it*' (Kringelbach & Berridge, 2010) – my emphasis is that we do not already have the means with which to develop that understanding. This is often driven by the misleading picture of the physicalist world-view that wants to reduce every explanation to physical causes. It is often coupled with a scientistic picture which leads such researchers to believe that the *only* viable knowledge possible is a scientific one. An illusory set of intuitions is built up so that scientists are seen to reveal the *hidden* nature of reality. But as Hacker (2007a: 46) affirms, human understanding is fundamentally of a conceptual (as opposed to metaphysical) nature:

> It is an illusion that scientific discovery can disclose what the words we use, such as 'gold' and 'water', 'fish' and 'lily', really mean. For what a word means is determined by convention, not by discovery.

Due to these common (gripping) kinds of false pictures, researchers and scientists can commit a scientific fallacy. They can over-inflate the role of scientific research and fail to see its limits. They can misunderstand *what it is* to provide an explanation for human psychology and behaviour, for no scan or analysis of molecular or neural 'behaviour' could contravene the everyday explanation that we can provide for human action. If I say I am happy, it is the public criteria of happiness that counts (taking into consideration the range of contextual factors relevant) and no scanning equipment could contradict it. Even with the widely known replication problems in analysing and making sense of the complexity of human psychology and behaviour aside, the greatest hurdle is that the way we use our words is so complex, that they do not admit to tight definition – and nor should they, they are *tools* not facts like the gravitational constant.[30]

One problem is that such researchers defer resolution of the problem to sometime 'in the future' when the science will allegedly catch up with the concept. For example, Kringelbach & Berridge (2010: 26) suggest that '[f]uture scientific advances may provide a better sorting of psychological features of happiness and its underlying brain networks'. The suggestion is that we will later understand the proper relations between neurology and psychology and the materialist 'hard problem' of consciousness, viz., the causal relation between mind and body, will somehow disappear with scientific advances. Kicking the proverbial can down road doesn't resolve a misconception, and no deferral of addressing a conceptual problem will (nor could it) advance empirical knowledge.

Summative remarks

As has been highlighted, human beings as agents, possess a range of powers. Using animals as an ongoing comparator, I discussed some important distinctions between conceptions of normativity and forms of life, powers, faculties and abilities – contrasting what I have called normative (A) – rule-oriented – vs normative (B) – axiological etc. This distinction is important in order to better understand the unique (and individuated) ways in which we, *qua* human beings, may seek out our own goodness, in particular, by finding ways to express our creative, emotional, moral, intellectual passions and interests (as permitted within our given contexts and abilities). This being the case, I would suggest that agency (and its ordinary cognate terms, such as autonomy, freedom, liberty, self-expression and self-direction etc.) is, therefore, the *central orienting* concept around which flourishing is made possible. By paying particular attention to it, we may provide meaningful conditions for the realization of human flourishing on both personal and political levels. Seeing as we are *all*, in one sense, individuals with virtues and vices, and yet in another sense, legal persons within social and political communities, whether or not we do indeed realize flourishing is a matter of both personal character and circumstantial luck.

Further, as suggested, our behaviour is fundamentally normative, rather than nomological or causal in orientation. As simple as it is, this insight can be a bulwark against the many forms of biological reductionism (cf. Hacker, 1995: 160). The explanatory force of good or bad reasons is a public and shareable matter. The degree to which there is logical warrant for attribution of the infinite and various forms of human action is laid bare as features of our language and a decent judgement of the occasion is what counts. The answers to so-called mysteries of human psychology, action and behaviour are therefore not locked away in some metaphysical location waiting for scientists and researchers to locate them. Believing such is akin more to 'science fiction' than science (cf. Hacker, 2021: 181). *Contra*, the key that unlocks our understanding is simply to grasp that 'nothing is hidden' (*PI* §435) but is explorable through our norms of use and conceptual mapping etc. This insight is what may help us to know *how* to go on, *how* to devise the right questions to ask, *how* to enrich our understanding on a given phenomenon, and *how* to go about dissolving our confusions.

Although we can act with or without reasons, and we share certain primitive ways of acting, unlike the animal kingdom, the development of our linguistic, imaginative and perceptual abilities affords human beings endless possibilities for reflection and creative arranging of pertinent concepts within an 'open ended array of forms of action' (cf. Hacker, 2013a: 103). This is not to use our powers and abilities to raise an anthropocentric hierarchy in nature, but it is to make salient distinctions for our benefit of insight under certain conditions and in certain contexts. The implications of a distinction conception of agency in both education as well as politics should be clear by now. For understanding the relations better between these powers and abilities gives us routes to see problems anew, by conceptualizing problems in diverse contexts and disentangling knots in our thinking and creating beneficent conditions for human autonomy and welfare. Thus, we have at our disposal immense conceptual and linguistic powers in which we may realize *our own* potential (including taking good care for the animals in our care and the planet on which we live). By ever better grasping the language-games that relate to our *own* flourishing, growth, and development, we are better enabled to grasp our duties to each other and to nurture conditions for a mutually beneficial relationship with other forms of life. The journey of discovery, however, begins within.

6

Personal Growth and Development

Although the concept of personal growth and development[1] has a certain trite quality about it (due to the proliferation of self-help books over recent years), there is something central and profound about the concept that often evades attention. My view is that this is because it has become associated with individualism, neoliberalism, and all the other problems normally associated with capitalism and the field of positive psychology. Yet, there an explicit moral and ethical imperative at the heart of the concept of personal development that is impossible to ignore in the context of human flourishing. Personal development is closely connected to the concepts of characterological growth, self-knowledge, skills and abilities, virtuous goals and crucially, wisdom. As Bates (2021: 6) has suggested, however, the instrumental and narrow pursuit of characterological virtues, such as resilience, can lead to an 'inflated self-perception of one's own capabilities' and an 'indifference' to the condition of others.[2] My conception of personal development, then, is not egoistic or focused on career development, wealth or spirituality, or indeed the gratification of the Self (though goals such as career development are obviously implied in a secondary sense). Rather, by virtue of the categorial remarks already made with regards to the nature of human beings, it is integrated into a complex, social and moral system of concepts. The focus of this chapter, then, will be on the development of character and self-knowledge *for* flourishing.

With this in mind, it will be useful to look at this range of conceptual relations, specifically, what it is to know the Self, what is desirable to know, how one might go about meaningfully improving oneself within the options available to us as individuals, and importantly, how one might go about developing a better understanding of what it means for us to live the 'good life', especially through times of adversity. Following Wittgenstein's set of methods,[3] this includes nurturing beneficent *ways* of thinking, such as gaining a new perspective over the concepts of interest, and their pertinent relationships (cf. *PI* §122). Although I won't have scope to explore this fully here, plotting some of the most important relationships in this network of concepts allows us to have some sense of oversight (*übersichten*)[4] on the related problems in the uses of a word. Such techniques can be quite transformational on a philosophical as much as a personal level. This is partly why Wittgenstein (*CV* 24e) suggests, '[w]ork on philosophy – like work in architecture in many respects – is really more work on oneself. On one's own conception. On how one sees things. (And what one expects of them.)'.

I acknowledge that professional philosophy is here correlated with ordinary practices in life, but I do so intentionally. Wittgenstein is also attributed with the aphorism that if one wants to improve the world, one should: '[j]ust improve yourself' (Monk, 1991: 17). This slogan might at once seem glib, but in fact it may help to highlight a conceptual insight with regards to the close relationship between morality, responsibility and agency (as highlighted by myself in Chapter 5).[5] Hence, following on my interpretation of Wittgenstein's integrated, moral approach to philosophy, I too am committed to the idea that any (often vague or woolly) notion of a 'good' for humankind must – by virtue of conceptual logic as much as the force of pragmatism – begin with 'oneself', one's understanding of one's duties, and one's responsibilities and place (predicament) in the world.

In aiming for our own growth, development and flourishing, we must first assume that we have some notion of the person (the 'Self') of whom is being developed. We can be tempted however, to ask questions such as: 'is it me that develops myself?'. Such questions can be misleading and can surreptitiously lead us into conceptual confusion for we can assume a division of selves. We can be led to assume that there is a *real* me (e.g. the Self, the mind that is me, or the consciousness that is me) who is acting on another entity, i.e. whether that be another side of me or the body. Further, when we associate certain words, or psychological concepts, with our feelings we can mistakenly conclude that these constitute the very meanings of these words themselves (*PPF* §174—6, §181–3, §214). This can lead to a form of epistemological privatism or solipsism which can further lead to metaphysicalizing confusions of human thought – even madness.[6] As Monk (1991: 25) has noted, in contrast to his earlier writings, '[m]uch of Wittgenstein's later philosophical thinking about the Self is an attempt once and for all to put to rest the ghost of this view' and hence, refocusing our minds on the normativity of knowledge and understanding. Nonetheless, hugely important to us here, as philosophers, is averting the risk of over-intellectualizing human growth and development which can also lead to a kind of what I'd like to call, inauthentic 'rational excess', the kind of development that is detached from some of the important ethical and experiential implications of our inner lives, and hence, detached from the *practice* of life. By the end of the chapter, it should be clear that separating thinking from action too sharply, though useful at times, can have a pernicious effect on self-knowledge and personal development. Heeding Wittgenstein, what we want, rather, is a recognition of the embeddedness of our linguistic practices in and *through* our unique form of life (*PPF* §335).

Chapter sections

Hence, in section one ('The absurdity of the 'Self'") I will explore some of these subtle confusions, in particular, the notion that we are private entities with private identities within our bodies. Conversely, I will make a case for normative identity and the importance of developing a well-informed concept of Self. This is important both to help demonstrate the public and sharable nature of knowledge (including self-knowledge), but also to provide a simple and workable framework for better understanding what it is to develop as a person with flourishing in mind.

In section two, ('Personal senses of identity') I explore notions of *personal identity*. This happens to be an area of philosophy with extensive attention. My focus here will be on addressing the nature of identity, its common association with memory and how this relates to personal development. My aim will be to de-mystify the concept and dislodge it from its metaphysical associations. Nevertheless, because the 'Self' is no essential thing, I will also show how memory and narrative play an important role in what I will address in section three regarding degrees in conceptions of the Self.

In section three ('A rough conception of "Self"'), building on the notion of a Self as a conception, I show how mastery of the Self-concept is part of what it is to mature as a human being with the capacity for using one's agency in creative ways for personal fulfilment. This helps to build an approach to personal development that is far more open-ended that we might otherwise assume (not least in the context of some of the arguments of biological determinism).[7]

In section four ('Ways of knowing oneself: knowing-*how* versus knowing-*that*'), building on insights from both Ryle (1946) and Cassam (2014), I look at *ways of knowing* oneself. I explore their critiques of intellectualism and rationalism respectively, in the context of what we might term as cognitive verses practical knowledge. In particular I pay attention to Ryle's notorious distinction between knowing-*that* and knowing-*how* suggesting that the latter is not reducible to the former. As I will show, this has serious implications not only for concept mastery and self-knowledge, but for what this looks like in practice too (i.e. the development of practical wisdom).

Finally, in section five, ('Knowing *how* to live the good life') I build on the previous sections under the focus of knowing-*how* approaches to gaining wisdom and insight into *how to* live the good life. I spend some time critiquing Grimm's (2015) conception of wisdom (which he sees as being epistemically motivated towards well-being). I suggest that his analysis is misleading and excessively reductive. If wisdom is anything generally at all, it is not a kind of knowledge per se; rather, as I will suggest, it is a kind of skill or *ability* to make good judgements.

Following Aristotle and others, I will suggest that the development of epistemic and moral virtues is also hugely important. I am not, however, interested in perfectionistic conceptions of human beings. As Cassam (2014: 9) suggests, '... it's helpful to distinguish real humans as we know them from *homo philosophicus*, the idealized subject of so much philosophical theorizing'. In this spirit, I will *not* be advocating for an idealized form of human perfectionism (à la Hurka, 1996); human beings are, after all, developmental by nature. Rather, my focus will be on the human being as *Homo loquens*: concept-deploying, moral agents.

I now turn to explore uses of the Self in the context of personal development and maturation. This will be important in order to explore further how confusions about our 'self-concept' can lead to epistemic, conceptual, metaphysical and essentialist confusions that have practical and deleterious consequences on human understanding and development.

The absurdity of the 'Self'

We often talk about the *true* Self, the *real* Self, *old* Self, *new* Self, the *future* Self, etc. These uses suggest the *states* of persons with each 'Self' having a distinct logical relationship to the present Self. For example, we say that we must find our true or real 'Self', both broadly assuming that we are *deceived* about our identities. We also talk about our past or future selves in the context of the development of human beings in the natural course of maturation. This humanistic ethic reinforces the creative force of human beings (to some degree at least) as masters or creators of their own destinies; a *Homo Faber*.[8] Hence, we also talk about self-employment and self-defence; self-promotion, self-development and self-improvement; self-acceptance and self-actualization. These are action-oriented things that we (seemingly) do *to* ourselves. When we are self-employed, it means that we work *for* ourselves; when we learn self-defence, we are learning methods of defending ourselves against attack. When we practice self-promotion, we conduct actions that work to raise our own profile or standing within a particular community. When we work on self-development or improvement, we assess our strengths and weaknesses and identify how we can improve ourselves in some practical sense (usually through upskilling or education). When we talk about self-actualizing, this is naturally *teleological* in nature for we aim towards some kind of beneficent outcome through some form of directed, purposive activity.

In everyday parlance such uses of the Self are normally unproblematic as long as we accept them as linguistic devices for making certain forms of distinctions. After all, in an ordinary sense of speaking about *my* job I am not actually talking about your job but *my* paid role with my employer. It is the surface grammar and contrast that can lead to confusion. In speaking about *my* goals, I am not speaking about your goals, I am speaking about *my own* targets, standards or aims. As long as we understand that when speaking of myself, my mind, my passions etc., we do not go awry, whereas if we assume that the contrast is an agent versus an operation that is where we do go awry. There are, then, *implicit* problems related to dualistic notions of the Self as possessor of a body; an inner Self who owns a body.

A confused notion of the Self will almost invariably lead to confused and damaging outcomes in life (though there are cases of benevolent self-deception which I'll discuss later). If we take our language to refer directly to objects in the world, then it is perfectly logical to see the world in ways that are confusing, that is, to see me as both a subject *and* object of my actions. As Wittgenstein alludes, '"I" doesn't name a person, nor "here" a place, and "this" is not a name.' (*PI* §410).[9] If I say: 'I am pleased about my new job', in saying this, I report my feelings on a given issue, it is not me saying that the *inner* (or real) me is happy about something that is happening to the outer me (my body); nor is it saying something about what I now own. Rather, in saying this I merely inform you how things are with me, ontology and location have nothing to do with it – though such notions are misleadingly implied in the *surface* grammar. The confusion for some philosophers, as Anscombe (1975: 143) suggests, is to view 'I' as a proper noun rather than a personal pronoun.[10]

What would it be for me to be known to myself as both 'Eri' (proper noun) and 'I' (personal pronoun). It is almost as if the uses we are discussing here take the form of an indexical. They have the function of a kind of relative placeholder in our grammar, but they are neither entities nor referents (so conceived on the model of the inner psychological world versus a putative external reality). They are linguistic devices, rather, used to contrast linguistic entities e.g. *here* rather than there, *this*, rather than that, *I*, rather than you – as opposed to metaphysical entities.[11] So, when I have an interest in my development, it is not something that *I* do (as a subject) to *myself* (as an object), it is merely something that I *do* (usually with some form of rationalization). Confusing a linguistic term of ownership for a metaphysical possession or entity is blindly running up against the 'limits of language' (cf. *PI* §119).[12] The root problem is as a result of some linguistic confusion; our aim is to dissolve such confusions rather than advance or ignore them.[13] Our motivation should not be to build a grand theory of the psychological, metaphysical or phenomenal human *Self*, but rather to distil a better understanding of the *Self* in the context of our particular questions regarding personal development. A great deal of this exploration, therefore, revolves around the related notions of the particularity of the 'person'.

As I will now suggest, it is important to explore some further issues with regards to notions of personal identity in the context of agency, goal-setting and development. In so doing, it would be remiss then not to explore Parfit's (1971) take on some of the relevant issues, including what it means to be a person as subject, and to have an identity and how we can make sense of such terms. As I will argue, having a clear sense of identity is crucial for building personal efficacy and development.

Personal senses of identity

The related notion of 'personal identity' can be traced to Locke who argued for a form of psychological reductionism. For him, the 'person' was a kind of self-awareness entailing various kinds of *memory* states, between selves of the past, present and future, an experiencer of continuous of memories. For example, Locke (1979: II.27.ix) stated that:

> [A person is] a thinking intelligent Being, that has reason and reflection, and considers itself as itself, the same thinking thing in different times and places.

As Hacker (2007a: 265) suggests, whilst Locke did not go as far as Descartes to assert the 'I' as a metaphysical Self or ego, he did seem to have a picture of the mind as a private entity in epistemological (rather than ontological) terms. So, where Descartes saw the unifying principle of human beings to be an essential and immaterial substance, Locke saw the essence in purely epistemic terms.[14] In his seminal 1971 paper 'Personal Identity', Parfit explores the necessary components of identity. He does so by using an example from Shoemaker (1963), cited in Wiggins (1967), namely the problem of identity in the context of a brain transplant error.

In Shoemaker's rendition (cited by Wiggins, 1967) he asks readers to suppose that in the future humans could perform brain surgery by removing it from the body, repairing the relevant damaged sections of the brain, reattaching the relevant structures and nerves and re-inserting it into the skull. In that future, we are asked to imagine two patients (Mr. Brown and Mr. Robinson) in need of surgical intervention and repair of some sort. The surgeon's assistant makes a dreadful mistake by placing the wrong brains in the wrong places and so the surgeon re-implants them into the wrong bodies. One body survives the procedure, namely, with the body of Robinson and Brown's brain. He has particular, subject-relative memories. Shoemaker then asks us to call this man 'Brownson'. Brownson looks like Robinson but has most of Brown's memories including those pertaining to Brown's wife and various other events. He retains much of the characteristics, traits and mannerisms of Brown as well. Shoemaker (1963: 23–24) suggests that there would be little question that 'many of us would be ... rather strongly inclined, to say that while Brownson has Robinson's body he is actually Brown'. Of course, the baseline assumption is that a person's subjective identity is a physicalist one because it assumes that somehow the Self has a location within the brain, so when the brain is relocated, so goes the person (and personality) with it. The question is then raised about the *identity* of Brownson; as Shoemaker observes, '... it would be absurd to suggest that brain identity is our criterion of personal identity'. But the problem that Shoemaker set up is a form of double-bind where we are logically asked to assume the absurd in order to conclude the equally absurd finding ourselves in an impossible predicament.

Parfit (1971: 5) asks us to re-examine the problem of personhood in the context of the swapped brain example that these texts (i.e. by Shoemaker and Wiggins) explore. *If* we accept the logic of the thought-experiment, (that is, a mind conceived as a bundle of continuous memories held within a skull) then the question of the identity of the Self is Brown, trapped inside another body (that of Robinson). Primarily, it is abundantly clear that the 'picture' of the Self offered to readers here is a dualist one underpinned by a form of physicalism. However, the problem is set up by already presupposing a reductive criterion for personal identity (using a naturalist explanatory framework, logically equating the brain with the mind, and then with the subject-agent) whilst then moving to a totally different criterion (e.g. behavioural) form of criteria, hence a categorial error ensues.

By way of an example, we can consider the case of Jane Dobs, an older person with advanced dementia and very few aspects of their personality intact. In a legal context, understanding what the 'person' of Jane might mean is somewhat clear, and someone may be afforded the same legal status of identity as before onset dementia. Naturally there are several pragmatic concerns here to do with legal responsibilities as well as the execution of her will and estate, all of which play a part in continuing a *legal* sense of identity in the absence of what might otherwise seem to be the presence of the person. Those who know Jane, however, are likely to see her differently if she changes her behaviour substantially. This is because in context, the features of her personality helped to distinguish her for who she is.

Let's say she had a cranky disposition, a belief in Judaism, a wry sense of humour, and goals to retire in Cote D'Azur, run a vineyard there etc. These are all facets of her personality that help to shape *who* she is (or rather, who she is 'seen as') to others. Of course, we may decide to *treat* them as the same person irrespective of their loss of individuated personality, perhaps as an act of faith or compassion, or because we love them. Nonetheless, her behaviour forms a considerable part of the criteria for our understanding for who she is – memory alone is insufficient. Once the criteria for Jane does not seem to be met then we may well not treat them as the *same* person. It does not necessarily matter that Jane might not live out her ambitions and goals for retirement (i.e. her internal, subjective, psychological goals of life), for many people fail to live out their dreams and do not lose their identity. What is important is that the criteria we are used to applying in speaking about her is more or less retained (or *not* as the case may be).

In cases where Jane might be losing her temper, her memories or even her mind, we have stock phrases such as 'She's not quite herself', or 'She's not been the same person since it happened' ... or 'She is out of sorts' etc. These amount to something like, 'She is not *behaving* like she normally does'; the focus is on the public criteria descriptions of her behaviour. This is not to suggest that if someone loses a large part of their memory that they cannot be a person (clearly, they can), it is merely to suggest that they would not necessarily be the *same* person (objectively, behaviourally). They become someone new and in so doing they lose some things whilst gaining others. They lose a form of objective identity, whilst they retain the same legal identity.[15] Relatedly, people like Jane will likely not see *themselves* in the same way as they did previously, though they may be the same Self (subjectively). If they have different goals, memories (or lack thereof), emotional responses, even dispositions, then it makes perfect sense that they might 'see' themselves differently. A change in self-conception need not have a medical problem as its source. It is also a perfectly ordinary occurrence in the context of the stages of life. As we learn, develop and grow, (or not, as the case may be), priorities change and as a matter of pragmatic alterations, our identities can change from stage to stage as we adopt new roles in life in new contexts.

For example, a child might be very inhibited and quiet in early years, but then grow in confidence and competence developing a sense for self-efficacy. Whether this amounts to a different Self or identity is subject to the criteria for the original Self so construed. What seems clear is that there is a necessity for *behavioural* criteria to be fulfilled in terms of how we might conceptualize any notion of a Self. In the brain transplant error case offered by Shoemaker (1963) and Wiggins (1967), we can see the absurdity of the kind of psychological reductionism offered by Parfit (1971) in the context of personal identity.[16] As Hacker (2007a: 271) suggests, 'a human being does not have the organism that he is'; s/he is the organism that s/he is. It therefore makes no sense to see ourselves as compartmentalized, discreet, moveable brains (biological reductionism), or indeed of selves contained with our minds consisting of memories and experiences (psychological reductionism). In other words, we are whole beings. Speaking in terms of distinctions between various aspects of the human being is merely one way of drawing attention to a salient feature of our conceptual grammar, in order to understand it better on a given occasion and for a particular purpose, with a given contrast in mind. That is a conceptual (as opposed to a metaphysical) exercise.

A rough conception of 'Self'

The distinction between me and others suggests that my self-identification (through my particular experience, memories, relations etc.) as a subjective agent is roughly equivalent to what Strawson (1999) suggests is the possession of the concept of Oneself, (or as Joplin (2000) suggests, a 'self-concept'). This possession is certainly not one of Cartesian entities nor of Lockean minds. It is merely a way of me operating with efficacy in this world as both a developmental person (subject to changes in experiences, goals, ambitions, reasons) whilst also remaining as an authentic one consistent to particular set of values important to me. It wouldn't make sense if I were to alter my values on a daily basis, because such values need defending *for reasons*. This going about with a coherent conception of myself permits me to develop somewhat of a folk theory of myself, a self-narrative, as an efficacious and authentic agent in the world; this moves from weaker conceptions to stronger ones as we possess our language to ever greater degrees of competence and self-knowledge. As Hacker (2007a: 240) rightly suggests:

> A creature that has mastered a language with demonstrative and indexical devices, including the personal pronouns, can acquire the self-reflexive cognitive and cogitative abilities that constitute self-consciousness ... only if he can reflect on his reasons and probe his motives can he strive for that self-knowledge that is attainable by self-conscious creatures.

Possessing the concept of Self (or of having a Self-concept) then is not necessarily the same as being self-knowledgeable. As developing human beings, we are prone to epistemic 'blind-spots', so the degree to which we can ascribe our development is warranted insofar as we are willing to push beyond our current conceptions of Self, personal identity, and personal limitations (e.g. self-limiting beliefs): development *logically* requires movement. A Self-concept is relative to where we have been (our past experiences, our stories that we tell ourselves about ourselves), where we are (how we feel about our present state of mind and affairs) and where we wish to be or go to (in terms of our hopes, goals, dreams and ambitions). Joplin (2000: 46) avers:

> There are many aspects of the self that are not fully accessible to the person whose self it is, and thus many aspects of the self that are not possible objects for conceptualization.

I think that Joplin is being quite right to draw distinctions between current and future selves. This linguistic strategy allows us to realize that we can arrive at major points of learning and change to the point that we become forever altered.[17] Being caught within some level of ignorance is the human state of affairs by default. What this implies, at least for me, is that a Self-concept is incipiently simple, thin and minimal. It is a diamond in the rough, a rudimentary concept of beginnings. Because of our two-way volitional powers, we have the power to decide, to judge, and to alter one's course and this then offers us a huge range of scope allowing for a range of possibilities for gaining self-knowledge within the parameters of the conception of the Self. We grow insofar as we allow ourselves the space for characterological development. Building on our almost infinite agential powers, the endless possibilities for personal development also suggest, at least logically speaking, that the somewhat partial notion of the Self propels us towards change.

This unfolding self-knowledge from various states of ignorance, suggests to me that we cannot know precisely what we do not yet know; there are 'unknown unknowns'.[18] This epistemic insecurity by itself *can* compel us to accept the logical and pragmatic truism of the need to adopt an attitude of epistemic pluralism (ways of knowing) or contextualism, for if we cannot know what we do not know then it follows that we do not yet know how to get ourselves out of such a predicament of ignorance. The good news about this is that no matter how dire our immediate conception of Self is there is always *logical space* for development; that is, precisely because of our state of ignorance (or ongoing development), there is *almost* always hope.[19]

So far, I have been exploring the various *uses* of the concept of the Self, and some of the related absurdities with the implications of dualist notions of Self. As I have shown, this is merely a feature of our language and our grammar. I have also tried to show that developing a coherent concept of the Self is vital for personal development because it allows us to conceptualize new possibilities outside of our immediate experience. This ability to play with conceptions of the Self, then, is a highly useful tool for personal development and maturation. No doubt, there are ways of knowing and ways of evaluating whether one knows. How we make sense of this is central to the issues raised in this chapter.

I turn now to discuss some of the epistemological issues which pertain to a conception of oneself as an epistemic, rational and moral agent. Specifically, to redeploying Ryle's (1946) distinction between knowing-that and knowing-how in the context of personal development. It is useful because personal development is not mental development, it is rather knowing-*how* to do something (action) that counts, and relatedly, knowing-*how* to go on (conceptual mastery) within the language-games of goal-setting and growth.

Ways of knowing oneself: knowing-*how* versus knowing-*that*

The distinction between knowing-that and knowing-how was made popular by Ryle (1945) in his presidential address to the Aristotelian Society. He was concerned with the 'prevailing doctrine' of intellectualism, a theory that posits that 'Intelligence is a special faculty, the exercises of which are those specific internal acts which are called acts of thinking, namely, the operations of considering propositions'. Ryle's account seems to, roughly speaking, amount to an undermining of the elitist notions of knowledge at the time, one that reduces practical knowledge to factual or propositional knowledge (hence the intellectualist label).

Following Wittgenstein, it also places knowledge (certainly knowledge about what is important in life) largely outside of the mind, and back within the practical realm of human action and ability.[20] Ryle's distinction between *knowing-how* (e.g. how to perform a practical skill) versus *knowing-that* (e.g. knowledge *about* things, propositional facts and truths) was an attack on the intellectualist dogma that knowledge somehow always needed to be cognitive or mental in nature first, and then applied. For example, Ryle (2009: 8) says: '... [w]hen a person knows how to do things of a certain sort (e.g. make good jokes, conduct battles or behave at funerals), his knowledge is actualized or exercised in what he does'. On the one hand this sounds like he is suggesting that there are two processes at work; one is at a level of factual knowledge, and then secondly, the exercise of *that* knowledge. However, in opposition to such claims, Ryle (1946: 1) suggested that:

> Intelligence is *directly exercised* ... in some practical performances as in some theoretical performances ... an intelligent performance need incorporate no "shadow act" of contemplating regulative propositions.
>
> [my emphasis added]

Ryle draws on numerous other examples including the cases of behaviour, etiquette, teaching, legal performance in a court etc. In each case he argues that knowing-how *presupposes* knowing-that. This is to say that for Ryle, the practice or the action comes first as a matter of developing skill. It is only latterly that we have the opportunity to reflect and reason on why we acted in particular ways, why this worked etc. The problem for Ryle is that we can often confuse a devised system of retrospective intellectualized learning about skills (knowing-that) for the learning process and inculcation of the relevant skill itself (knowing-how) which he suggests is the vastly superior, '[e]ducation or training produces not blind habits but intelligent powers' through *practice* not intellectualization. In doing so, he suggests that knowing-how is the exercise, actioning, execution, manifestation, even 'actualization' of a different kind of knowledge and understanding, not of propositions per se, but of 'principles', norms and standards of behaviour, or in 'learning how to act'.[21]

To begin with then, what kinds of things might count as 'knowing-*that*' in the context of self-knowledge? Building on Ryle, Cassam (2014: 43) offers some examples:

- Knowing that you are generous (knowledge of one's character).
- Knowing that you are not a racist (knowledge of one's values).
- Knowing that you can speak Spanish (knowledge of one's abilities).
- Knowing that you are a good administrator (knowledge of one's aptitudes).
- Knowing that you are in love (knowledge of one's emotions).
- Knowing that a change of career would make you happy (knowledge of what makes one happy).

The kind of self-knowledge outlined above certainly seems useful for personal development. It's harder to go about one's life if one is deluded about one's abilities, beliefs or characteristics in a fundamental sense because you will (normally) face a life of even greater challenges then you would otherwise face. Facts seem important in pragmatic ways, not purely intellectual ones. Some argue, however, that all knowledge is reducible to knowing-*that* (including knowing-how).[22] This is at least partially true because experience shows us that we grow in knowledge about ourselves and the world through time (at least in principle). The central question is whether self-knowledge is even possible outside of a knowing-*how* ability. It is one thing to know that an arrow is an arrow, prima facie as a fact, but seeing as what is to count as an arrow is primarily to know what *kind* of thing an arrow is (knowing-that), we can see how it could be argued that knowing-how could be reducible to a knowing-*that* kind in one sense; there doesn't seem to be one without the other.

In the case of the arrow, however, the concept is meaningless outside of knowing-*how* – namely, to think about the role that an arrow plays in the language-game of archery. This includes knowledge of what to do with it, where to place it on the bow string, how to use it and how to use it well. To try and reduce that knowledge to propositional knowledge (e.g. the arrow rises and falls, will pierce flesh etc.) is simply misleading. Typically, knowing-how might suggest a practice of some sort, which seems to imply the application of both mental knowledge and practical *skills*, though not necessarily the discreet mental knowledge supposed by some intellectualists. Broadly construed such skills might include,

- Language skills (learning facts, grammatical rules and idioms)
- Reflective skills (ability to reflect and gain knowledge about yourself, strengths, weaknesses, values and goals)
- Career skills (knowledge)
- Interpersonal skills (surface relations/ people management)
- Interview skills (interpersonal skills)

- Relationships with others (deeper relations, emotion regulation)
- Health insights (physical and mental well-being)
- Practical skills (tricks on a bike/ art/ magic/ climbing trees/ fishing/ play-fighting/ card tricks/ DIY/ making rope swings/ fires/ bows and arrows), and
- Practical wisdom (good judgement in everyday matters).

Wittgenstein draws a related distinction between technique (learning fixed rules in systems of knowledge) and judgement (knowledge gained through experience and intuition). In the context of knowing the feelings of others, Wittgenstein states:

> Can one learn this knowledge? Yes; some can learn it. Not, however, by taking a course of study in it, but through 'experience' ... Can someone else be a man's teacher in this? Certainly. From time to time he gives him the right tip. – This is what 'learning' and 'teaching' are like here. – What one acquires here is not a technique; one learns correct judgements. There are also rules, but they do not form a system, and only experienced people can apply them rightly. Unlike calculating rules.
>
> PPF §355

A telling remark is that 'these do not form a system'. Here Wittgenstein is alerting us to the impulse towards generalizing about that kind of knowledge too tightly. There is only so far that a rule, a proposition, or a fact can take us, the real benefit lies in the ability of a person to perform good judgements of how these 'facts' fit in to a given system of concern appropriate to answering the question at hand in a given situation. Similarly, as Ryle suggests in the context of practical wisdom, 'Aristotle was talking about how people learn to behave wisely, not how they are drilled into acting mechanically' (Ryle, 2009: 15). This distinction has huge implications, for pedagogical practice among other areas. Crucially of interest for us here, is how we *learn* to develop as a person. It might seem sensible to suggest that it is not through the learning by rote of the principles of life, or in repeating mantras, or in forcing certain behaviours that we learn how to live a good life.

Ryle's critique does throw a criticism at disciplinarian approaches to teaching which he equates with teaching a seal. For example, he contrasts a 'recruit' (i.e. a student, initiate) with an animal: 'Unlike the seal he [the recruit] becomes a judge of his own performance – he learns what mistakes are and how to avoid or correct them' [parenthesis added]. This seems to be the very mark of intelligence (or perhaps 'insight') for Ryle. This helps to support arguments that suggest that agency and autonomy are crucial in the context of meaningful learning and development. I may have the potential as a human being to develop musical talent, and indeed the ability to master it, but I may choose to do nothing with it for an ability (once learned) need not be strengthened and may be subject to neglect. If someone struggles with motivation, they may even choose not to apply their vocational abilities to work, for example. Winch (2006: 74) too agrees with Ryle in this important sense:

> ... autonomy requires one to be able to engage in a form of practical reasoning concerning one's own ends in life. The outcome of the exercise of autonomy should be a course of action based on *one's own motivation*.
> [my emphasis]

Although the concept of knowing-that is useful in fundamental ways, knowing-how seems to require of us greater intelligence and insight. Further, as Hacker, 2013a: 3) suggests, the 'former is not in general reducible to the latter'. The duality of knowing-how is perhaps akin to learning a language on paper. Whereas knowledge of verbs and cases is important for general rule-mastery, it is the *practice* of speaking a language (learning all the idioms and body language that helps to communicate effectively), that is more important.[23] This indicates a broad range of knowing abilities for sure. On this view, know-how seems on one hand to be a *background* knowledge or range of assumptions about how to go about with knowledge (e.g. awareness of concepts and schemes and how to operate within them). On another, it is a kind of *practical* knowledge (or skill) which might typically include activities such as riding a bike, handwriting, drawing, or playing a musical instrument etc. I'd like to suggest that *both* uses are forms of practical judgement. This seems to be a position that intellectualists like Stanley & Williamson (2017) may also, recently, be willing to concede.[24] Nonetheless, Hacker (2013a: 153) articulates at least three central uses of *know-how*, and these will be relevant here:

> What is possessed when one has achieved mastery of an art or craft is practical knowledge or know-how. We may distinguish, in Aristotelian spirit, between the know-how of making (mastery of a craft) the successful exercise of which produces an artefact that is good of its kind, the know-how of educating (of cultivating analytic powers, teaching intellectual and practical skills, inculcating virtues), and the know-how of doing (e.g. mastery of the art of medicine, the arts of politics or of war, the performing arts). All involve acquisition of information and principles to a greater or lesser degree. But neither information nor maxims suffice for mastery of a craft or art.

Hacker's 'know-how' schema seems to suggest 1) mastery of a craft, 2) mastery of analytic powers, and 3) mastery at work. Self-knowledge and understanding, then, seem to be evidence of maturation in a given domain of knowledge, what seems to differ is a matter of degree in the level of maturity, skill and ability. Hence, whether or not someone masters a particular skill-set will rely hugely on the degree to which we (as a culture) *value* such skills.[25] Ryle (1946) and Cassam (2014) both articulate their own distinctive version of conceptions of knowing-how, and both are targeted to avoid rationalist or intellectualist excess in their conceptions of knowledge. Hacker (2013a) builds on these insights to help form a richer schema for know-how. In the final section I will explore these 'know-how' themes a little further in the context of the closely related terms of wisdom, well-being and flourishing.

Knowing *how* to live the good life

Grimm's (2015) explicit aim of his paper is to contrast his account of wisdom with the kind of wisdom that Ryan (2012) has advocated, one based on a 'rational beliefs'. The rationality criterion has a long and well-established history.[26] Grimm's strategy is to contrast 'theoretical' wisdom (which he associates with the rationality criterion) with 'practical' wisdom (which he associates with practical knowledge-how).[27] This all seems sensible. In terms of areas of agreement with Grimm according to his theory, it makes perfect sense to me to suggest that the kind of knowledge that is conducive to wisdom entails (at least in part) knowing *what* is good for well-being, one's standing in relation to beneficial goals, and knowing-how one might go about attaining such goals. Further, Grimm also suggests that knowledge of how to live well admits to degrees (I made a similar point earlier in the context of self-knowledge). However, I take the following issues with his approach.

Firstly, Grimm (2015) frames wisdom in terms of the kind of know-how that centres on what is important for well-being. He proposes a three-fold framework for his 'partially articulated' theory; specifically:

1. Knowledge of what is good or important for well-being,
2. Knowledge of one's standing, relative to what is good or important for well-being,
3. Knowledge of a strategy for obtaining what is good or important for well-being.

The epistemic focus for Grimm leads him to see knowing-how to live well as 'a complex state', which he seems to mean a mental state. He goes on to give examples of wise people. For example, he contrasts what he terms as an 'ideal state' of knowledge (such as the state of knowledge claimed by some of the writers in the Bible about the God of the Abrahamic religions)[28] with so-called 'progressors', discussed by some of the Stoics like Seneca, or as he prefers, the 'incipiently wise' (Grimm, 2015: 141–142).[29]

However, Grimm's notion of this wisdom as being a 'state' is misleading. Firstly, because states of mind are fleeting and transitory. We can be in a state of bliss, or sadness, or happiness, or desire, but not of knowledge. For one, we do not have a use for that particular phrase, but in any case, what would it be to be in a state of knowledge? A state of 'nirvana' perhaps (implying total knowledge, according to the Buddhist system of beliefs) but not knowledge in the sense that we are talking about here. One's knowledge that one is wearing socks does not refer to some mental state of 'sock-on-foot' knowledge, it merely means that I remember putting them on, or see that I have socks on. Equally, if I forget that I have socks on it does not mean that I have lost my state of socks-on-foot; it simply means that I have failed to recall a former action or event for whatever reason. After all, we do numerous humdrum activities quite automatically, 'without thinking', and this can contribute to forgetfulness of the detail, but that is not losing a mental state. It is related to our ability and skill to recall events and actions.[30] Hacker (2013a) identifies the tendency to view knowledge as a 'mental state' with the contention that grammarians tend to view first person avowals of knowledge in the stative form. For example, one would not normally say 'I am knowing' or 'While I was knowing' – for this would sound incoherent. Rather, we say, 'I know', which sounds like I am in a state of knowledge (Hacker, 2013a: 153).[31] States imply passive and transient modes of consciousness, whereas knowledge is fully conscious, active, and engaging. If Grimm's claim is that wisdom is a form of knowledge, then, whatever such knowledge is, it cannot be a kind of mental state.

Grimm (2015: 150) also makes quite a radical move in reducing wisdom to 'knowledge of how to live well'. As he argues, 'Knowing how to live well is what we might call the "focal meaning" of the concept wisdom.' But it is not at all obvious that the goal of wisdom is well-being. Even by his account, he cites a number of exemplars such as Martin Luther King or Mahatma Gandhi and I do not think that, though wise, these figures could be considered to be wise *for* their ability to know about what is good for well-being or how to secure it; after all, both were assassinated for championing their ethical and political beliefs which doesn't seem at all wise if well-being is the aim of wisdom.[32] Rather, the source of attributions of wisdom for characters of history like Gandhi and others seem to centre, at least partially, on their *foresight*; that is, on their abilities to see beyond immediate political expedience, to bring about positive social change, and to exemplify virtue to others in the process. But this is not at all a concern for well-being, quite the reverse. On their example, rather than knowledge, *virtuous action* (such as transcendence, courage, selflessness, compassion etc.) is what seems to contribute to an assessment of wisdom. Of course, whether or not such action or wisdom is epistemic in nature largely depends on your conception of the virtues (e.g. as knowledge, skill or practice). It is not that Grimm discounts the value of the virtues in ascribing wisdom, his conception of wisdom as cited above, is epistemic; more to the point – it is epistemically *directed* towards well-being. This claim is somewhat utilitarian in ideological orientation. Yet it is not at all clear why a virtue should be classed in such reductive, egoistic or consequentialist terms.

Finally, Grimm often focuses on 'knowledge-*of*' (i.e. good) which seems at least to me to be a form of knowledge-*that* rather than knowledge-*how*. For example, he notes that 'there is no such thing as "being wise in general"', and advocates for a 'genus-species view of wisdom' (Grimm, 2015: 149); however, this is to confuse different *uses* of wisdom. Whilst it is perfectly sensible to suggest that no man is perfectly wise, we have a use for the term 'wise people' in a 'general' sense. What wisdom means in a context will be specific, but 'general wisdom' or 'generally wise' is a perfectly feasible way to go about describing some states of affairs for the very reason that it is *not* epistemically focused (at least not in the knowing-that sense); indeed, there is no end to knowledge of that factual kind.[33] Nor indeed is the use of 'general wisdom' concerned with any notion of 'perfection' (although there are some religious or philosophical traditions that do draw that association).

It is not particularly complicated or 'deep' to observe that general wisdom is attributable insofar as someone has a particularly striking ability to make good judgements about a wide array of affairs relevant to life. Although one must develop abilities (i.e. they are learnt through formal and informal education) wisdom is transferrable across various domains of knowledge and action. In arguing for the 'genus-species view of wisdom', Grimm (2015: 149) claims that the, '… generic notion of wisdom needs to be relativized to a domain—made specific—before it has any reality'. In doing so, he seems to undermine the crucial element in knowing-how which is about *skill* not epistemic content; agential judgement, as opposed to discreet epistemic value. The criterion of success here in my view should be the development of *human* skill and ability. Although the distinction is not always as clear as we might think, and although we can definitely talk about the attainment of developmental wisdom (through experience), wisdom amounts to a knowing-*how* kind of knowledge, an *ability* to think with agility, capability and judgement. The kind of wisdom that we are interested in here is one focused on human ability as opposed knowledge.[34]

This is partly why Wittgenstein's insights on the practice of philosophy have such a significant bearing on a profound range of epistemic, personal, ethical and moral issues, because they may help us to be motivated to 'see' and frame things aright, to *want* to develop beneficent perspectives and frameworks where genuine moral insight, personal development and transformation can meaningfully occur.[35] The goal, then, can be nothing less than *liberation* from either philosophical or else personal problems that might have a philosophical root (though these are often related).[36] What could be more personally or professionally transformational than that. This is why Wittgenstein's ethically orienting maxim to first 'improve yourself' is as profound and meaningful today as it ever was, and why, I suggest – it has powerful liberatory potential in both philosophical and personal contexts. It cuts deep into our ways of thinking as a complex human being embedded within complex contexts that we need to learn how to navigate if we are to flourish.

Summative remarks

In this chapter, I have aimed to show that one of the crucial skills in personal development is developing conceptual clarity with regard to conceptions of the 'Self'. I have also suggested that even though we can be aware of our ignorance and lack of self-knowledge, through greater awareness of our human agency and abilities we can (and should) adopt a positive disposition by default to personal development. I have also shown that possession of the kinds of knowledge that are useful to personal development and flourishing are indeed related to knowing-how to live a good life; but this is not comparable to knowing-that something is the case, or even how to ascertain and attain well-being, because what the good life consists in is first and foremost practical as opposed to epistemic.

The kinds of skills and practices relevant to achieving overall goodness of life is *action* oriented (where 'action' includes developmental conceptual mastery). This is where thinkers like Wittgenstein (2009), Ryle (1946) and Cassam (2014) are rightly sceptical of accounts of self-knowledge and well-being that focus too heavily on the role of the intellect or the rational aspects of our lives. Although my focus has been primarily conceptual, distinctions between mental concepts and performative ones need not be so sharp. I hope to have successfully demonstrated that extending some of Wittgenstein's central methods of analysis to the 'problems of life', particularly those that have a misconception at their root, can be transformative and liberatory on a personal as well as a professional level. Getting *oneself* aligned rightly, as Wittgenstein advises, seems to be the most sensible place to start if we truly care about positive social change. Yet, the moral dimension of personal growth and development *for* flourishing is also crucial to discuss. We are after all social beings. In the final chapter, then, I will explore our conceptions of meaning and happiness, in the context of our moral duty to others, especially because of the pernicious power of self-deceit to cause harm to ourselves and others, and thereby inhibiting genuine prospects for meaningful human flourishing.

7

Summum Bonum: Happiness and Meaning

In this chapter, my interest is in the relations between the concepts of happiness and meaning(fulness). These are intimately connected to each other; indeed, it is hard to imagine happiness without a person having attained a sense for what is meaningful in their life. Equally, it is difficult to consider a meaningful life without a degree of happiness. It is for these reasons that happiness and meaning are so intimately connected and important to analyse together for they are not merely interconnected, but closely *interrelated*; they are partly reliant on each other. This will also, hopefully, help to mitigate the potential for banal or narcissistic conceptions of happiness from gaining a footing in our minds; after all, we are most interested in forms of happiness that contribute to flourishing lives. This is to say that we're interested in the uses that are most relevant to human growth, success and betterment of both ourselves and of others.

As mentioned in Chapter 6, there is then, a moral imperative at the heart of our interest in this chapter too; we cannot merely *choose* what is meaningful, worthy, enjoyable or satisfying independent of the normative standards for what counts as meaningful. Nor indeed outside of the axiological, social and moral contexts within which we are situated. We must be able to orient ourselves towards these noble and fulfilling goals in ways that are *morally* defensible and integrated into the whole of life. As Cottingham (2005: 31) has rightly said:

> ... nothing about the idea of the meaningful life as integrated presupposes that every human has to lead the same kind of existence, or that there is not room for many varieties of human flourishing – artistic, athletic, intellectual, and so on. What is presupposed is that to count towards the meaningfulness of a life these varied activities have to be more than just performed by the agent with an eye to personal satisfaction; they have to be capable of being informed by a vision of their value in the whole ... by a sense of the worthwhile part they play in the growth and flowering of each unique human individual, and of the other human lives with which that story is necessarily interwoven.

Finally, because '[t]he notion of a good life *for* a human being is linked problematically with that of the life *of* a good human being' (Hacker, 2021 – emphases added), there are complicated normative tensions and relations for happiness and meaning in the context of key issues raised in epistemology as well as ethics, and on the proper relations between subjective and the objective norms and values.[1]

Chapter sections

In section one ('Happiness – an initial taxonomy') I sketch out some of the key *uses* of 'happiness' including exploring the relations with pleasure, joy and satisfaction with one's life. This is important to highlight the *subjective* dimensions to happiness, in particular, some of the relations with satisfaction in life. I also explore Tatarkiewicz' (1976) four-fold taxonomy of happiness (satisfied, experiences of greatest joy, success, and the highest good) with reference to recent work by Hacker (2021) on happiness. In particular, I pay attention to some of the problems between subjective and objective dimensions of happiness, with a brief exploration of the concept of *summum bonum* in light of the importance of aesthetic value. Further, I explore the diversity of criteria for success and the importance of morally defensible reasons in qualifying whether success contributes to happiness or not. I will then finish with a brief note on tackling the misleading notion of first-person epistemic authority with regards to subjective ascriptions for emotions like happiness.

In section two ('The delusion of circumstantial happiness') I explore attitudinal possibilities in the context of the struggle to attain meaning *through* suffering and absurdity. I therefore explore these issues further through Camus' (2013) use of 'The Myth of Sisyphus' in his rendering of meaninglessness and absurdity paying attention to his justification for the apparent absurdity of human existence. I then contrast his view with that of Frankl's (2006) in order to highlight the importance of attitude in the face of the challenges and vicissitudes of life.

In section three, ('The delusion of "The" meaning of life') I begin to explore the variety of uses for the word 'meaning'. This is important in order to develop some clarification for what kind of question/s we are asking when we ask what *the* meaning of life is, or indeed, whether life is the kind of thing that can have a meaning. I tackle such confusions through an exploration of teleology; as I suggest, it is likely one of the roots of confusion as to whether life has a meaning.

For example, I draw distinctions between *purpose* and *causative* conceptions of teleology with the aim of clarifying what is wrong with the question of *the* meaning of life. I finish by drawing a correlation between a conceptual common problem between epistemic scepticism and axiological or normative justification in terms of life's meaning. Moreover, I address ways of seeing that support notions of *the* meaning of life, drawing distinctions between two central kinds of value (trivial and substantial), for example, comparing pleasurable and transient activities with (possibly unpleasant but important) altruistic activities. As I suggest, the latter contributes greatly to one's sense of purpose in life and provides space for epistemic and characterological transcendence.

In section four, ('Meaninglessness and the hazy life of the "Blob"') I explore a case raised by Wolf (2007) with regards to a paradigmatic meaningless life. I explore what that life might look like and compare two conceptions of the Blob arguing that whilst both lives may be redeemable, one leads to a life that is morally justified (which I argue is what meaningfulness hinges on) and the other is not. I therefore explore the importance of moral orienteering through one's characterological weaknesses. I will adapt Wolf's case using a comparative approach, with what I call 'Good Blob' versus 'Bad Blob', in order to help highlight an important piece that is missing from Wolf's analysis of meaning. In the concluding remarks, I will tie lessons learnt from these various strands of delusion to suggest that *ceteris paribus*, our human predicament of ignorance actually provides endless possibilities and logical spaces of hope for anyone leading what appears to be a meaningless life. Finally, in section five, ('The importance of attending to one's delusions') I reaffirm the possibility developed in Chapter 6 regarding the logical space for hope that ignorance provides. Following Wittgenstein's insight with regards to overcoming an illusory problem, I suggest that the way forward is not necessarily an epistemic one (at least not in isolation) but rather one of the 'will'. Thus, I propose that *attitude* plays a critical role in liberating oneself both epistemically as much as characterologically. As I suggest, such a move plays a central role in developing happy and meaningful lives.

Happiness – an initial taxonomy

Happiness is a complex and 'disputed' concept for a number of reasons. Firstly, it is first and foremost a psychological concept and as such it can be a report of how things are with oneself (subjective happiness). We can say that we are happy *about* something (like a football team winning); happy *that* something is the case (e.g. our friend got married); happy *with* somebody (i.e. we feel loved and contented). Just these few examples suggest a huge range in emphasis with conceptual connections extending from ecstasy, joyousness, pleasure (being pleased about), delight or indeed bliss. In these cases, happiness is a report for how things are with oneself (subjectively speaking) and so, we say, that a great deal hangs on what *makes* one happy – or what do we do that we find pleasure or joy in etc. Hence, these uses suggest one taking *pleasure* in some goal or activity, something or someone. In a different sense, it can also mean being *pleased with* some state of affairs (e.g. in terms of career, relationships or finances). These connected concepts might suggest a sense of temporality or transience, but meaningful happiness is more than that. In declaring that we are happy we do not always mean something that is transient like a mood, but rather we mean a *lasting* state of affairs of reasonable duration. There is a sense that things are *generally good with me*.

The sense for overall happiness here, is not to imply an insight or satisfaction with every aspect of our own lives, clearly, we don't have that. We may be happy about certain aspects and unhappy about others; indeed, we may be deceived about what happiness is, or else intentionally deceive ourselves about whether we are in fact happy. Context helps us to clarify the meaning of a use of happiness, for in speaking of happiness with relationships, jobs or hobbies etc., we do not mean happiness per se, but rather, *satisfaction* with the aspect of my life. In speaking about happiness as a state of affairs, we make an overall assessment for how things stand *with me* as the kind of being that can be said to have a good, including, for example, the goodness of biological health. Although no form of value can be rendered intelligible save by reference to 'living beings' who can act for reasons, in asking about someone's goodness in terms of health, this is not merely a biological question.[2] We are, rather, primarily interested in their *overall* well-being – and only a sentient creature may possess a state of wellness.[3] This indicates, then, a complex set of relations between subjectivity and satisfaction (*my* state of mind, affairs, or sense of being), as well as longitude and totality (*my* assessment for the overall state of affairs for my life over a reasonable duration).

Figure 5 may help to see the connections between the issues that I raise in this chapter. It will be useful now to explore happiness a little further, for in doing so, we may be able to better glean some of the important nuances that help us to better understand some of the key confusions we may be prone to (whether in research or on a personal level) when speaking about happiness, particularly in

Happiness	Tatarkiewicz' analysis of 'happiness'		I. Is satisfied,
			II. Experiences the Greatest joy,
			III. Is Successful, or
			IV. Possesses the highest good.
	Success & the 'highest good'	Summum bonum	Blessedness
			Goodness
			Love
	Issues		The role of 'success' evaluated
		Authority & objectivity	Sense & meaning
			Cultural change
		Delusions	Circumstantial happiness
			'The' meaning of life
		Dereliction of responsibility	The Blob (case)
			Moral orientation
			Addressing delusions

Figure 5 A taxonomy of 'happiness' and related issues.

the context of our Western culture that is captivated by materialism, consumerism, individualism, scientism, and some might say, narcissism.

Tatarkiewicz' analysis of happiness

One of the most comprehensive (yet largely unknown) analyses of the concept of happiness was undertaken by Tatarkiewicz (1976). Beginning with Aristotle's treatise, '*Nicomachean Ethics*', Tatarkiewicz traced the concept of happiness through the ages citing happiness as one of the most prominent 'problems' in Western philosophical thought.[4] In his analysis he proposed that there were *four* central uses of the concept of happiness. Namely, a (wom)man is said to be happy if:

I. S/he is satisfied,
II. Experiences the Greatest joy,
III. Is Successful, or
IV. Possesses the highest good.

The first two categories relate to the subjective senses already alluded to, regarding pleasure, enjoyment and bliss. Tatarkiewicz' latter two categories of success and the highest good, are of the objective kind. I have already noted that concepts (even ones that relate to subjective feelings) are normative, subjected to public criteria, and thus epistemically objective.[5] The degree to which success and happiness are related is problematic and we might be tempted to think that confidence in the close association between the two are somewhat misplaced. After all, almost everyone has heard of someone having a 'midlife crisis' which, though can mean a number of things, among them is the notion of regret and the pressures of aging which propel some to live a life for a *new* set of reasons. Because we may grant that certain conceptions of success seem to be associated with materialism, it's not at all clear how we might defend such a conception outside of either an egoistic or materialist framework.[6] Tatarkiewicz' taxonomy highlights aspects of happiness that relate to human flourishing and success (use III) and satisfaction (use I). Equally, however, if we were conducting a teleological analysis of spiritual or philosophical ideals, we might be more interested in notions of the 'highest good' (use IV) and the greatest joy (use II).[7] These need not be mutually exclusive or contradictory but simply reflect a range of applications, uses or *conceptions* uttered in a plurality of contexts. This is partly why Hacker (2021: 243) has suggested that happiness is a source of 'systematic disagreement'. Axiological conceptions of happiness wax and wane with the fickle fashions of history and are relative to the cultural value set in a given age.[8]

Success and the 'highest good'

Notions of both success and the highest good are subjective in orientation. They signify a particular value set and yardstick by which we tend to measure ourselves, whether in materialist or religious (or quasi-religious) senses respectively. We would do well to remember that Tatarkiewicz' taxonomy is summarizing happiness from an *historical* perspective, and classical notions of the good life and the good citizen were influential over recent history. Such writers often conceived of a hierarchy of goods and values, so, although there was a degree of disagreement on the detail of attainment (for example, whether pleasure, civic duty or morality were the greatest contributory goods) many of the major classic thinkers seemed to agree that possession of *eudaimonia* was itself the very embodiment of the highest good for which we should aim i.e. the *summum bonum*.[9] The notion of *summum bonum* was introduced by the Roman philosopher Cicero,[10] although the term was also central in Aquinas.[11] Perhaps this is why *eudaimonia* remains the most influential concept in neo-Aristotelian philosophy and related fields.[12] These diverse aspects of happiness suggest that the word has a wide array of loosely connected *uses* that include notions of blessedness and goodness in various forms (e.g. financial, psychological, aesthetic etc.).[13] I am here reminded of Browning's (1892) elegant, romantic, but controversial poem. Written in his old age it recalls what the notion of 'summum bonum' meant *to him*:

> All the breath and the bloom of the year in the bag of one bee:
> All the wonder and wealth of the mine in the heart of one gem:
> In the core of one pearl all the shade and the shine of the sea:
> Breath and bloom, shade and shine, wonder, wealth, and—how far above them
> Truth, that's brighter than gem,
> Trust, that's purer than pearl,
> Brightest truth, purest trust in the universe—all were for me
> In the kiss of one girl.

For Browning, the simplicity of this 'kiss' encapsulates much of what is important in *life*, including: social connection, love, mutual trust, illumination, sensuality and bliss.[14] In Browning's poem, then, we have at least two routes for the relation of success and happiness: one historical and one etymological. On the one hand success seems important to a happy life, for what would a happy life be without a sense for success and the affirmation we get from self-competence, motivation, goal-setting, performance and the development of effective strategies.[15] Indeed, it is difficult (or impossible) to imagine a flourishing life without a degree of success, through the practical application of insight and skill. Yet, we also know that success, if sought for narrow reasons (e.g. materialist reasons) can lead to self-deception and can have a corrupting effect on character, at least on most accounts in ethics and philosophy. Not everyone, however, can enjoy success. It would seem odd then that this might preclude them from happiness. *Contra* Aristotelian accounts, Tatarkiewicz was alert to the subtleties and nuances between happiness and success, and this is why he discounted the relation as necessary. As Tatarkiewicz noted (1976: 7),

> One can be satisfied with life without good fortune or intense joy and, conversely, good fortune and intense joy are no guarantee of satisfaction with life. Happiness in the sense of 'good fortune' is not essential to make a man happy.

This acknowledgement seems to support the centrality of occasion-sensitivity. The problem of an apparent paradox lies in our conflicting conceptions (and thereby criteria) of success. These vary from culture to culture, and we need to be aware of our tendency to project our values onto others. I'll avoid patronizing any particular cultures,[16] suffice to say for our purposes here, it's logically justifiable for cultures (or sub-cultures) to have completely alien frames of reference for what might count as success. Thus, merely using the word is insufficient outside of an apt orientation towards the specific occasion and context of normative values and linguistic forms of expression.[17] As Hacker (2021: 16) has suggested, '[s]ince prospering and flourishing are goals of human beings, the concepts of the beneficial will readily find a place in the conceptual scheme of any user of a well-developed language'. So, even though there will be localized *conceptions* of happiness, generalizations as to the broad parameters for happiness (such as meaning, joy, pleasure) can be found through our shared human forms of life. Hence, as the concept of *summum bonum* helps to exemplify, questions of happiness are questions of subjective and aesthetic value. But what might it mean to have an 'objective' conception of happiness? It is to that issue that I now turn.

Whose authority?

A final point worth making in this section, is that there are also epistemic problems with *some* notions of subjectivity. There is a temptation to think that *I* am an epistemic authority about what is meaningful or happy to me. As the thought goes, only *I* can know how *I* feel, therefore what I say must be the case for me. Hacker (2007a: 246) tackles this confusion below:

> The subject's sincere word is an expression or manifestation of his thought or experience. Its special status is grammatical, *not epistemic* – the agent is not an authority on his pains and thoughts as he might be an authority on something which only he has seen and studied. Rather, his utterances are logical (non-inductive) criteria for how things are with him, and his sincerity, in cases where self-deception can be excluded, guarantees truth.
>
> [my emphasis added]

On the one hand, there is a logical preclusion to knowing certain things (such as one's own pain) this cannot be doubted so it cannot be known, it just is. But on the other, any utterances or reports for how things are with me must always be weighed against other, primarily behavioural, evidence. When we aver or report how things are, we are merely describing or expressing using (public, sharable) linguistic norms. As Wittgenstein states: '... even if it is a report, he does not learn it from his feelings' (*PI* §5). My first-person claim to happiness is limited in these important senses. This is what helps the philosopher to distinguish between cases in terms of how to diagnose a given problem at hand and to consider which strategies to use in helping someone who might be confused, deceived or both in terms of their own happiness. This is where we see somewhat a blurring between subjective and objective aspects of happiness – for on the one hand, they are *my* feelings, but on the other they are subjected to public criteria.[18]

The delusion of circumstantial happiness

Whilst such an assessment can be as a result of aspects of life that justifiably provide me with satisfaction, whether on subjective or objective criteria, such assessments can be in *spite* of the absence of such aspects of happiness. In this important sense, happiness is *attitudinal* and a matter of choice, agency and free will. For example, I can be in the middle of a relationship break-up but instead of *seeing* the break-up as bad news, I could see the possibilities for other more fruitful relationships. My job could be ending, but I can look ahead to taking on a new challenge and learning new skills. These are rather ordinary circumstances that impact our lives. Most of us *must* develop an ability to address these problems in life positively (that is, we must become resilient) in order to flourish, for without this flexibility of attitude we will, no doubt, flounder. Human existence is simply too problematic to manage evading problems, no matter how wealthy or seemingly protected one is from such harms.

Further, even in the direst of circumstances happiness is possible. For example, Frankl (2006) an Auschwitz survivor, relates how in the early days of his being held prisoner in a Nazi concentration camp, '... how content we were; happy in spite of everything'. One can imagine the survivors nurturing a mindset that seeks for reasons to be happy and goodness wherever it may be found. It is also, of course, testament to the resilience, faith and dignity of the human soul in the face of what might appear as meaningless suffering.[19] This is not an empirical claim relying on testimonies of Auschwitz survivors like Frankl, but it is a case that exemplifies the importance of context in ascriptions of happiness. Finally, it happens to be a source of absurdism, and this is what I will explore next through some of the key thoughts of Camus on meaning. This will highlight the role of character and attitude when dealing with the challenges or 'problems' of life.

Flourishing Under Fire[20]

In the Myth of Sisyphus (Camus, 2013), Camus sees the problem of absurdity for human beings stemming from the 'impossibility of reducing this world to a rational and reasonable principle'. Camus suggests that there is a gap between human concerns and the world of 'reality', thus conceived as everything outside of the human mind. He sees no way out from this predicament and so in finishing he declares the only option is existential abandon, a form of cynical acceptance: 'The struggle itself towards the heights is enough to fill a man's heart. One must imagine Sisyphus happy' (Camus, 2013: 90). Camus' suggestion that Sisyphus could be happy is itself an affirmation of this absurdity, albeit a heroic one. Camus suggests that once we go through the process of 'absurd reasoning', adopting a position of acceptance and meaning towards one's life is all that is left, but that this is fine. Meaning is bravely created by human beings *despite* the fact that life is apparently meaningless. Whether or not this counts as a good reason for living is debatable, but for Camus, it certainly counts as a 'reason for dying'. For Camus, this dilemma of the will to life forms the most 'fundamental question of philosophy', namely, the question of suicide. Camus bases his assessment, however, on an expectation that there *should* be an explanation to the fundamental problems of life for human beings and that these will be discoverable (at least potentially) 'out there'. Camus (2013: 17) cites the engagement in meaningless forms of work as an example of pointless existence:

> Rising, tram, four hours in the office or factory, meal, tram, four hours of work, meal, sleep and Monday, Tuesday, Wednesday, Thursday, Friday and Saturday, according to the same rhythm – this path is easily followed most of the time.

He suggests that this 'unillustrious life' is filled with wishful thinking about a hopeful but unlikely future. He relates the pointlessness of routine work with Sisyphus' pointless daily grind of pushing the rock uphill at the whim of the gods. The point of redemption comes when one day the 'why' question 'arises' in the hearts of human beings; it's the question that drives us.[21] Camus' problematization is therefore based on a particularly alienating way of seeing the world. One that aims to address many of the problems of his time, including doubts about whether life can be meaningful outside of a religious framework.

For Camus, the dilemma is driven by an assumption that social relations are not enough and in lieu of an intelligent being that might be able to *explain* the reason for human existence, without which we are left to arbitrarily design our own meaning. It's for this reason that Camus suggests that our lives lose any explanatory force, we become *lost* in wonder and captured by misapprehension. Camus suggests that human beings are caught in the absurdity between the self-consciousness that makes them aware of their own predicament, whilst lacking the conceptual tools to reason or find a way to justify their own existence.

But Camus seems somewhat constrained by his choice of analogy. Whilst Sisyphus is useful perhaps to demonstrate resilience, determination and courage in the face of powerlessness and the possibility of an apparent sense of absurdity, Sisyphus' life is about as one-dimensional as one could imagine. This is not at all like the life of an actual human being. As Hacker (2021: 326) observes, Sisyphus is not a 'social creature', neither does he have a 'self-transcending task'.[22] To contrast, for example, Frankl (2006), an Auschwitz survivor, appeals to the reasons for living *outside* of the self (friends, family or God) and although suffering in and of itself is meaningless he suggests that rather than robbing human lives of meaning, the meaning we get is found in the way in which we *respond* to suffering. For Camus the very fact that we must choose meaning seems to be a source of absurdity but for Frankl it is a source of redemption. Adopting an *attitude* of gratitude and a willingness to transcend one's circumstances affirms the importance of life and acts as a buffer against the worst experiences imaginable.[23] As Frankl (2006: 131) avers:

> A negative attitude intensifies pain and deepens disappointments; it undermines and diminishes pleasure, happiness, and satisfaction; it may even lead to depression or physical illness.

Frankl's (2006) use of happiness must of course be relativized to the appalling circumstances he had to face where *ordinary* conceptions of happiness, fulfilment, enjoyment and pursuit of one's goals or abilities must abate. It is misguided then to think that our purposes are 'uniformly meaningless' or indeed uniformly meaningful. What matters most is how we *choose* to address the challenges of life. For lives to be absurd and meaningless they would need to be 'unreasonable, preposterous, ridiculous, silly, ludicrous, or farcical' (Hacker, 2021: 324). The notion of absurdity does not seem to turn then on the indifference of the world to the lives of human beings, as Camus infers, but rather on our *attitude* to life.

A case: the 'Kindness Pill'

Consider the possibility that we can peer into another galaxy, and that in that galaxy was a planet with a civilization quite like ours. One of the main behavioural differences is that they smile at each other incessantly because they think that this is being kind. We know that kindness is rightly a virtue, and we know that smiling is a form of kindness, but imagine if they were kind *only* because they were given some kind of pill which was designed in order to produce certain virtues (such as kindness, compassion, conscientiousness etc.).[24] Aside from the fact that there are a priori reasons which preclude making humans virtuous by external means such as pills (because virtue requires the very possibility of vice and moral choice). If these human beings did exist, I think that they would lose a fundamental feature of what we currently consider to be human, namely: agency and free will.[25]

This is not a straightforward assertion however, because much may turn on the degree to which such medication induces, alters or enhances human behaviour. We know, for example, that there are mood enhancers presently that human beings take, and this does not negate humanity (though they may diminish it). Nevertheless, it is enough to highlight that such human beings might exist, and as such, could be considered an absurdity (at least *to us*). So, although life is not the *kind* of thing that could be absurd or meaningless (outside of a subjective way of seeing it as such), this does not preclude the possibility of meaninglessness for humanity as a whole, for example, if we were all medicated en masse in this way in perpetuity. It would not, however, be fundamentally meaningless, only contingently so. As long as there is the *logical possibility* for human agency, there remains hope for redemptive or mitigating reactions to alleged absurdism in life. This requires a personally transcendent perspective within which we may assess the problems of life.

There are therefore aspects of happiness that relate to transient states of *mind* (feelings and emotions), states of *affairs* (good luck, fortune) as well as *attitudes* towards life (how I choose to see life, despite the circumstances).[26] The former two classes being more susceptible to the whims of luck and good fortune, the latter consisting in a position that one can adopt, for *reasons*. This latter aspect is one that elicits lasting satisfaction and meaning for it is one which I *shape* and rationalize as a moral agent in the world. Although there are many ways in which we may see the world or adopt a particular attitude towards it, what Frankl's and Camus' contrasting perspectives help us to see is that *ways of seeing* the world carry their own logical and practical commitments. We may each have good reasons for our commitments, but some reasons are better than others. This is an important correlation with Wittgensteinian philosophy, as he suggests:

> How much we are doing is changing the style of thinking and how much I'm doing is changing the style of thinking and how much I'm doing is persuading people to change their style of thinking.
>
> Wittgenstein, 1967: 28

One way to help to explore further the complex relationship between happiness and meaning, along the axes of subjectivity and objectivity, is by having a look at the confused notion of 'The' meaning of life, a notion that is bound to lead to absurdity because it is fundamentally confused. Before I address that confusion, I will sketch out the plurality of meanings in the context of the misleading notion of 'The' meaning of life. This will help to build a reasoned approach for addressing these tensions over 'authority' in the context of *meaningful* conceptions of happiness.

The delusion of 'The' meaning of life

According to Leach & Tartaglia (2018), the question of the 'meaning of life' is considered to be a relatively modern concern.[27] To understand the question properly, however, we need to first understand the kind of presuppositions that support *that* kind of question. For example, the word 'meaning' itself can be used in a number of ways. When we say, "What is the meaning of this interruption?", we are interested in knowing what possible *reasons* you might have for being insolent (justificatory). Whereas, if we ask, "What is the meaning of beach walks?", we know that this is patent nonsense, for beach walks are not the kind of thing that can have a meaning (although the experience of walking on a beach can be meaningful). Why then do we ask what 'the meaning of life' is? Is it not equally obvious that it is not the kind of thing that can have a meaning? Part of the problem is that because of the plurality of related but distinct meanings of meaning it is quite easy to be perplexed by such a question.

We could, for example, re-phrase the question in order to make it more intelligible. One can imagine a psychotherapist speaking to a patient and asking: 'What was the meaning of *that* beach walk for you?', or 'What do beach walks mean to you generally?' (eliciting a subjective response). We can also use meaning to ask questions that require an objective answer: 'What is the meaning of this calculation?', e.g. 'What is the meaning of the mathematical formula of Pi (π)?'. But if we were to ask, 'What is the meaning of Macbeth?', it might not be clear what we were asking. Perhaps, something like 'What does the text signify *to you*?'.

But if we were to ask what the plot of Macbeth is, then we could answer that perfectly lucidly in objective terms. In other words, questions of a certain order require subjective responses alone and framing such a question *as if* an objective answer were possible leads us into confusion. As Wolf has rightly suggested, 'the question … is extremely obscure, if not downright unintelligible. it is unclear what exactly the question is supposed to be asking' (cf., Wolf, 2007).

It's interesting to note that Shakespeare uses this word 'signify' to articulate Macbeth's doubts about the purpose of human existence. When Macbeth receives some news that the queen 'is dead' (by suicide), this causes Macbeth to sink into deep despair; being close to his end, he laments:

> … Out, out, brief candle!
> Life's but a walking shadow, a poor player,
> That struts and frets his hour upon the stage,
> And then is heard no more; it is a tale
> Told by an idiot, full of sound and fury,
> *Signifying nothing*'.
>
> Act 5, scene 5, *Macbeth* [my emphasis added][28]

In analysing the text, then, we might ask 'What is the central message?', 'What is the moral of the story?' etc. (which could elicit both subjective and objective responses). Even better then, to ask: 'What is the meaning of the text, to *you*?', then we know a subjective response is required – or else, 'What *is* the story of Macbeth intended to convey?' (eliciting an objective response regarding Shakespeare's deliberate crafting of the story for a given purpose), obviously subject to evidence and warrant. The roles, definitions and ways of reading literature, poetry or prose are complex and contested. As Eagleton (1983: 6–7) suggests, literature does not operate with ordinary uses of language so recognizing that forces us to question what people do with writing as much as 'what writing does to them'. Literature then can be seen as 'non-pragmatic' discourse, as opposed to academic topics, aimed rendering problems in life 'more perceptible' than they might otherwise be.[29] In each case, the meaning of 'meaning' is somewhat distinct, or at least, requires distinct kinds of more particularized questions and responses. In other words, as suggested, questions of a certain order require subjective responses alone and framing such a question *as if* an objective answer were possible is one major contributory factor which helps to explain why we are prone to be lead into confusion. But there is more to be said on this misapprehension, in the context of the Greek concept of *telos*.

One possible root of the problem: *telos*

Part of the problem here is in identifying and clarifying what we are asking. The question of *the* meaning of life seems to be interested in two kinds of teleological explanation, causative (backward looking and explanatory) as well as functional (goal-oriented and purposive), i.e. it is retrospective as much as prospective; it looks in both directions.[30] The notion of *the* meaning of life can mean either the purpose or ultimate goal, whilst also looking for a causal explanation or reason for life and existence. In this way, the concept of the meaning of life seems to track at least partly along ancient Greek conceptions of *telos*, which was seen as the causative end or goal of some *activity*.[31] In the English language, ends and goals differ in important senses. For example, causative ends imply the result of something else (like a ripple in the pond being the end result (*telos*) of a pebble being thrown into it). The pond could not choose to ripple as a result of the pebble landing on its surface; the ripple is the ultimate result of an event or process. Simply put, it's a matter determinative of cause and effect. In this sense *the* meaning of life amounts to an explanation for the inception of existence (e.g. creation or the Big Bang) as much as its end (in both religious and scientific terms seen as the destruction of the universe). This can be contrasted with *purposive* ends which are rational and agential in nature.[32] The further link with *eudaimonia* or flourishing (as the highest good, or *summum bonum*) is also clear from a teleological perspective to help explain what is most worthy of our attention.

Although we usually understand teleology in terms of 'goals' and 'ends', this bidirectional perspectivism need not be contradictory. For example, Hacker (2007a: 162) gives a case to consider in terms of human behaviour that may help. If we imagine how we might explain a revenge act, we could explain it in both retrospective as much as prospective terms. If we imagine a murder has taken place, we can say that the *goal* (G) of a murderer was to kill a person (P). But we can also say that the reason for that goal (G) was revenge for another murderous act (M). In this way we can arrive at a point of teleological explanation for the murder: i.e. G was *caused* by M. In other words, there is a 'pattern of reasoning' which explains a given outcome causally; the backward-looking component 'renders the *purpose* of the action perspicuous' (Hacker, 2007a: 163, my emphasis). This works fine for human behaviour but cannot be applied to life as a whole – we have no God's eye perspective.[33] In asking *the* meaning of life along this line of inquiry too, we want to know not just *what* brought life about and where we are going but importantly, *why*. This has naturally led to endless religious (theist) as much as scientific (rationalist) speculations and theorizing.[34] Indeed it is sometimes hard to tell the difference between religion and science. I suggest that it is this speculative element that is so attractive and alluring for romantics as much as rationalists. It is possible, however, only within a certain way of thinking about the world, rooted in religious or scientific speculation. It's useful in a number of ways (not least to help in terms of self-knowledge and concept development) but as soon as we take the question too seriously, we err; a fortiori when we infer meaninglessness from a putative state of ignorance. This is partly why Wittgenstein said that:

> It appears to me as though a religious belief could only be (something like) passionately committing oneself to a system of coordinates. Hence although it's belief, it is really a way of living, or a way of judging life.
>
> *CV* §64

Wittgenstein draws a distinction between commitments that might provide meaning in life, that is, a way of seeing and attending to life – an *attitude* – as opposed to applying standards for knowledge typically used in addressing concerns that are epistemic or philosophical. This is at once a tighter definition of 'philosophical' but also a loosening (and clarifying) the reasons for our beliefs and action. Essentially, although conceptual schemes and language-games differ substantially, with religion and science, the world-views often demand similar *attitudes* to life; it is for philosophy to help to unravel them both where needed.

Now that the relations between happiness and meaning are clearer, I will now address a fundamental delusion with regards to 'The' meaning of life. I will do this by conducting a brief exploration of the plurality of the concept of meaning in order to highlight some important distinctions that may assist in dispelling this particular form of delusion. I will then build on this with an exploration of other roots to confusion through an analysis of the Greek concept of *telos* and the existential notions of the 'otherness' of existence.

The meaning of life: What's wrong with the question?

In this case, for example, the use of the 'What?' interrogative implies that meaning is a kind of describable *thing*. In a religious sense, we could indeed come up with a form of meaning (e.g. in a Christian sense, the meaning of life could be to worship and to have faith in Christ). Adoptees of these religious philosophies tend towards a *cosmic* picture of meaning in life, often opposed to reductionist accounts seen in naturalist philosophies (cf. Hosseini, 2015: 3).[35] However, outside of a specific religious context for the question it is hard to see what sense it would make. A better question could be, what is the meaning of life for a Christian, a Sikh, a Jew etc. As Schinkel (2016: 401) suggests, there is a kind of plurality of meanings and 'people searching for meaning are not always searching for the same thing'. But even this is incomprehensible *if* we are speaking about *The* meaning of life in an objective, cosmic sense, that is, not in a literary or metaphorical sense.

For example, although Schinkel's (2016) notion of 'life' is taken to mean the overall experience of human existence, being, consciousness and all that this entails including thought-life, activities and relationships etc.[36] But is it hard, then, to know what could not count as 'life'. Its reach includes everything. What sense can be made of such an all-encompassing parameter? The trouble is that just as nothingness is incomprehensible, so is everythingness (e.g. all of 'life'). In order for a question or a doubt about existence, that is, in order for it to be debatable, we would need to have something to contrast it (all of existence and life) with. If no distinction is drawn, then it's hard to know what is being communicated. So, although we can express a doubt regarding our subjective *reason* for our individual existence in causal terms (for example, why was my birth accidental or intentional, natural or via *in vitro*, should I continue living etc.), what would it be to doubt the reason of *all* existence?

Perhaps these kinds of questions make sense in the context of my death, i.e. my *non-existence*; as Camus claimed, 'suicide' is the fundamental question in philosophy. But in that case, I am merely asking whether I should live, i.e. whether my *reasons* are good enough *for me*. This expresses an existential crisis for an individual person, not a state or condition of human beings more widely, a fortiori, for the whole of existence.[37] The very notion of the possibility for there being a meaning for all existence seems fixed by a certain way of seeing the world, one where humanity is somewhat at odds with everything else outside. For example, Schinkel (2017: 546) states:

> The paradigmatic example is the 'philosophical' wonder at the bare fact of existence, the fact—and the mysteriousness of that fact—that there is something rather than nothing.

Interestingly it is this inner/outer dualist picture of humankind existing in the 'bare fact of existence' that is a source of *both* despair (à la Camus, 2013) and idealized deep wonder in the case of Schinkel, (2017). The wonder, mental cramp, or aporia, that either everythingness or nothingness elicits should help us realize that the concepts are flawed and the question of the *reason* for the existence of life is poorly framed. Certain 'facts of life' just are as they are. This proposition is not a tautologous form of fatalism, it is evidence of an attitude of acceptance that one may adopt towards the diversity of the human species and the lived experience of existence, it is a reasonable assumption given that we have no choice over existence.[38] If we use one of Wittgenstein's metaphors, 'nothing in the seed corresponds to the plant which comes out of it—this can only be done from the history of the seed' (Z §608), that is, there is no essential end to the plant which could express itself in any number of ways, for example, subject to environmental factors. Wittgenstein's interest there was human behaviour, but I think it is a useful metaphor for life in general as well which is quite chaotic (or so it seems to *us* from *our* perspective).

The meaning of life for animals is similarly incomprehensible. Hacker (2021: 328) explains: '[a]nimal life as such has neither purpose nor meaning. Animals (contrary to the book of Genesis) were not made for us, nor do they exist for a purpose'; however, for obvious reasons, they can have their own purposes and pursue their own goals. Nevertheless, indulge me for a moment and imagine that animals, say caterpillars, could reason. Perhaps they began doubting the reasons for their own existence. What would it be for a caterpillar to question the meaning (reasons, purpose) of leaves, rain or gardens? Those things obviously have a purpose *to them* as in a function (food, shelter, sustenance etc.) but outside of religious metaphor, they have no 'once and for all' purpose. This is why I suggest that the question of doubting *why* something exists (their function, purpose or reason) is related in *kind* to the sceptical question of doubting *that* something exists (or at least whether I can know that it does); both forms of query (why and that) are based on misleading analogies. The former is based on the cosmic nature of reality with human beings (as agents) pitted against the real world and the otherness of existence. Similarly, the latter is based on the misleading notion that my consciousness or awareness is pitted against an external and unknowable world. But as Wittgenstein suggested: 'The questions that we raise and our doubts depend on the fact that some propositions are exempt from doubt, are as it were like hinges on which those [doubts] turn' (*OC*, §341–344).[39]

Of course, Wittgenstein's insight was targeted at epistemic scepticism. It was intended to lay bare that there are some things that you cannot doubt, and thereby, cannot be said to know. Further, it was intended to lay bare the fact that our entire game of knowledge, and its logical possibility, depends on the very fundamental facts we take for granted (like I am alive, am an agent, and have power over various affairs in my life etc.). In the context of the meaning of life, its goodness or badness does not consist in our ability to know *whether* it exists or indeed *why* it exists, both of which are, strictly speaking, nonsense; one is beyond epistemic doubt, the other is beyond perceptual purview, *both* are beyond the limits of sense through language. Rather, our evaluations are only possible from a particular vantage point, a view from 'somewhere' within which to evaluate it.[40] This is not to say that we do not have a use for such a *concern*, as suggested, in religious (or literary) contexts which adopt a religious kind of metaphysics (in some cases as metaphor, in others as claims to knowledge).[41] After all, we have innumerable problems in philosophy and who is to say that a given set of problems are to be barred from troubling us as thinkers; quite the opposite, philosophy gets its purpose from such problems.[42] The religious metaphysical picture of the world provides the kind of framework within which such an idea could gain a footing and we can learn some lessons from within it. But, outside of those cosmic frameworks of meaning, we would do better by asking questions like why things exist in this *particular* way – e.g. *why* is the earth spherical – or, *why* do we worship these kinds of gods – or *why* do we have these kinds of religious practices – or indeed, *why* do we think it important to ask these kinds of questions etc. These questions are comprehensible, explainable, and thereby, answerable in philosophy.

Now that we have addressed the incomprehensibility of notion of *the* meaning of life, it remains clear that life may however be assessed in several more particular ways. Not so much as a whole but from the perspective of an individual. It will be helpful to explore now how this fits with subjective and objective value, assessments of *a* meaningful life and meaning in life *to me*.

Sources of subjective meaning and value

Religion, spirituality, ideology and affiliations to significant causes obviously provide us with sources, and resources, for developing subjective value. But not all are of equal value. This is why we must distinguish between something's meaning something *to a person*, and something *lending* meaning to a person's life (cf. Hacker, 2021: 311). I suggest that the difference can be seen as a distinction between what is *trivially* valuable or meaningful, versus what is *substantively* meaningful; the latter is objective, the former is not.[43] For example, in terms of the meaning we get from altruistic activities, we may compare helping a neighbour put out the bins with more substantial acts such as volunteering for a local orphanage or supporting children and families in war-torn parts of the globe. In terms of memories, we might be able to recall a teenage crush or lover, as opposed to falling in love with the woman (or man) of one's life with whom one is settled and committed. In terms of their contribution to one's happiness, these activities are weighted according to the *substance* they entail, so the more trivial the activities, the more likely they are to give you a transient pleasure; whilst the more substantive, the more likely they are to offer you a lasting sense of meaning.

The dichotomy between these cases then, is not merely triviality and substance, but also *transience* and *transcendence*. There is nothing more transcendent than either giving up one's life for another (in terms of transcending one's own self-interests), or indeed entering into danger where one may lose one's life, e.g. as a soldier, martyr or medic. This is why Jesus is attributed as saying to his disciples: 'Greater love has no one than this: to lay down one's life for one's friends.' (Book of John 15:13). It is the *ultimate* sacrifice. Indeed, it is the reason why we celebrate and glorify the dead each year on Remembrance Sunday. It is also why we glorify heroes in epic tales of battles between good and evil.[44] Yet most of us will not place our lives in harm's way quite like that yet we manage to find meaning in life.

Most human activities, whether trivial or substantial, are rather humdrum activities that we do in the course of life. Anyone who has had children or been a carer will be able to tell you the sacrifice that parenting or personal care of any sort entails. Even teachers, tutors and lecturers will be able to comment on the personal sacrifices made for their students. This is why I think Hacker (2021: 331) suggests that there are 'no mysteries about how to live a meaningful life – it is above all blinkers that stand in one's way, and misfortune that drains one's spirits and weakens one's will'. Sources of meaning are somewhat obvious (even platitudinous): to say that love, deeply held belief, friendship and personal achievement are all meaningful, is a rather disappointing insight for a philosopher to make. What is, however, of philosophical (and ergo, practical) interest, is developing understanding of one's areas of confusion, blind-spots or 'blinkers'. Despite the common phrase that 'ignorance is bliss' (which amounts to the truism that sometimes we might prefer ignorance), ignorance is itself a source of meaninglessness and nihilism, worse still, when the blinkers are intentional. Such blinkers are as much epistemic as they are characterological:

> ... deadly human vices of selfishness, such as greed, lust, envy, and jealousy, and the equally deadly vices of cruelty, hatred, callousness or indifference to the suffering of others, arrogance, and the unfortunate intellectual flaws of stupidity, ignorance, and lack of understanding.
>
> (ibid.)

Self-knowledge, then, is not merely a useful tool for understanding our way about language but is *itself* a critical source of meaning in its own right. As a practice, we must be 'at home' in the chaos of pain and suffering in order to have a shot at transcendence (cf. *CV* §65); there are no cheap options available.

By way of contrast, I will now explore subjective conceptions of meaning *in* life through a case study of Wolf's (2007) 'The Blob' where she advocates for 'significance' as a primary means of evaluating meaning in life. In contrast, I will suggest that in being human (a social, moral and rational creature), there is a moral imperative to develop one's moral compass. Hence, moral orienteering is what truly counts when making assessments of value and meaning 'in' life.

Meaninglessness and the hazy life of the 'Blob'

Susan Wolf is one of the most prolific writers on the topic of meaning in life. For example, she is the author of a variety of books including *The Variety of Values: Essays on Morality, Meaning & Love* (Oxford, 2015), and *Meaning in Life and Why It Matters* (Princeton, 2010). She has also published a number of papers including 'Meaning and Morality', *Proceedings of the Aristotelian Society* (1997a); 'Happiness and Meaning: Two Aspects of the Good Life', *Social Philosophy & Policy* (1997b); and 'The Meanings of Lives', in Perry, Bratman, Firscher, eds, *Introduction to Philosophy: Classical and Contemporary Readings* (2007). She is also known for her 'hybrid theory' of meaning aiming to bridge the apparent gap between objectivist and subjectivist conceptions of meaning in life.[45]

Let's therefore consider a case that Wolf (2007) raises that challenges our conception of meaningfulness on the subjective route. Her aim in that paper is in locating 'the possibility of finding meaning', through the lazy and 'hazy' life of 'The Blob'.[46] The Blob spends his days and nights in front of a television set, drinking beer and watching sitcoms. Wolf argues that this is paradigmatic of a meaningless life because it consists in a life disconnected from everyone else. It's not an 'unpleasant level of consciousness', rather, it's quite comfortable. He is not hurting anyone either (at least not directly). Yet, his life seems meaningless – or at least, seems to lack meaning. Blob seems to be existing like the lotus eaters discussed in the introduction by Edgar & Pattison (2016), a life of pleasure and indulgence. We might justifiably deem such a life quite useless and meaningless, both to the Blob and to others. Other than the most degrading consumerist of reasons for living, Blob's existence is one which certainly lacks *substantive* meaning or purpose; even trivial meaning is doubtful. We don't have a rich picture for the Blob's life, but he seems to be living somewhat of an automated existence without any substantive engagement with life, for example, pursuing goals, activities and relationships. Indeed, Wolf (2007: 4) suggests that '[i]f any life, any human life, is meaningless, the Blob's life is.' So, what can we say about the Blob in terms of meaning in life (trivial) or a meaningful life (substantive)? What's wrong with it?

Wolf makes some effort in arguing against a moral focus to meaning. She states that 'it is debatable whether even the Blob deserves specifically moral censure', by which she means that we should think a bit further before we judge or prohibit such a life. She says so partly because of the apparent lack of negative impact on others for the Blob harms no one through his one-dimensional existence – he only seems to be harming himself.[47] But her strategy is to detach the notion of morality almost entirely. She contrasts 'paradigms of meaningful lives' which seem to exemplify 'great moral virtue or accomplishment' such as Gandhi and Mother Theresa. However, she contrasts such lives with other 'morally unsavory' figures of history like Gauguin, Wittgenstein and Tchaikovsky (Wolf, 2007: 8).

This is an interesting list. I'm not sure anyone would argue with her exemplars. However, the trouble is her inferences for a deflationary account of the importance of morality. Whilst we know that Gandhi, Mother Teressa and others *typify* a meaningful life because they gave a great deal of their lives up for others, we do not actually know everything about their lives, nor do we need to. But our watered-down pop conceptions of them are problematic *if* we are going to then compare them with other figures of notoriety, for what we know about them is equally dubitable. Assuming they were not superhuman, the moral exemplars may well have had equally dubious lives to those in the list of morally 'unsavory' characters like Wittgenstein. For sure we know that he made some serious mistakes,[48] but he also showed depth of character in giving up his fortune and living a somewhat simpler existence as a philosopher – and this is not to mention the transformative impact he has had in helping philosophers to overcome their own confusions. These seem to be indicative of the admirable character traits such as generosity, humility, courage and insight. That is not to say that these are sufficient for an attribution of meaning (far from it), but it is to throw a light on a diminished and impoverished account of meaning based on what we might know about someone in the public eye.

The missing dimension of moral orienteering

Wolf's (2007) comparisons don't seem to work for her in drawing attention to the apparent lack of connection between meaning and morality. Quite the opposite, a meaningful life is one imbued with moral activities and substance. We should recognize that the fame or success one achieves is not a *measure* of the value or meaning of one's meaningfulness in life in isolation. No matter how well recognized that person's activities are they are only 'token' of the substance (cf. Hacker, 2021: 319). That is, they are dubitable *indications* of deeper characterological strengths and virtues being applied in meaningful contexts within one's life. Where there is incongruence between the apparent reputation of a person and their real life (for example, where they have been shown to be abusive or cruel to others) their achievements pale into meaninglessness, a fortiori, where the meaningfulness of their lives is based on a moral assessment of their achievements (rightly or wrongly). This is not to place morality of too high a pedestal, but it is to affirm, *contra* Wolf (2007) that without it there is no meaningfulness in life.[49]

Wolf's focus on activities and significance in her conception of meaning, leads her to miss an important distinction between personal achievement and a morally defensible life. I think if she went a bit further, for example, by comparing Gandhi to Hitler, then that would have been a clearer comparison for it would rightly locate meaningfulness in terms of what is *valuable*. As Hacker (2021: 312) has suggested, '[n]othing that is evil can give meaning to a person's life, for evil is the paradigm of disvalue'. This is why the aspect that gives *substance* to a given conception of meaning is one that has a characterological hallmark. I suggest that this is what is wrong with the Blob's life: through characterological weakness, he is failing to live up to the moral imperative implied in his being the kind of creature he is, namely, a human being with immense rational and moral powers. This suggests to me that *awareness* of one's own abilities matter, at least in terms of harnessing the implied importance of moral *responsibility*, notably that social creatures with moral and rational powers have to others in community.

So, bearing in mind this hallmark, what may we infer in terms of Wolf's case of the Blob. I think we can see his case in at least two ways. For example:

1. We can imagine the Blob being somewhat unaware of what is important or valuable, so he may be innocent or ignorant about what is meaningful in life.

Perhaps the Blob had poor role models, parents or experiences which helped to shape his character. It may also be the case that he is somehow impaired (e.g. through having some health issue). In such cases I think we can agree that his behaviours do not amount to meaningless living per se, but rather, a *limited* life. In other words, he is either innocently deceived or mentally disabled. I'm going to call this Blob, 'Good Blob' because the major factors in his life that helped to shape it are largely out of his control.

2. We can also imagine that the Blob is fully aware of his meaningless existence and carries on regardless even in the face of such knowledge.

The Blob seems to be a clear case for exemplifying the vices of laziness, avarice and cowardice. Worse still, Blob may be in self-denial about his predicament with a tendency towards epistemic insouciance and bullshitting others.[50] I'm going to call this Blob, 'Bad Blob'. In such cases we might be happier to condemn Bad Blob for failing to live up to his own potential and, as a result of his lack of honesty with himself, to be somewhat trapped in a cycle of vice, self-deception and vicious behaviours. The normative standard suggested here requires no heroism per se, certainly not as conventionally conceived.[51] But it does require the practice of ordinary virtues like diligence, patience, self-control and moral courage, even on a minimal level. On this basis we could rightly consider Bad Blob's life as quite absurd and meaningless for he has forsaken his most basic of duties, the exercise of his powers and abilities as a human being.[52] In terms of the logical features of meaningfulness, what seems to matter is that a person has a sense of foresight and responsibility over the choices s/he has, and – being guided by a well-informed moral compass – the bravery, determination and persistence to pursue those challenges through to their natural conclusion (insofar as one has genuine possibility for action).

The importance of attending to one's delusions

The good news is that, as suggested already, the very 'predicament of ignorance'[53] provides the logical space for hope, maturation and transcendence. Hope is only required under problematic conditions, it is therefore pointless without having the need to address challenges in life. Further, because we are developmental creatures we can change. Wolf (2007: 16) makes a related claim in her final assessment: '... [there is] no reason to doubt the possibility of finding and making meaning in life – that is no reason, in other words, to doubt the possibility of people living meaningful lives.' A life without meaning, even a meaningless life (so conceived) is logically redeemable, whether in fact it manifests that potential is a matter of individual character, and to a degree, circumstantial luck.[54] This is important to remember because it affords us a degree of mercy to others and humility regarding our own flaws of character.

In either case, however, in terms of *both* Good and Bad Blobs, such patterns of living can have vicious impacts on one's life with real effects on health, relationships, financial independence, conceptions of personal efficacy, confidence and happiness etc. Crucially, if we fail to pay sufficient attention to our own vices, which *all* of us have, we can become exemplars to others for meaningless living (as the Blob has); this is, ordinarily, something which we want to avoid if nothing else but for reasons related to maintaining one's credibility and reputation – an important factor in succeeding in one's life or career whatever that may be.[55] If we are not very good at this iterative process of learning, and importantly, if we do not *attend* to our delusions and blind-spots, then our development can be a 'hard-won' self-knowledge'.[56] Thus, breaking free from vicious effects of ignorance, or delusion seems important for developing well or indeed, flourishing, as human beings – certainly *not* to do so impairs such development.

A major route to this 'upskilling' that I suggest is nurturing an awareness of the role of ways of seeing and seeing aspects, a kind of perceptive pluralism. The interrelated notions of 'ways of seeing', 'aspects' and 'seeing-as', can be great gifts for personal transformation. They encapsulate the importance of developing one's *abilities*, namely, through know-*how*, insight, and the ability to grasp a variety of language-games. But also, as I have been at pains to reinforce throughout this book, *attitude* – by divesting oneself of epistemic bias, dogmas and prejudices. This amounts to a change in 'aspect' and thereby, a new 'way of seeing'. As Wittgenstein (2005: 301) highlights, this is not merely an epistemic aim, but a shift in *attitude* or 'will':

> What makes a subject difficult to understand — if it is significant, important — is not that some special instruction about abstruse things is necessary to understand it. Rather it is the contrast between the understanding of the subject and what most people *want* to see. Because of this the very things that are most obvious can become the most difficult to understand. What has to be overcome is not difficulty of the intellect but of the will.
>
> [my emphasis][57]

The added good news then, is that if one is interested in understanding these concepts, then this very activity (or praxis) will already put one in a very good position to adopt them.[58] Once grasped, developing a set of key insights can help to initiate profound and emancipatory effects on the way we think, giving us tools to deliver *ourselves* from the ensnaring grip of illusory pictures in life, and thereby providing the conceptual space for human beings to build more meaningful and happy lives. After all, happiness 'cannot be pursued' for its own sake; it must 'ensue' from a life well lived (cf. Frankl, 2006: 9). One of the key skills that are important here then, is being able to navigate all the vicissitudes of life. This is a practical skill. It is about nurturing the ability to know intuitively and conceptually (through mastery of concepts and reflexivity about one's own habits of thinking). It is knowing *how* to play the language-games related to life, happiness, meaning and flourishing.

Summative remarks

I have suggested that happiness and meaning are so closely related that to separate them would amount to their disintegration. The factor that pulls them together is one of substance, goodness and morality. Through the particular kind of therapeutic philosophy advanced here, I have shown how asking the wrong kinds of questions often leads to confusion; in particular, I explored the Greek concept of *telos* and how this translates into English as meaning, purpose and explanation. Further, I argued that there is a tendency to see existence in terms of the 'other' and that this, too, is another source of confusion. In particular, by pitting human consciousness and existence against everything else, we artificially distance ourselves from that which we are embedded within. We have no possibility for a 'view from nowhere' as Nagel supposed. Our subjective viewpoint is the only one that we may access. This is not to discount the importance of objective perspectives (in terms of the normativity of concepts) but it is to lay bare the confusions regarding the assumed possibility for objective knowledge regarding any notions of a singular purpose or meaning of life.

Finishing, then, with an exploration of the Blob, I developed Wolf's (2007) case by comparing Good Blob with Bad Blob. As suggested, *contra* Wolf, the role of morality and character are central features of subjective meaning in life, for in asking these perfectly reasonable questions we are most interested in what is valuable in life (as the epitome of goodness). I have also shown how responsibility plays an important role and, by implication, knowledge. A life without meaning, even a meaningless life is logically redeemable, whether in fact it manifests that potential is a matter of individual character and, to a degree, circumstantial luck. This is important to remember because it affords us a degree of mercy to others and humility regarding our own flaws of character.

In either case of both Good and Bad Blobs, such patterns of living can have vicious impacts on one's life with real effects on health, relationships, financial independence, conceptions of personal efficacy, confidence and happiness. What seems important, then, for our flourishing and development is a therapeutic praxis. Specifically, I suggested that *summum bonum* is where we are ever more self-enabled to understand what is *valuable* in life. By attending to that most vital of iterative processes, we can break free from our ignorance and the power of delusional thinking – certainly not to do so may preclude our epistemic and moral development *qua* human beings, and therefore, our flourishing as persons.

Concluding Remarks

How does this book contribute to debates in the field?

The confusions I have identified in this book are not discipline or field specific, but conceptual in nature. A contribution to understanding on this concept may well prove useful in terms of how we think about these issues across a *range* of academic disciplines and policy-related fields of inquiry that deploy the term for their own interests. As outlined, the concept is deployed in various zones of public policy. If research agendas become divorced from actual use then either something *else* is being said, or else, nothing is being said at all. Both eventualities require elucidation. Notably, I have expressed an interest in the projects of positive psychology and positive education, but also in diverse areas that use normative terms but place a high regard for a scientific methodology at the centre of their projects, such as Transhumanism, positive neuroscience, public health, political science, and some forms of hybrid-philosophy.

A contribution to human understanding

With this in mind, it is worth making a distinction between a contribution to knowledge (so conceived as a series of theses, theories or empirical claims) versus a contribution to *understanding*. My claim for the originality of this book and the contribution to understanding (as opposed to knowledge, so conceived) has been two-fold:

I. One is a direct contribution to understanding of the concept itself (and related conceptions; including setting us reminders for how language works as a practice), and,
II. The other is an indirect implication of the problems raised and addressed on wider fields of knowledge.

In this book, there is no new knowledge or theory being developed; the elucidations I highlight merely explicate certain practices and workings in our language. Following Hacker (2010, 2013a) I take philosophy to be concerned with the process of clarification of pertinent features of our language and directed at human understanding rather than knowledge. Philosophy neither explains nor discovers the essence of things in the world, it sets out to remind us of what is already in 'plain view'. (cf. *PI* §89 and *PI* §126), though the 'plain' quality of our terms is often obscured by the diverse ways in which we use our words, the games we play with them, and thereby, our misapprehensions of surface grammar.[1]

This has implications for the kind of *conclusions* we can draw from such an investigation for there will not be a final concluding account of human flourishing here – nor is that possible in the context of the complexities of the human life; we all come with our preconceptions, biases, blind-spots, self-deceptions etc, and we all have our own questions and motivations that drive and interest us. Any advancement in understanding is, as Baker (2004: 192) suggested, a 'person-relative' development. I have therefore aimed at providing the right balance between a general level connective analysis so as to provide a sketch for one possible ordering,[2] punctuated by the more subtle conceptual elucidation of cases. The point is so that we can all know *how to go on* in employing the concept of human flourishing in different cases on specific occasions (*PI* §154). This is a *human*-centred focus that is sensitive to human life and human linguistic practices.

Understanding the concept of human flourishing

With regards to my contribution regarding understanding of the concept itself, to date there is no piece of research addressing the fundamental conceptual confusions on the concept of 'human flourishing' (and cognates), certainly not with this level of focus; yet this is sorely needed. This book is the first systematic analysis of the concept. It therefore fills a significant lacuna in the research, one that is currently characterized largely by grossly misleading and misguided research. My hope is that this book can provide somewhat of a useful reference point for a clearer understanding of the term/s of interest to us here. Even though human flourishing is itself somewhat of a philosophical concept aimed at the human good, there are also perfectly ordinary uses that pivot directly from these traditions.[3] I therefore hope to have contributed to a process of *clarification* and a degree of liberation from the kinds of personal and/or philosophical anxieties that may tend to trouble those aiming to address important questions about the concept (and related conceptions) of human flourishing.[4] Specifically, building on the aims and concerns outlined in the opening Introduction chapter,

'Introducing the Problem', I hope to have elucidated our understanding of the following key concerns:

1. The broad nature of conceptual confusions in the use of the concept of human flourishing (e.g. scientism, reductionism, essentialism and subjectivism) and why we should pay closer attention to context, purpose and use;
2. The key features and connections in the conceptual landscape of human flourishing (e.g. humanness, agency, personal growth, happiness and meaning). Specifically:
    a. The extent that any claim to knowledge is reliant on a putative human nature, what that nature is, and how we can better understand such notions;
    b. Why it is important to draw a distinction between two forms of description for the centrally important concept of 'agency', specifically: normative (A) – criterial, logical, conceptual and normative (B) – axiological, political etc.[5]
    c. The implications of conceptual mastery over allegedly 'contested' terms through insights into the pertinent language-games that relate to ways of knowing, human or personal development, moral orienteering, and notions of meaningful 'happiness'.
3. How to evaluate claims to knowledge about the concept in terms of how we can *know* that a person is flourishing (or not) i.e. relevant criterial implications;
    a. Where the proper domain of this kind of inquiry lies (i.e. conceptual work as opposed to empirical research);
    b. Whether flourishing can be 'measured', as is commonly claimed, and, where the concept of human flourishing can be meaningfully deployed in research programmes.

As I have aimed to show, paying attention to how language is embedded within the diverse contexts and practices of our lives, in '[t]he things we do and why (reasons, motivations) we do them',[6] matters.

On methods: The problem with a scientific conception of knowledge

My central aims in this book have been to support the untangling of certain conceptual knots with regards to our thinking and use of the concept of human flourishing and related terms. What has been clear to me at least is that multiple fields and disciplines invoke the concept of human flourishing to their own ends and for their own purposes, including within the various fields of psychology, policy, education, epistemology, ethics and others. As I have shown, the concept is used interchangeably with other related notions such as health, welfare, well-being, happiness or indeed, *eudaimonia*. There is then a range of theories, models and empirical (or hybridized) approaches to attaining knowledge about human flourishing which are studied using various forms of qualitative, quantitative and even biological methods. However, as suggested in the Introduction chapter and elsewhere, the problem and the method often 'pass' one another by. This is because questions about concepts are addressed through conceptual analysis rather than empirical investigations, which would only entail further conceptual presuppositions.

Importantly, then, failing to grasp the conceptual issues adequately (founded upon a range of scientistic, essentialist, reductivist, subjectivist presumptions) inevitably leads to poor quality, or worse, misleading research. At best such research enterprises offer minimal insights that can easily be gleaned already from conceptual work. Yet it is the glimmer and shine of science that pulls in the interest of many who (perhaps misguidedly) seek robust claims to knowledge about normative matters through scientific methods. To the lament of many who work in philosophy, perhaps the humanities are viewed on par with religious or historical studies as cultural artifacts that are part of our past, not our future. This is a shame, and we are personally, culturally, educationally and epistemically impoverished for it. Advances in knowledge require not only innovation, intuition and creativity, but also philosophical insight.

I have also aimed to highlight that reducing a complex concept (or set of interlaced family resemblance conceptions) like human flourishing to related concepts and terms such as virtuous-rationality or practical reason, well-being, happiness, success or whatever, belies the contextual nature of our use of terms. As I have endeavoured to make clear, there is a fundamental misunderstanding of the nature of such terms and how we may understand them. Such conceptions are driven by assumptions that we can reduce one concept to some essential element or another, or that we can derive an *essential* aspect of all conceptions. The motivations for such projects are often driven by an 'craving for generality' (*BB* 19; also, *PI* §89, §109); that is, an attempt to settle a once-and-for-all account of these concepts. The good news is that once we are able to identify where we may have gone array – that is, by understanding the complex use of language as tools for particular purposes, in contexts, and on particular occasions – we are better able to identify the relevant network of conceptual relations, problems and resolutions to those problems.[7] Even better if we can dissolve them and opt to ask entirely different questions. In so doing, we are better able to identify the kinds of presumptions that belie what may appear to be hidden in the grammar of our terms. This is not to suggest that such *grammars* are fixed and thereby subject to a theoretical account, rather, they are made perspicuous through developing a sensitivity to such contexts so that a word that may appear in one sense to mean one thing, will show itself to be something entirely in another.[8]

The primacy of normativity

The notion of normativity is essential if we are to properly understand why some uses of a word make sense, and why others do not. Although there is a great deal of permissibility and possibility with our use of terms like human flourishing, it is the logical grammar of a concept that gives it meaning, sense, and the possibility of utility as a tool in our conceptual toolkit. So, in speaking of the flourishing of human beings we must first and foremost be sensitive to the categorial *kind* of being that we are, generally speaking; this should be uncontroversial and straightforward. What is good for persons is not the same good as what is good for plants or machines, obviously. As Korsgaard (1996: 46) suggests:

> Normative concepts exist because human beings have normative problems. And we have normative problems because we are self-conscious rational animals, capable of reflection about what we ought to believe and to do.

But knowing *why* this is the case is just as important. In other words, we should be sensitive to the 'reasons for good reasons';[9] we should be sensitive to the kind of normativity that we rely on in language for sense-making and meaning. Specifically, human beings are the kind of being that use language possesses complex two-way powers. As suggested in Chapter 5, these powers are closely related to two central forms of agency: one which is normative in the linguistic, rule-oriented and categorial sense – normativity (A) – and the other, is normative in the socio-cultural norms sense – normativity (B). Where it matters, we must also be sensitive to the particular person that we are, our dispositions, strengths and weakness, and our blind-spots. We must be sensitive the multifarious reference points of use (cf. *PPF* §7; also, Baker, 2004 and Sandis, 2015).

We should then, if willing and interested, no longer be gripped by the same kind of concern that aims at a 'discovery' along the lines of a scientific inquiry, but can become attuned to the complex, normative dimensions that imbue such terms with meaning. Hence, because of the tendency for language to go on 'holiday' i.e. when we do not pay attention to the particularity of a given grammar, there is an imperative in research to move towards a certain clarification of thought or thinking. This is, I suggest, a moral and ethical concern because outside of such a way of developing understanding, we risk adopting misleading pictures and, thereby, producing poor quality and misleading research on the topic. Seeing as flourishing and related terms are deployed in concrete senses by policy-makers, there is a significant ethical duty to get our conceptions in order before operationalizing them in public policy or related contexts.[10]

As outlined in the early sections of this book, 'scientistic' assumptions elevate the scientific method in areas that are more suited to philosophical inquiry. The neurological, etiological and scientific approaches to understanding the meaning of terms, like human flourishing, (as seen through the lens of studies in positive psychology and education) are examples of categorial confusion and scientific over-reach, par excellence, because no amount of empirical study could possibly address a conceptual problem such as 'What is human flourishing?'. The 'What is...?' grammatical form misleads, but as I have endeavoured to highlight, the superficial appearance of words as fixed entities is illusory. Rather, such concerns should better be understood in primarily conceptual or criterial terms.[11] In other words, what is to count as flourishing is a *normative* as opposed to 'nomological' concern.[12] Professional and ethical practitioners of the sciences are well-equipped to undertake the tasks that fall within the nomological sphere, it is when they attempt to then apply nomological approaches to normative issues that the waters of clear thinking get muddied, and thereby, genuine understanding goes with it.

Methodological distinctions

Further, as I have aimed to illustrate, certain conceptions of philosophy which conflate empirical and conceptual investigations (intentionally or otherwise), develop a hybrid methodology that makes little sense when pressed. As such philosophy is also not immune to these kinds of methodological or categorial error. As exemplified in the Introduction, Cassam's recent suggestion that '[p]hilosophical claims about extremism require empirical support' (cf. Cassam, 2021: 29) is misleading because it fails to distinguish between psychological and philosophical concerns. Research that is driven by a concern into the so-called motivations of extremists is of a distinct psychological category when compared with what we mean (conceptually) by such terms as 'extremism'.[13] Understanding about the latter is logically prior to the former and we must pay close attention to these distinctions if we are to actually understand complex phenomena, like extremism. This is not to say that the sciences cannot inform our understanding of a given phenomenon (like 'happiness', 'flourishing' or indeed 'extremism') – of course they can. New contexts elicit new ways of seeing a given problem, so something that may have seemed settled is challenged under the freshness of a new context and new problems. Sometimes this can amount to an alteration in conception or a new concept entirely too. The very nature of language (so conceived as tools) means that it is subject to change.[14] But it is to say that philosophical understanding is logically *prior* to empirical investigations, and further, that philosophical investigations are *not* logically reliant on them.

Contra Cassam (2021), the framing for our research questions and concerns must not fail to draw this distinction. It is problematic, even nonsense, to seek a scientific answer to the *nature* of flourishing as if it were a law of the universe like the gravitational constant. It isn't. Further, empirical research enterprises could not alter the concept or the logical criteria for use of a conception in a given context, though researchers may technicalize a concept, often erring on the way (cf. Putnam, 2012, and Egan, 2002). Empirical research sheds some light on the *interpretations* of a particular conception as used in practice by a given community within specific set of cultural and other reference points. But even then, claims applicable to a community would be limited by the specific characteristics and dispositions of individuals within that community. In short, what I have tried to make clearer, is that in terms of normative concepts, what is 'generalizable' is not in any way scientific, but rather, categorial and criterial (with all the constraints that this implies).

As Hacker (2007a: 449) suggests, we do not need empirical research to tell us about the nature and relations of concepts any more then we need to conduct social surveys of the 'moves' of chess-pieces. The implicit 'rules' for use of such terms are ordinarily taken as a given – we 'just know' intuitively what makes sense and what doesn't. What we do in philosophy is to make those implicit rules more explicit and perspicuous through skilful conceptual analysis, connective analysis and conceptual elucidation. This insight forms a background knowledge and insight into the workings of our language which we ordinarily are able to do; the problems largely occur when we want to research, theorize and generalize.[15] Hence, on a general level, we do not speak of 'flourishing murderers' for good reason: because the criteria for flourishing suggests that which is good for both the person as well as the community. It would make no difference if one person found it made them happy to self-harm or kill others, it would amount to a misattribution (or perversion) of the term.[16] We are language-speakers situated within normative communities of moral agents and as such, this places a great limitation on what may count as 'the good' for us, in a general 'common good' sense as well as what may be attributed more locally or on a personal level. As suggested, this places great *constraints* on what can meaningful be said or asserted from empirical research on the topic.

Hence, developing mastery over our concepts and nurturing a sensitivity to how context and occasion alters our understanding of the words we use has practical import for the research or policy programmes that we undertake on the concept, as much as the wisdom and self-knowledge that we need in order to flourish. This is not merely a concern for *Homo sapiens*: human beings as wise-knowers, but human beings as moral agents and persons – *Homo loquens*: language-deploying, socially-situated, living beings. As suggested, this places human beings at the centre of our interest. As such, the nature of this book may be broadly construed, to coin Hacker's (2007a) term, as a 'philosophical anthropology', that is, conceptual work which makes more perspicuous and lucid the criterial relations (possibilities and limitations) of human flourishing, goodness, and growth for human beings. This could be seen as a form of 'naturalism'. If so, it is certainly not one that is scientific in orientation, rather, on the Aristotelian approach to conceptual analysis, it amounts to a recognition for distinctions that need to be made in terms of 'kinds' (and categories).[17] Combined with Wittgenstein's language-game method (or some related approximation), this is how we may know our way about the concepts of interest.

Personal and professional implications

The somewhat fluid and creative ways that we use words and language, and the embeddedness of those expressions within our practices, and our use of multifarious language-games, suggests that there is more than one way to see the world (i.e. more than one way to conceive of it). In short, we should avoid what Hyslop-Margison & Naseem (2007: preface) term as the 'hegemony of the habits of mind'. Such a dogmatic attitude is antithetical to a pluralistic conception of knowledge and understanding (central pillars of value in our Western, liberal democracies) and is deleterious to genuine human understanding. This is because it frustrates its very possibility of understanding by relocating epistemic agency elsewhere, outside of the moral agent.

We have little say over the criteria for a given use, but we can use our understanding for the social and personal good. In other words, we should allow as much space as possible for epistemic, social and political agency. These values create the very possibility for discussion, agreement and social cohesion within societies that would otherwise tend towards an almost unmitigable epistemological and political tyranny. The price of apathy towards the status quo is immense and felt most by the vulnerable, often voiceless members of our communities.[18] I suggest, therefore, that we have a moral duty to engage with our communities or the socio-political sphere in some way or another. Certainly not to do so is deleterious to our *own* moral development as well as the wider community that we belong to. Naturally, this places ethical responsibilities on those who are in a position to help, advise or mentor others, including educators, parents, life-coaches, etc.

Social, political and ethical implications

The social, political and ethical aspects of this analysis of the concept of human flourishing, then, are also important, Centrally, because flourishing has a criterial connection with moral agency, and thereby, moral responsibility.[19] Together, the 'cultural grammar' of flourishing, is rooted in certain shared values, practices and behaviour. This helps to highlight some interrelated aspects of what flourishing means between cultures that are rooted in the nature of what it means to be 'human', as a social being.[20] The roots here are not merely normative (B), culturally-speaking, but fundamentally normative (A) (criterially-speaking). Although there will be important differences in what it means to be human between these conceptions (e.g. for me, this analysis has a distinctly 'Western' focus), certain shared forms of life help to mitigate against differences on a wider linguistic level where many concepts will be shared across cultures, but with different words being used.[21] As I have suggested, alongside the rather humdrum conceptual constraints on the general level, what truly matters is that we should be concerned with fixing the purpose and question at hand, and then we can begin to develop a coherent conception from which to work with and apply, as opposed to seeking some general conception applicable across diverse cultures or sub-cultures. What matters is asking the right questions and applying the appropriate methodologies. This is, in my view, the key to unlocking our understanding on complex philosophical and social problems like 'human flourishing' and generating quality research and policy which have a meaningful bearing on people's lives whether in education, social policy or science.

The ethical duties of policy-makers

It is, however, important to note that it is *not* in the gift of policy-makers and others in positions of authority to insert some flourishing into their populations as if flourishing were something one could add to top up a glass of water. Flourishing is first and foremost agent-led. But it is in their gift to provide the *conditions* for human flourishing. Berlin's (1969) distinction between positive liberty (what an agent can do) and negative liberty (the absence of obstacles) is useful and conceptually insightful here. It highlights our fundamental relationship with freedom and liberty. I therefore suggest a slight adaptation to Berlin's innovation: two ethical duties for decision-makers and policy-makers:

1. A positive ethical duty: namely, a duty on policy-makers to *nurture* the appropriate social and cultural conditions for human flourishing;
2. A negative ethical duty: namely, a duty on policy-makers *not to do harm* and to learn lessons from past mistakes.

How we conceive and recognize human agency in our democracies therefore matters hugely. It has a direct and cogent bearing on the flourishing of human beings. We have responsibilities to others, to each other, to avoid doing harm. Human forms of life are also predicated on a healthy, thriving ecosystem. This means we also have responsibilities to work symbiotically with the natural order, with the natural world and with other species; this is also vital in order to meaningfully honour the dignity of human beings who live within such environments. Of course, we need not leave things to decision-makers; from a grassroots perspective, we can and should do more *ourselves* within our communities too. This requires active citizens who are able to think clearly, find courage, and tackle the problems of our times with leadership, skill and resources. It has been done before and it can be done again.

Because of the truism that '[t]he welfare of the people in particular has always been the alibi of tyrants' (Camus, 1955), there are wider implications on various aspects of public policy where notions of 'well-being', 'flourishing' or claims for 'the common good' are deployed – at times for confused, dubious or nefarious purposes. Within our Judeo-Christian, Western-Liberal context, the role of our education system in nurturing autonomy has been crucial for some of our most positive developments as a civilization, at least at times (cf. Winch, 2006). Indeed, I would suggest that this is our crowning civilizational glory.[22] As Meerloo (2021: 164) infers, then, respect for humanistic, moral, and ethical concepts (such as agency[23] and political pluralism) can be vital bulwarks against some of the worst atrocities in our troubled, recent history:

> Our human strength lies in our diversity and independence of thought, in our acceptance of nonconformity, in our willingness to discuss and to evaluate various conflicting points of view. In denying the diversities of life and the complexity and individuality of the human mind, in preaching rigid dogmas and self-righteousness, we begin gradually to adopt the totalitarian attitude.

Our developmental knowledge, understanding and humanistic cultural and political practices are not merely couched within the 'contested' realm of normative (B), as is commonly presupposed, but is first and foremost *predicated* on normative (A). There are solid reasons (informed by our developmental conceptual and ethical understanding of what it means to be human) why we should respect the centrality of pluralistic 'ways of seeing' the world.[24] Failing to pay attention to the logical centrality of agency (and related ordinary terms such as autonomy, liberty, freedom), could, therefore, have serious, deleterious and dehumanizing consequences for both individuals and societies, particularly so as we enter a new era of conceptual, social and political contention over the influential role of technological advances.[25] This suggests to me that there is at least the potential for this book to act as a prescient 'reminder' for researchers interested in the concept of flourishing (or conceptions of flourishing), to look a little further than we might otherwise tend to look; in 'philosophy, the winner is the one who can run the race most slowly' (*CV*, 34e). We should, as I suggest, respect the multifaceted *normativity* of these kinds of concepts; indeed, we have a duty to do so.

A Call to Action

This book is therefore an invitation to think differently about yourself, and your relationship with others and the world around you. This has personal, professional and political ramifications. By aiding concept mastery and conceptual development within educational, academic or informal contexts, this analysis could conceivably assist in the mitigation of significant epistemic, political and social harms. Importantly, it may help to inculcate a healthy scepticism towards the moral claims of those in positions of power and authority, whether in research, education, politics or elsewhere. The ability to develop cogent and coherent conceptions of human flourishing is therefore potentially transformative on every level, from root to branch.

Most of us are doing the best we can under difficult circumstances. My central hope with this book, however, is to challenge dehumanizing research and practices on the topic and to encourage those interested, to begin take human flourishing seriously, in the various endeavours we undertake, whether in research, policy or personal life. This suggests for me some possible actions that we can all consider:

I.   **As citizens, community activists, and those engaged in helping others**: to *take time* to better understand how concepts like flourishing operate within our language. In part this entails nurturing academic and other virtues such as curiosity, humility and moral courage. It is also about nurturing within society spaces of constructive dialogue and inquiry, thereby reinvigorating our civic societies and democracies. We can do this independently of decision-makers and we should, wherever possible.
II. **As researchers, policy-makers and citizens**: to *realize our duties* to ourselves, to each other, and to the eco-system. This is a direct consequence of seeing flourishing aright, in context of the immense moral and rational powers we have as human beings. Developing conceptual insight comes with a price, and the price is *responsibility*. Recognizing and responding to that renewed sense of responsibility is the imperative of our age.
III. **As leaders**: for those who can, to *lead through ethical action*. Politics should be effective, but centrally, it should be ethical. The humdrum decisions of policy-makers have a huge impact on the prospects for human flourishing. There is no greater honour than being able to contribute to society in a leadership capacity. If our leaders become more willing to develop robust ethical frameworks for action and decision-making, it will be nothing less than *transformative* for our human species and form of life; we should expect nothing less.

Human flourishing is a fascinating concept intellectually. Yet it is also potentially one of the most powerful concepts in the English language. It has the power to transform lives *towards* the good; towards the conditions for genuine and meaningful happiness, welfare, and prosperity for all. My hope is that the conceptually-informed insights articulated in this book might, therefore, help at least a little to nurture genuine positive change in you as a person, your profession, your community and in society. The challenge is that *not* to do so could be a dereliction of one our most fundamental duties as human beings. One of the central weaknesses of our society lies in our inability to nurture spaces of transformative inquiry. i.e. spaces that allow us to speak about meaningful subjects in ways that translates into genuine positive change. As *Homo loquens*, I believe that we need to reason and reflect together on the concept and the implications for better understanding of the concept, in order to see it and bring about much needed change *as it emerges*. I have great faith in reason, education and dialogue (perhaps naively). This is *our* generation and *our* time to realize human flourishing for ourselves and our future generations. It is time to take human flourishing seriously. We have the appropriate conceptual tools at our disposal, all we need is the *will* to do it.

Notes

Preface

1 Wittgenstein, cited in Gasking & Jackson (1967: 51).

Acknowledgements

1 Originally coined by John Donne (1572–1631). See Donne (1636).

Introducing the Problem

1 For example, according to MacIntyre (1998) the ancient Greek concept of *eudaimonia* is 'badly but inevitably translated by happiness'. As he notes, a 'change of language is also a change of concepts' (MacIntyre, 1998: 39), where language means the particular set of relations between concepts in given contexts.
2 Seligman uses the PERMA model, which is an acronym for P = Positive emotion, E = Engagement, R = positive Relationships, M = Meaning, A = activities or achievements (Seligman, 2011).
3 Adapted from a combination between Bloom's Taxonomy (Bloom et al., 1956) and VanderWeele's (2017) 'Human Flourishing Index'.
4 For example, see HM Treasury (2021) for the policy rationale for well-being measures in the UK. Also see Seligman (2011: 205) who, adopting a pragmatic approach to instrumental government policies suggests that: '[p]olicy itself follows from what is measured, and if all that is measured is money, all policy will be about getting more money. If wellbeing is also measured, policy will change to increase well-being'.
5 Wittgenstein (2009) – *Philosophical Investigations*, standardly cited as '*PI*' from here on.
6 'normative' in the sense of being 'rule-governed'.
7 Read (2005) has suggested that using Wittgensteinian 'jargon' can become a problem in itself. He suggests that scholars should (where apt) use them as an 'obstacle to be overcome' not an end in themselves. I aim to use such terms without fetishizing

them or suggesting that these form some kind of regular methodological framework. As insightful as these terms, they merely form a useful starting place, but once their elucidatory function is complete, we may dispose of them entirely. We may kick the proverbial ladder away. (cf. *TLP* 6.54).

8 I will elaborate on this point further in my Concluding Remarks chapter. You may also read Hacker (2010, 2013a) for a helpful explanation of this distinction in general.

9 This is quite standard in terms of the assumptions guiding research projects on human flourishing. For example, Lee et al. (2021) suggest that the more we can know about well-being, by which they mean the more we 'study' it empirically, the better we can know what it is and how to promote it by 'measuring the unmeasurable'. Similar approaches have recently been deployed by Cassam (2021) as well. He recently suggested that: '[p]hilosophical claims about extremism require empirical support'. (cf. Cassam, 2021: 29). But this seems to me to be prima facie mistaken. Believing that philosophical research can be (or needs to be) hybridized with empirical knowledge is to misunderstand the nature of a conceptual problem and it is to conflate two modes of analysis. It also demonstrates a misguided optimism with regards to the alleged empirical foundations of the epistemology of well-being (or indeed, 'extremism' as the case may be), even within prominent philosophical discourse.

10 The problem of a narrow, instrumentalist policy approach is implicitly acknowledged by Seligman (2011: 26) where he suggests that well-being policies driven by subjective measures are: '. . . vulnerable to the Brave New World caricature in which the government promotes happiness simply by drugging the population . . .'

11 More's distinction between dualism and functionalism also fails to address the Cartesian fallacy evident in dualism between mind and body. It merely exchanges one error for another, all the while retaining the Cartesian dualist frameworks intact (cf. Hacker, 2007a, Bennett & Hacker, 2003 for related discussions of this fallacy within neuroscience).

12 The kinds of problems I raise here are not intended to provide an authoritative critique of Aristotelian thinking on the problem of flourishing, but rather, indicative of the kinds of issues an Aristotelian (or neo-Aristotelian) account might have to respond to. More on the various *uses* of 'flourishing' in Chapter 4.

13 I will revisit the Greek concept of *eudaimonia* further in Chapter 4, by way of introducing some salient distinctions, contrasts, and comparisons with the central concept of interest to us here, 'human flourishing'.

14 Cf. De Leeuw, R. & Buijzen, M. (2016) and Seligman & Csikszentmihalyi (2000).

15 For example, Parsons famously posited that the patient enters into a sick role and the Doctor emerges, as the 'guardian of the established order, as the gate-keeper of deviance, and as the embodiment of the "sacred" order of normality' (Parsons, 1951: preface). Parsons rightly posits that such a conception of health (mental or physical)

is one of 'dependence'. Naturally, a conception of health which posits professionals as the ultimate arbitrators of human wellness cannot be consistent with a conception of flourishing and health which promotes the inherent goods of autonomy and human ability.
16 I explore this point on the conceptual problems of a neuroscience of happiness and well-being further in Chapter 5.
17 Readers may well find it useful to read Hand (2023) who provides an excellent set of arguments for why a view of education being centred on flourishing is problematic. For example, he suggests that 'flourishing is not the sort of thing a person can acquire by learning'. Whilst I agree with much of Hand's remarks and criticisms, I do not entirely agree with this claim because flourishing necessarily entails personal growth, development and learning. This will become clearer in Chapter 6. Nevertheless, Hand's chapter will be very useful reading for those interested in the kinds of issues that emerge as the aims of flourishing and education are conflated together in ways not particularly helpful for educators.
18 Also see *PPF* §371: 'The existence of the experimental method makes us think that we have the means of getting rid of the problems which trouble us; but problem and method pass one another by'.
19 For example, Rogers (1961: 23) stated:' Experience is, for me, the highest authority. The touchstone of validity is my own experience. No other person's ideas, and none of my own ideas, are as authoritative as my experience. It is to experience that I must return again and again, to discover a closer approximation to truth as it is in the process of becoming in me.' This raises the spectre of private insight and knowledge in ways that fail to recognize the primacy of the normativity of language and the public role of concepts that aid self-knowledge and understanding.
20 Of course, on the one hand we do have a use for that picture of the Self in specific circumstances. The concept of a 'person' for example is related to such an outer conception of the Self, originating from the word *persona* (a mask) worn by ancient Greek actors. cf. Hacker (2007a: 286).
21 Hacker (2007a: 241) attributes to the conceptually confused legacy inherited from both Locke (regarding introspection) and Descartes (regarding privileged access).
22 '… one might speak of a subjective understanding. And sounds which no one else understands but which I 'appear to understand' might be called a "private language"' (*PI* §269).
23 Iago's monological machinations (from Shakespeare's Othello) spring to mind here as an example.
24 I pick up on some of these themes relevant to discussions later in this book, specifically, Chapter 3, section four and Chapter 6, section one.
25 Nevertheless, the problem could be alleviated somewhat if we were to have fewer questions and the possibility for follow-up probing and clarification through

complementary methods. Once we have the conceptual frameworks pinned down for both the questions and responses we can then draw out (potentially) some valuable knowledge and inferences from such research. Still, the quality of such research remains limited at best and requires researchers that possess philosophical and conceptual skills that are often absent due to the limitations of disciplinary boundaries, experience and training.

26 Wittgenstein (2009) – Philosophical Investigations: Philosophy of psychology, a fragment, standardly cited as 'PPF' from here on.

Chapter 1

1 This may be one of the reasons why Professor Guy Longworth facetiously quipped on Twitter that one could '[r]uin a work of philosophy by inserting "normativity"'. (Longworth, 2020).
2 As Thomson (2008) suggests normativity amounts to 'normative judgements' about, for example, the nature of the 'good' (cf. Wedgewood, 2007).
3 I will explore more explicitly a distinction I draw between these conceptions of 'normativity'; that is, normative (A), rule-governed linguistic behaviour, and normative (B), moral or social norms – which is the more prevalent and widely known use, certainly in philosophy.
4 This merely highlights the fact that a kind of being that did not suffer in those kinds of ways, would have no relation to our particular kinds of joking (not unless the jokes were based on *similar* fundamental facts of life).
5 See Baker & Hacker (2005a): 152) for further analysis on the exceptions that Wittgenstein raises here.
6 I will argue this more explicitly in Chapter 4.
7 For example, Hacker (2007a: 121) highlights that 'the categorial term "agent" articulates a general pattern in the use of subject-referring terms in sentences ascribing acts, actions or actions on another thing to a subject', thus distinguishing between other categories of concepts related to human beings, such as that of substance causation, powers, mind, body, and person (cf. Hacker 2007a: preface, xi).
8 'Perhaps the word "describe" tricks us here. I say "I describe my state of mind" and "I describe my room". You need to call to mind the differences between the language-games' (*PI* §290).
9 Also see Monk (1991: 536–537): '"Hegel seems to me to be always wanting to say that things which look different are really the same", Wittgenstein told him. "Whereas my interest is in showing that things which look the same are really different." He was thinking of using as a motto for his book the Earl of Kent's phrase from King Lear (Act I, scene iv): "I'll teach you differences."

10 The term 'use' here is not to be confused with empirical surveys for *actual* use in society. The insight is intended to highlight the need for analysis of the logical relationships of our words, in contexts of use, and as features of our language. Hence, a better simile (as opposed to an epistemic miner) would be one of a logico-topographer surveying 'semantic' landscapes of meaning in given cases, rather than one of a socio-linguist conducting empirical surveys (see Hacker, 2007a: 14 and 2013a: 444–448).

11 This quote from Glock is rather dense. See *PI* §92, and the editors' note for that remark, for comments on the apparent 'hidden' nature of words, leading us to being misled into seeking out their real or true meanings. Also see, *PI* §315 and *PPF*, xi §315 for Wittgenstein's clarificatory remarks on the relationship between essence and grammar. Finally, see Forster (2004) for an in-depth analysis of the senses in which Wittgenstein's notion of a 'grammar' is arbitrary and the senses in which it is not.

12 Hacker (2015: 16) posits that categorially, the concept of a 'form of life' is not predominately a biological one; rather it is 'cultural' (though it is specific to the *kind* of being that we are). Also see Moyal-Sharrock (2015: 25) who has suggested: '... a "form of life" is not a single way of acting, albeit characteristic of a group of organisms (such as speaking, calculating or eating animals), but must include innumerable other such shared ways of acting that cohesively form the necessary background or context or foundation of meaning' [emphasis added]. This delineates important conceptual boundaries, but also hints at the possibility for pluralistic ways of being human, an aspect that Moyal-Sharrock & Sandis (2019) have since extended into the debates on gender identity.

13 Cf. Hacker (2007a: 40) and (2013a: 268). Also see (Glock, 2009): 'Wittgenstein's functional conception of grammatical rules: the logical status of a sentence is due not to its linguistic form, but to the way it is used, and for this reason it can change.' (ibid: 660).

14 Cf. Travis (1989), Hacker (1986), Hacker (2015)

15 Cf. 'When a sentence is called senseless, it is not, as it were, its sense that is senseless. Rather, a combination of words is being excluded from the language, withdrawn from circulation.' (*PI* §500). But we can be blinded to this fact. As a result, philosophical problems, questions and concerns can arise whilst language goes on 'holiday' (*PI* §38). This is a crucial insight from Wittgenstein that helps us to draw our attention to what (and indeed whether anything) is actually being asked.

16 See Sharrock & Dennis (2008) for some further discussion.

17 Cf. Baker & Hacker (1990) critiquing Malcolm's (1989). The central position of dispute between them seems to amount to a difference over what 'agreement' means.

18 Hacker (2007a: 171) highlights a related contrasting point when he speaks of the normativity of 'normality'.

19 However, one might be tempted to accept, as William Blake has suggested, that if 'the fool would persist in his folly he would become wise' (Blake, 2011: 225); or as

Wittgenstein advises, not to be 'afraid of talking nonsense! Only don't fail to pay attention to your nonsense' (*CV*, 64). However, counsel assumes in the listener an ethic of self-improvement, moral and personal development, moving from misunderstanding to understanding; there is no room here for a permanent attitude of acceptance towards foolishness, senselessness, guile, meaninglessness or dogmatism.

20 It is important here not to imply a kind of excessive epistemic constraint or dogmatism. There is more than one way to see a given thing, phenomenon, or problem, but sense is always necessary for anything to be said at all. This is addressed through Wittgenstein's use of the notion of 'ways of seeing', which I will explore in the next Chapter 2.

21 As Hacker (2013a: 462) averred, '[t]he ancients did not have to confront the conceptual problems posed by quantum mechanics.' Our conceptual problems are particular to us, they are framed by our situatedness, our conceptual schemes, and linguistic practices and the degree to which we are capable thinkers and agents.

22 For a more comprehensive account of the concept of meaning from a Wittgensteinian perspective, see Baker & Hacker (2009), especially Chapter VIII (pp. 129–152). In that chapter Baker & Hacker provide an exposition of Wittgenstein's latter thinking on the topic. Specifically, they provide a ten-fold set of criteria on which we may use for determinations on the meaningfulness of terms, including the importance of (public) 'shareability'. This should not, however, be taken to imply a theory of meaning. Wittgenstein's insights were first and foremost conceptual, addressing common philosophical issues of his time (many of which beguile us still today).

23 See Baker (2004) for analysis on the distinction between concept and conception. Here, following Baker & Hacker (2005) I simply suggest a kind of problem-oriented pragmatism; we can see things in ways that are more useful and better suited to a given task in a specific cultural, socio-political space, place and time.

24 NB: neatly categorizing terms is not a possibility because, as highlighted, the concepts that words signify are not discreet entities that may be categorized like words, rather they are 'abstractions'. They signify logical *relationships* between words. The upshot is that *use* (practice) is what matters. Hence, the seemingly endless possibilities for use are only limited insofar as we (as linguistic agents) a) have imaginative limitations for use, e.g. as a result of education and enculturation etc., and b) such uses operate within the bounds of sense.

25 See note to *PI* §122 for a clear description of the original German term.

26 I use Hacker's term here: 'web of words' (see, Hacker 2007a: 11) to highlight the interconnectedness of grammars.

27 See Glock (2009) for further discussion on concept change.

28 Also see Travis (2008: 2–9) for his explication on various uses of 'blue', where is explores a debate on the nature of 'truth' conditions between Austin and Strawson;

specifically, on the problematic relation between our use of words and the world (including the agent making the utterance).

29 No moral judgement is made or required here on the ethics of pantomime performances in family environments, nor indeed on the possibility of sexist connotations. It is merely to illustrate that language-games are multi-layered and contextual with a host of points of 'reference', including linguistic, personal, tonal, physical, cultural etc.

30 This is partly why Sandis (2015: 131) states: 'If to understand a language is to understand a form of life, then to understand a person is to understand a whole life'. We can understand people or cultural features in theatrical practices generally by understanding our specific cultural context (linguistic understanding). Relatedly, by understanding someone's personal life story, we can understand their reference points and what they 'mean' by an utterance (linguistic as well as psychological understanding).

Chapter 2

1 For a fuller explanation of the relevant methods of analysis here, readers should attend to the tetralogy by Hacker (2007a, especially Chapter 1) and (2013a, especially the Appendix), but readers may also enjoy the further analyses in the final two volumes in the set, 2018, and 2021.

2 'Therapeutic' in the sense of assisting with providing clarity over conceptual confusion, particularly the kind that leads us into delusion. It is worth briefly noting here, however, that there has been some debate between, notably, Gordon Baker and Peter Hacker on how the term 'therapy' is to be used. I will explore this a little further in section 2 of this chapter.

3 Also, see Hacker (2013a: preface) where he outlines his intentions in crating the four volumes on human nature as a 'comprehensive' essay in 'philosophical anthropology'.

4 'The name "philosophy" might also be given to what is possible before all new discoveries and inventions' (*PI* §126)

5 Of course, it's important to note here that this is not a criticism of literary discourse or mythical narrative. Although it is not within the scope of this book, there is also a powerful and unique role for metaphorical and symbolic language e.g. in folk, religious, literary or artistic discourse. I'd suggest that we need those discourses as well for meaning and sense-making of human experience. A fundamental problem emerges (e.g. psychologically, epistemically, socially or politically) when we fail to identify the language games being deployed and get caught up in a category error, the kind that contributes to delusional thinking. A great deal hangs on what is at stake and whether claims to knowledge (or a distinct form of folk narrative knowledge) are problematic, or not.

6 Also see *LFM* 44 for original citation direct from Wittgenstein's writings where he alludes to the task of the philosopher, metaphorically, as a topographical 'tour' guide so that we may learn our way about.

7 NB: After working closely together for many years, Baker and Hacker had a disagreement on the methodological matter of 'therapy' as a method. For Baker, it was clear to him from Wittgenstein's earlier writings that Wittgenstein was influenced by Freud's conception of psychoanalysis (cf., Baker, 2004: 140). Conversely, for Hacker, Wittgenstein's discussions of Freud and therapy were anecdotal, incidental, and unimportant. Baker was, according to Hacker, 'deeply mistaken' (cf., Hacker, 2007b: 90). My view is that this dispute is largely a matter of emphasis in terms of the problems identified. Hacker concedes that '[n]o one, I think, would dispute that Wittgenstein's later philosophy has a therapeutic goal – analogically speaking' (ibid., 99). But Hacker also dismisses the idea that a therapeutic approach is fitting as a description of Wittgenstein's philosophy. Hacker is after all right that Wittgenstein saw the *fundamental* problems of philosophy consisting in problems in the forms of our representation in language (cf., *PI*§109), i.e. wider than the personal level. That said, Baker is also right that Wittgenstein was acutely aware that beyond the rational debates on the nature of language, there is a personal or psychological dimension to addressing philosophical problems, and that these influence how – or whether – we see a problem (Also see McFee, 2015, especially Chapters 2 and 5 for a defence of Baker). My view is that both Hacker's and Baker's insights are important. This issue does have methodological implications, however, and this apparent duality between philosophical and personal dimensions will become important later in the book as we consider the importance of self-knowledge, personal development, attitude, moral orienteering and delusion in the context of the flourishing life.

8 Again, see note to *PI* §122 for a clear description of the original German term.

9 The term, 'elucidation' is often used by Hacker to help to outline Wittgenstein's elucidatory aims of philosophy (cf. Hacker, 2007a: 11–17). In *PI* §90, Wittgenstein compares 'light' with 'purpose', and in doing so suggests that in problematic cases, the sense and meaning of an utterance are together understood best when compared and contrasted with vivid pictures of 'hidden' non-sense.

10 Originally coined by Strawson (1992) to highlight the complex interconnectedness of concepts in their relationships with one another. Hacker also uses this term extensively to suggest the possibility of a conceptual 'map' (cf. Hacker, 2007a: 438 and 448).

11 It's important however not to make too much of the phrase 'depth grammar' itself because it could lead one to see the hidden grammar as having some fixed nature (as our surface grammar does). That is a view attributed to the early Wittgenstein and it amounted to an essentialist and representationalist way of seeing language as rooted

in a putative metaphysicalized 'external' reality. As Baker & Hacker (2005a: 61) suggest, although 'our conceptual scheme is conditioned in various ways by the regularities of the world and the regularities of natural human reactive and discriminative behaviour', it is not 'regular' in the way that scientific laws are. Though our world is partly shaped by our perceptions of it, and ergo, our limitations – these contingencies are by no means governed by what might be conceived of as hidden 'super-rules'. Neither are they fixed to logical or metaphysical features of the world or indeed to human nature. In other words, our conceptual schemes and the network of rules across our range of concepts in natural language could be otherwise. Nevertheless, I do find it useful because it highlights the fact that we do need to look and see beyond the surface in order to see what's going on in a sentence, what is essential and what is not in order to convey meaning; more specifically, what is misleading.

12 The example echoes Best's (1978) example of the problem of audible sunsets which are simply logically precluded due to the incommensurability between the language-games of *hearing* (concepts regarding audibility) and *seeing* (concepts regarding perception or sight).

13 Watts (1977: 30) also once said, 'you can't get wet from the word water'. The obviousness of the point is not intended to be profound, merely clarificatory.

14 'To suppose this is to confuse the scaffolding from which we describe the world with the shadow the scaffolding casts upon the world. The world has no "scaffolding", and what looks like scaffolding belongs to our means of representation.' (Hacker, 2013a: 445).

15 I refer to the kind of sentimentality seen in Schinkel's (2017) paper where the line between metaphysics and concepts is not clear, and the style is literary, misleading and opaque. I have written a paper entitled: 'Lost in wonder: a response to Schinkel's concept of "deep wonder"'. In that paper I compare and contrast two aspects of wonder: one which is focused on wonder as *experience*, and another which I propose as more defensible in educational settings, based on *inquiry*. (cf., Mountbatten-O'Malley, 2023b).

16 cf. notes to *PI* §122

17 I will explore the problematic concept of 'Humanness' further in Chapter 3.

18 Also see Hacker (2007a: Ch. 1) and Hacker (2013a: Appendix) for a comprehensive defence of the critics of this particular form of conceptual analysis which he terms as a 'philosophical anthropology'.

19 The concept of the 'unconscious', though popularized by Sigmund Freud, was originally coined by Friedrich Schelling (in Germany) and later introduced into English by Samuel Taylor Coleridge (Bynum et al., 1981: 292).

20 For the original source see Fliegende Blätter (1892).

Chapter 3

1. E.g. Fredrickson & Losada (2005) is an extreme exemplar case of one form of reductive approach to humanness and human flourishing. It may be worth skimming Brown et al. (2014) for a critical analysis of the problematic application of mathematical concepts in the original piece. Also see a defence from Fredrickson (2013) where she conceded some errors but maintained the value of the key empirical findings, and a further rebuttal from Brown et al. (2014).
2. See Tomasello & Herrmann (2010).
3. Wittgenstein (1991) *The Blue & Brown Books* (standardly cited as *BB*).
4. The human predicament is incredibly similar to that of the animal kingdom. That said, because of our diverse and particular human forms of life, it is also distinct in important senses ... '[i]f a lion could talk, we wouldn't be able to understand it' (*PI* §327). Our terms have the force that they do, partly because of our biology, but also because of our unique and shared histories, cultures, powers, limitations and interests as human beings. See Hacker (2015).
5. Also see Winch (1990)
6. Naturally, this seemingly almost endless inquiry can be frustrating. When might we know we have reached a sufficient end point? That depends on the nature of the problem at hand, and a judgement about what exactly is needed in order to address it.
7. In Chapter 6 I will further explore what I call the 'absurdities of the "Self"', in the context of personal identity and the *normativity* of the Self.
8. Remember that human beings cannot be reduced to an essence like 'dignity'. However, it is clear to me that politically, dignity is of central importance to human flourishing. Firstly, this is because it has a close relationship with the concept of 'agency'. It also has practical import, by affording us basic human rights, needed because, historically, the dignity of human beings has been abused by tyrants and autocrats. It is therefore both a normative as much as an axiological term that helps to crystalise why legal protections and moral practices are necessary, at least in terms of human welfare. I will explore the political role of dignity and agency a little further in Chapter 5. Also see Neill & Nevin (2021) for a political and philosophical account of the role of dignity with human flourishing in the Canadian economic context.
9. Begum had been through a lengthy legal appeal process against the withdrawal of her UK citizenship, which has only just concluded on 26 February 2021. See The Supreme Court (2020).
10. See Graso et al. (2021), who from a multidisciplinary perspective, discuss what they term as 'asymmetries in human cost evaluation' (i.e. when comparing different strategies for virus mitigation), which they argue is partly due to the tendency for

moralizing discourse during the pandemic. The harms implied are not merely personal or social, but also epistemic.

11 Of course, the notions of danger here will always be context sensitive because a thrill-seeker who enjoys adrenaline sports (like snow-boarding, bungee-jumping or BASE-jumping) is normally deemed acceptable by most in society yet may or may not meet the criteria for carelessness or precariousness. In such cases the judgement of precariousness will be closely tied not so much to the activity itself (*contra* drug-taking) but to the *way* in which the activity is undertaken.

12 Even if by using the word 'love' in this context, someone actually meant 'I thought about how much I love you' then it would still amount to a different concept because the logical consequences would differ substantially (i.e. it might be the concept of 'thinking about loving'). The concepts related to love here (e.g. thinking, intention) would still be subject to public criteria for what is to be counted as 'thinking about love'. Thus, on the one hand, through insight into the actual use we have clarity over the kind of concept being deployed, and on the other we have the force of normativity that is in play either way.

Chapter 4

1 Hacker (2013a) distinguishes between *focal* concepts (e.g. 'health'), *family resemblance* concepts (e.g. 'game') and *multi-focal* concepts (e.g. 'belief', 'imagination', 'consciousness'). I'd like to suggest that the concept of human flourishing can be *both* a family resemblance concept (in the sense that diverse uses have some loose resemblance to one another) as well as a multi-focal concept (in the sense that when our direct interest is the growth and goodness of a living being, this still has multiple centres of variation e.g. persons vs animals) which are neither members of a family, nor are they focalized.

2 We must be weary of fetishizing or reducing the virtues as well. A virtue is not a separable, digitized feature of the human being any more than flourishing is, but it is a kind of activity embedded within a range of contexts and complex life conditions.

3 The apparent family resemblance link is likely tied to the Latin history of the word in which those more archaic uses share a common etymological root 'flor'– cf. Pearsall, 1998: 706.

4 E.g. The flourishing of an empire that is deemed to be evil in nature is understandably conceived as morally deleterious to entire populations. A framework of norms (and other contextual reference points) will help decide whether the moral dimensions for flourishing societies or civilizations is relevant.

5 The term, 'conspiracy theories' are generally defined in relevant literature as attempts to explain the ultimate *causes* of significant social and political events and

circumstances with claims of secret plots by two or more powerful actors (cf. Aaronovitch, 2010; Byford, 2011; Coady, 2006). There is a distinction to be made between 'theories' and 'beliefs' one can consider a theory without subscribing to it (cf. Goertzel, 1994). It is worth noting that one can believe that a given theory has 'some' weight (empirical or logical evidence) without generalizing about the reductive conclusions associated with many conspiracy theories.

6 We could learn something from the plant applications of flourishing, especially in terms of the focus on *conditions* of growth (although there is far more at stake when dealing with human beings, i.e. more than mere material conditions).

7 The implications are that we have scope to manage our own flourishing, albeit in a limited sense, as responsibility is shared. However, as will be explored later in Chapter 7, attitude and *will* matter, especially under unfavourable social or political conditions.

8 See Hull & Pasquale (2018) and Davies (2015) for a thorough critique of instrumental, neoliberal and corporate approaches to happiness.

9 Also, in light of the damage of corporations on the environment, or well-being of the populations that are impacted by corporate growth and development, it is worth mentioning that the moral dimension of corporations has been developed through the lens of 'social responsibility'. although logically amoral, human beings do lead corporations and so can imbue corporate strategies with some central values as an acknowledgement of the socio-economic impact of corporate growth and development. See Aluchna & Idowu (2017) for further discussion of the increasingly important notion of corporate 'social responsibility'.

10 Of course, human beings also behave instrumentally to one another, and corporations are made of persons, but when they do, we rightly attribute them as having sacrificed an important aspect of their own humanity. The inherent structure of corporations (as outlined) can encourage this kind of irresponsible and unethical behaviour.

11 This is where context of use is important because if Jack were the name of a robot or super-computer then we wouldn't be concerned about connective analyses related to agency or character development for example, because robots are not the *kind* of thing that we ascribe moral agency to.

12 I coin the term: 'specieal' as an adjective describing that which relates to *species* because 'special' is too ambiguous.

13 For the purposes of clarity in this section, I will use the concept of 'eudaimonia' even though it is most often translated as 'happiness', certainly in modern translations.

14 As Crisp (Aristotle, 2004: xiv) suggests: 'Greek culture was one of excellence, in the sense that young men were encouraged to compete with one another in many spheres of life, including athletic, intellectual, and aesthetic activity.'

15 Aristotle's (2014) *Nicomachean Ethics* – abbreviated to NE from here on

16 In conceptualizing the 'soul' here, although Aristotle will have had 'divine' in mind, for our purposes here it is sufficient to say that the 'soul' for Aristotle broadly equates with our modern notion of the 'mind' or mental faculty (cf. Crisp, in Aristotle, 2004: xiv)
17 I also build on this with further discussion of success in Chapter 7, in the context of happiness and flourishing.
18 It may be useful to clarify here that there is a patent risk in making an artificial judgement or demarcation between what could be considered as 'normal' and 'abnormal' psychological states for human beings. This is for obvious reasons, premature. After all, all human states are standard, 'illness' and 'health' are shared by us all. The point regarding 'standard' and nonstandard simply relates to our concepts, our uses of words and their related conceptual shades or *foci*.
19 I explore 'failure' in the context of a meaningful life in Chapter 7.
20 I will explore the relationship between success and happiness further in Chapter 7.
21 There are exceptions of course. We can, for example, attribute simple or primitive forms of happiness to an infant, for example, after they have been fed. What we mean in that sense is something like content, satisfied, satiated, feeling good etc.
22 Cf. MacIntyre (1999: 67), where he suggests that judgements of human flourishing are those where 'we judge unconditionally about what it is best for individuals or groups to be or do or have not only *qua* agents engaged in this or that form of activity in this or that role or roles, but also *qua* human beings'.
23 Where to 'fail at life' amounts to a failure to engage with the relevant activities of life, and hence, a failing to use our innate human powers. More on this in Chapter 7.
24 As usual, we need to be aware of the risk of implying an essential feature of a concept by asking what a concept 'is'. In fact, this phrasing simply amounts to: what does it *mean* in *this case*. For example, sometimes affirmatively: they *look* like they are living life successfully; sometimes negatively: they *don't* look like they are living life in a bad way. The context dictates the dominant use.

Chapter 5

1 I use Alvarez's (2010) conception here illustratively. I find her conception of practical reasoning being oriented towards goodness idealistic in a similar way to how Grimm (2015) idealizes wisdom being oriented towards well-being (I will discuss this in Chapter 7). You can, for example, reason quite practically about how to commit evil yet evil practical reasoning still counts as practical reason, though perhaps not in a way that reflects the central interests of philosophy in general. What may be happening here is a form of evil-denialism where reason is seen to be incongruent with evil. But as Hacker (2021: 93) suggests, animals are excluded from moral

agency, whereas human beings are indeed able to perform acts of evil. This is because moral acts require '... reason and reasoning, deliberation and intention formation, reflection on deeds'. Indeed, responsibility based on reasoning capacity is a crucial element in terms of culpability and the justification for ascriptions of evil (or not, as the case may be).

2   To be fair to Descartes he also thought of human behaviour to be psychologically reducible and explainable mechanistically where complex responses to perceivable objects could be 'conditioned by the passions and by memory' (Cottingham, 2008: 345). Nevertheless, because Descartes suggested that animals were mere 'automata' without a soul, he has been criticized for helping to legitimatize instrumental attitudes to them and an indifference to their suffering (cf. Moriarty, 2008: xxxvii).
3   Frankfurt uses spiders as an example where the implication is that agency admits of degrees between different sentient beings.
4   I discuss practical reason and wisdom further in the context of personal growth and development in Chapter 6.
5   I will discuss the prospects for effective user of Wittgenstein's notion of 'seeing aspects' as a device for gaining moral and epistemic insight in Chapter 7.
6   As is widely known, modern culture is a particular form of societal organisation that was shaped over relatively recent times, dated roughly from the growth of civilizations in the Near East and Fertile Crescent c. 4,000 BCE (cf. Toynbee, 1987).
7   For example, when we say that chemical substances acts on the surface of a particular metal. However, this is a different use of 'act' – loosely related but distinct.
8   However, inferences should not be drawn here for the favouring of an automated work life as well. The point here is on the most fundamental level of maintaining existence which our body 'does', *ceteris paribus*, relatively automatically.
9   Also see Reid (2010) for an earlier exposition of the concept of 'two-way powers'.
10 This is not to suggest that all good decisions need always to be well-reasoned. Some decision-making may be intuitive and derived through tacit knowledge and experience. The criteria for such decisions are difficult to describe to oneself, certainly at the time; they are somewhat hidden from plain view. In other words, in terms of behaviour, action often comes first, and then possibilities for reflection and justification after the fact. See Standish (2017) for an excellent discussion of the problems between language and understanding in the context of Wittgenstein's discussions of 'primitive' language games: 'The primitive form of the language-game is certainty, not uncertainty ... for uncertainty could never lead to action. The basic form of the game must be one in which we act' (*OC* §421).
11 See Boesch & Tomasello (1998) for an influential view from anthropological studies.
12 See Nida-Rümelin & Özmen 2012 for further discussion.
13 See Glock (2019) where he defines 'lingualism' as the suggestion that because animals lack language (like a human language) this precludes animals a priori from

possessing mental capacities at all, or at least the 'higher' mental capacities required for agency.

14 Berlin's (1969) distinction between positive (what an agent can do) and negative liberty (the absence of obstacles, barriers or constraints) is insightful for the very reason that it highlights the Janus-faced relationship that we have with freedom and liberty in social and political contexts.

15 As explored in Chapter 1, there are two central uses of 'normativity' of interest to us: 1) the kind which is used to suggest ethical and other norms, axiological concerns etc., and 2) the kind which is used to highlight that language is practice and rule-based. I am here interested in the former, though the latter is dominant in general throughout this book.

16 The moral status of human beings with impaired degrees of ability (e.g. those with 'cognitive disabilities') has quite understandably become quite a controversial topic of debate in ethical and philosophical literature. cf. Singer (1993, 2009); Carlson & Kittay (2009).

17 This must (both in a criterial sense as much as ethically speaking) include the full and diverse expression of human genetic variation. See Garland-Thomson (2019) for more on the ethics of diversity in gene expression.

18 A clarificatory point could be made here that has implications on both aspects of agency (biological and social), for those who do not have mental capacity, for example, but may be granted the benefits of agency through third party carers or custodians who act in their best interests. This is a well-established norm that is based on the understanding that all human beings are due a degree of fundamental 'dignity' *qua* human beings irrespective of their individual capacities. See Evans, (2019) and Gaymon Bennett (2019) for an exploration of dignity in the context of capacity, bio-ethics and human flourishing.

19 Wittgenstein was also highly critical of the practice of 'dogma', which he thought restricted human thought in highly vicious ways. He accused much of philosophy as a discipline, as well as the Catholic Church – as an authority – to be guilty of these vices (See Wittgenstein, 1980: 26 and 28 respectively).
More recently, in a scandal involving the publication of the Fauci emails, (BBC, 2021) Fauci accused his critics of attacking 'science' itself when they undermined or criticised him (Porterfield, 2021). This is perhaps a rather crude, example – certainly of the practice of hubris that appears to be propped up a reification of the voices for one vision of 'science'. Nevertheless, a plethora of applications of 'scientism' seems possible. See Beale & Kidd (2017) for a thorough exploration of the concept of scientism in terms of Wittgensteinian thinking. They broadly construe it as the 'overestimation' or over-extension of science through dogma leading to a corruption of philosophical thought.

20 Male rabbits, for example, can become terrifyingly aggressive to one another after being separated. But they can equally re-bond through gradual re-introduction.

21 However, for clarity, the suggestion of degrees here is not to suggest that animals have a lower end kind of the *same* intelligence compared with human beings. Arguably because of our disparate 'forms of life' (as in Wittgenstein's example with the lion), dogs and humans have qualitatively (not quantitatively) different potentialities for experiences of mind, emotion and agency. cf. *PPF* §1 and §327.
22 In fact, all manner of addictions may be considered here; even ideological, religious etc. The notion of false pictures is also relevant as something which compels us, which Wittgenstein compares to superstitions and illusions (*PI* §110; *CV* §83). Also see Baker (2004: 208) a human transfixed by a false picture is 'compelled to say something which seems, even to himself, empty, self-contradictory or meaningless'.
23 See Baker (2004) for some very powerful exegesis on Wittgenstein's philosophical method.
24 In an insightful and sensitive exploration of some of the genetic variation in the human genome traditionally labelled as 'disabled', Garland-Thomson (2019: 24) provides an analysis that weaves through the biological and social aspects of the human being. She suggests that we need not see human variation in terms of deficit. By avoiding stigmatizing discourse (like disabled), she suggests that we contribute to a healthy 'moral ecosystem', one that respects and cherishes diversity.
25 Although as Hacker (2007a) points out these in turn are rooted in ancient classical and Judaeo-Christian ways of thinking, cultural practices and traditions.
26 Although like many of the researchers in this field, they qualify their findings suggesting that they 'barely scratch the surface' of understanding on (in this case) the biological bases of paternal care (cf. Greene et al., 2016: 30). The deep knowledge, always of an empirical nature, is yet to be found sometime in the future.
27 See Rubin et al. (2019).
28 For example, children often feel irritable when hungry or hot and it has a direct impact on behaviour. This seems to be largely out of their control until they reach a stage of maturation (including developing skills of self-restraint). Although this counts as an explanation it isn't a 'reason' for action in the sense explored above. Reasons require reflection and at times we all act impulsively due to the influence of our biological conditions. This can be congenital or contingent.
29 Sandis (2012b) has published a thorough analysis of the central problems with the conflation of various kinds of explanation rife in interdisciplinary research; in particular chapter 7 of Sandis' book ('Spheres of explanation') where Sandis draws on the useful distinction between causal explanation and agential reasons for acting.
30 Putnam (2002) has argued against the 'fact/value' dichotomy showing how 'facts' are not objective, independent features of the world but are shaped by norms and practices; they presuppose normative values and concepts. Although much depends on the particular framing of a given question, seeing as we ascribe the language of 'facts' as descriptions for certain states of affairs, what counts as a fact is not fixed but

contextual. As he suggests, 'if we do not see that facts and values are deeply "entangled" we shall misunderstand the nature of fact as badly as logical positivists misunderstood the nature of value' (Putnam, 2002: 46).

There are also pernicious 'real world' consequences to viewing the world through the dogmatic lens of alleged objective 'facts'. Eugenics is perhaps one example where science can be used as a tool of abuse. More recently, the Executive editor of BMJ journal suggested that politicization of the science during the COVID-19 pandemic has been used to support policies geared towards profit at the expense of lives (See Abbasi, 2020). This is another way that certain forms of discourse can become pernicious, scientistic and totalizing in their orientation.

Chapter 6

1 For practical reasons, I will refer to the shortened term of 'personal development' from here on.
2 Bates (2021) is here alluding to the problems with 'ethical egoism'. This is an interesting ethical problem broadly defined as 'the doctrine that each person ought to pursue his or her own self-interest exclusively'. *Contra* that view, Rachels & Rachels (2014) suggest that 'our morality must recognize the needs of others', not as separate but in equal measure. This is consistent with the approach I have advocated for, though for different reasons, which rests on a conceptual remark with regards to the *kind* of being that we are (social and moral agents). As such, this provides an ethical framework within which we may be better equipped to judge what we deem as moral action or behaviour. It is also roughly equivalent to one of the central Christian tenets 'Do to others as you would have them do to you' (Luke 6:31).
3 See Baker (2004)
4 cf. Wittgenstein (2009: 252), notes to *PI* §122.
5 As McFee has suggested, 'exceptionless claims' have no role. In their places, slogans are deployed since '[s]logans are easy, and stick in the memory' (McFee, 2000: 24)
6 Please see Kusters (2020) for an incipient philosophy of madness. Advancing and extending Sass's (1994) exploration of mysticism and madness, Kusters explores useful aspects of solipsism of interest to the nature of self-knowledge in ways that might redeem it (somewhat) from the pejorative senses that we might be used to. Also see Borlotti (2023) for an exploration and defence of delusion in terms of the 'positive' role it may have in a person's life. It is, however, important to bear in mind that although madness and delusional thinking might have *some* redeemable characteristics or effects, and that we are *all* prone to these experiences from time to time, these states should be a transitional, at least in the context of a flourishing life.

7 I do not specifically address biological determinism due to space, but it is a useful comparator here to help highlight two ways of seeing oneself.
8 The term is attributed to the Roman proverb from Appius Claudius Caecus. Original Latin phrase: *Homo faber est suae quisque fortunae*. Cited in Cochrane (1958).
9 Wittgenstein also said: 'It is correct, although paradoxical, to say: "I" does not refer to (bezeichnet) a person' (*MS* 116, p. 215). Also, as suggested by Glock & Hacker (1996), whether or not 'I' is a referent depends entirely on the context; we cannot simply ascribe reference to the first-person in all cases, neither can we deny them in all cases.
10 Anscombe (1975) outlines that getting hold of the wrong object is logically excluded. The trap however, according to Anscombe (ibid: 59) is: '. . . that [it] makes us think that getting hold of the right object is guaranteed. But the reason is that there is no getting hold of an object at all. With names or denoting expressions . . ., there are two things to grasp: the kind of use, and what to apply them to from time to time. With I there is only the use.'
11 As Hacker (2012: 164) suggests, '. . . in philosophy, there are no mysteries – only mystifications and mystery-mongering'. What is needed then is to bring words back from their 'apparent' metaphysical nature and back to their perfectly ordinary and everyday uses (cf. *PI* §116 and Baker, 2004: 93).
12 Also related to confused notions of solipsism, subjectivity and an alleged 'ownership' of a mind; cf. de Gaynesford (2006).
13 Wittgenstein explores the pernicious effects of misleading pictures or 'features of our language' at length. For example, see *PI* §2–6, §291, §317 and §337. Also see Baker (2004) and Beale (2017 and 2020) for a contemporary exploration of this concept and its impact on human understanding in the context of misleading pictures, scientism, and the elucidatory role of philosophy.
14 Nevertheless, this focus of personal identity as a kind of epistemic and psychological continuity continued well into the twentieth century (e.g. cf. Grice, 1941; Wiggins, 1967; Shoemaker, 1963 and 1979; Parfit, 1971 and 1984). Parfit in particular spent a great deal of time on the issues related to this concept.
15 This opens up interesting conceptual matters in the context of multiple personality disorders, for in some cases, someone with DPD would have distinct dispositions for each of their personalities (or selves).
16 Cf. Parfit (1984), (1995) and (2012) and Shoemaker (1984). For a recent critique, see Ward (2019), where he makes a distinction between persons (as a subject of experience) and (life) experiences with the implication that identity cannot therefore be reduced to the mental because it entails a broader framework of phenomena outside of the mind.
17 Also see Paul's (2014) conception of 'transformative experiences' where she explores the power of making decisions in the unknown, and what bearing such decisions might have on our conceptions of ourselves and the world.

18 The phrase was brought into popular attention by U.S. Secretary of Defence Donald Rumsfeld when he said (in connection with the impending Iraq war) that there are 'known knowns, known unknowns, and still unknown unknowns' cf. Emiliano (2015).
19 I made a related remark in Chapter 5 in the context of Arendt's (1976) affirmation of hope for humankind, in spite of our pull towards maleficence and ignorance.
20 Cf. *OC* §51: 'In the Beginning Was the Deed'.
21 In Wittgensteinian terms this might approximate to learning a language-game, that is: '... consisting of language and the activities into which it is woven.' (Cf., *PI* §7).
22 Cf. Stanley & Williamson (2001).
23 This is also relevant to current debates about the educational challenges and issues raised by the emergence of Chat GPT. However, whilst AI can mimic ordinary language, it cannot replicate contextual insight. As Professor Korkontzelos (2023) recently conceded in his inaugural lecture, no matter the potential of AI, at best, we are a 'long way off' from it being able to interpret and communicate cultural and other nuances in the kinds of contextual communications that indicate true human-like intelligence [quoted remark paraphrased]. This suggests that there is potential for a re-focusing of educational practice, away from simple regurgitation of 'facts' (knowing-that forms), and towards a re-evaluation of the importance of criticality and insight (knowing-how). Also see remarks in Chapter 1 (section 5) on the contrast and distinction between 'following' a rule and 'according with' a rule.
24 'Knowledge depends on skill. A scientist knows that one theory is better than another, through her skill at assessing such theories. A wine-taster knows that the wine in front of him is a Bordeaux, through his skill at wine-tasting. An outfielder knows where the fly-ball will land, through his skill at fielding.' (Stanley & Williamson, 2017: 713)
25 In an era where scientism is one of the underlying forces of modern culture, and where knowing-that kinds of knowledge is privileged in the school-system (and even in the academy), it is not hard to see why the humanities are being undermined, (e.g. through loss of funding or reduced access to humanities degree programmes).
26 Ryan's (2012) position, though reductive, is not particularly controversial. She discussed Aristotle's approach to virtue epistemology in the Nicomachean Ethics, focusing on his theory of 'phronesis' (cf. Aristotle, 2014). For more recent scholarship on wisdom and related epistemic concepts see Nozick, R. (1989), Whitcomb (2011) and Baehr (2014)
27 This distinction is very close to the ancient Greek distinction between *sophia* and *phronesis* cf. Preus (2007). Also see Curnow (2011) for an up-to-date exploration of this distinction in the context of human development.
28 NB: I use Biblical citations in various places for illustration purposes only. They help at times to contextualize some thoughts that may have had a significant degree of

influence on Western philosophy, religion and culture – albeit often problematically (e.g. at times, by contributing to dogmatic traditions that can at times perpetuate misleading pictures and various forms of conceptual incoherence. cf. Hacker, 2007a: 13).

29 This notion of incipience is close to what I have been arguing in the context of developmental self-knowledge.

30 Hacker (2007a: 197) has spent some considerable time on this issue in numerous of his volumes on human nature. In his first volume he outlines: '... *to assert that one believes that p is normally to take a stand on whether it is the case that p. So to believe something (a fortiori to know something) is not to be in any kind of mental state*'. In other words, a propositional assertion could not be logically possible if knowledge were a state of mind; for there to be any basis to knowledge, per se, we need context, criteria, judgement and acceptance. Knowledge is then not the kind of thing to be in the mind, it is a public feature of our language.

31 Of course, the next step in the statist view, might be, as Hacker (2007a: 26) suggests, to confuse mental states with 'brain states'. I appreciate that Grimm is not going that far here but this is certainly one of the possible mishaps that could occur if one adopts a statist conception of knowledge and the mind without making the distinctions suggested by Hacker here.

32 I do not want to be dismissive here. Perhaps Grimm intends to point to a transcendent form of well-being that goes beyond how we might typically conceive of it in terms of self-interest. However, he does not indicate this in his paper (though he could have).

33 Cf. Book of Ecclesiastes 12:12: 'Of making many books there is no end, and much study wearies the body.'

34 In attributing wisdom, we can also say that a wise person knows how to ask and answer questions. Watson (2018) makes a case for advancing the human skill of good questioning. In her paper she suggests that there is a pedagogical value of what she terms as 'educating for good questioning' for character development – thus drawing a distinction between skills and virtues (the former nurturing conditions for the latter). This is I think very useful because it helps to show that the know-*how* kind of ability is foundational to virtuous characterological development.

35 Strictly speaking, Wittgenstein's focus is on philosophers philosophizing – but I take an developmental approach to his point here because, as I suggest, the same lessons can be drawn in order to bring one to a point of personal transformation; this requires a shift in perspective (cf. *PI* §155).

36 Also see Read (2020) who extends Wittgenstein's liberatory philosophy for critiques in social and political contexts. Read prefers the term 'liberatory' to 'therapeutic', and in so doing politicizes Wittgenstein. However, if Wittgenstein's philosophy of language is anything at all it is first and foremost oriented towards dispelling conceptual confusions *common* in philosophy and science.

Chapter 7

1. Here I mean normative in terms of common standards of 'moral' norms and agreement. That said, the notion of linguistic normativity on the Wittgensteinian understanding is one of the fundamental methodological assumptions of my analysis in this book, as I hope, should be clear by now.
2. Cf. Von Wright (1968: 50) and Maslow (2013).
3. On this use of 'wellness', it is good for both human beings as well as animals but not for plants. That said, we do have a use for whether a plant is 'happy', but this amounts to a different concept i.e. healthy. We need to see beyond the surface use of words and look at the underlying 'depth' or conceptual grammar of the particular application in context.
4. For example, he cites Aristotle to Seneca ('*De Vita Beata*', including a volume of the same title written by Augustine), to St Thomas Aquinas ('*Summae*') and into the enlightenment and beyond. Obviously, his work was written before the advent of positive psychology as well so there is a considerable and growing literature in that area (as already noted in the introduction).
5. Here the use of 'objective' is somewhat different in that it suggests objective attitudes to value judgements (i.e. axiological matters) rather than criteria for meaning (though these are closely linked).
6. NB, I mean here axiological materialism (monism), the misled belief that having money and possessions is *the* most important thing in life, as opposed to philosophical materialism.
7. Not that pure joy is excluded for the unreligious but that the concept here used is often associated with the pure joy of religious bliss in the face of suffering. For example, see James 1:2: 'Consider it pure joy, my brothers and sisters, whenever you face trials of many kinds'.
8. Tatarkiewicz (1976: 18) also said that '... no man is happy who does not hold himself happy'. Similarly, Hacker (2021: 246) has suggested, '[b]eing weighed down by a sense of the meaninglessness and pointlessness of life likewise precludes happiness'.
9. NB: The notion of *summum bonum* was introduced by the Roman philosopher Cicero (see *De Finibus*, Book II, 37ff), although the term was also central in Aquinas and his synthesis between Aristotelianism and Christianity. On his conception, *summum bonum* was defined as a righteous life of a believer in God; see *Summa Theologica*. There is no scope to explore these aspects here but MacIntyre (1981) discusses these concepts at length in 'After Virtue' though in a modern context of social practices, which may be of interest. This influence has extended even into analytic philosophy, notably through Moore (1903). For example, Moore had an aesthetic conception of summum bonum. For example, Moore (1903: Chapter VI, §110) suggested that the 'Highest good' was the 'ultimate end towards which our

action should be directed', and that this consisted in the 'knowledge of the reality of the beautiful object cognised'. Moore therefore developed an ethics of aesthetics.

10 see *De Finibus*, Book II, 37ff
11 see *Summa Theologica*. There is no scope to explore these religious aspects here but MacIntyre (1981) discusses these at length in 'After Virtue' though in the prism of 'social practices'.
12 See Frankel et al. (1999).
13 There were also a number of related Latin words including 'beatitudo' (success, pleasure and satisfaction) and 'felicitas' ('luck' or 'good fortune'). The relations carry into the English language, as Hacker (2021: 245) has noted, the English word 'happy' has roots which imply designations for people who have enjoyed 'good fortune, who is lucky, successful, and fortunate'. See Tatarkiewicz, 1976: 5; also, Clark (2007: 228).
14 Remembering the period in which it was written, Phelps (2018) suggests that this poem was Browning's 'most audacious poem'. This is because perhaps the style in which it was written was subversive and reminiscent somewhat of Pope's mock-epics. As such it served to deflate the values of his peers (reputation, success, happiness, God etc.); but instead of doing so for comic effect (as in the case of Pope), Browning does so for aesthetic and sensual reasons. Nonetheless, the subversive critique of contemporaneous axiological norms is clear. Also see Alexander Pope's 'The Rape of Lock' (2007).
15 See, Uusiautti (2013) for an analysis of the concept of 'success' where she argues (controversially) that happiness is a 'by-product' of the 'pursuit of success'.
16 As Monaghan & Just (2000: 26) suggest, '[e]thnographers are not always successful in guarding against a temptation to romanticize the 'otherness' of the people they study'.
17 See Sandis (2012a). He states that '[t]he English-speaking French person does not understand the Brit. It can take years to overcome the cultural differences, but it only takes seconds to explain how each phrase is to be "really" understood' – hence, those differences are not so difficult as to be intractable. However, the problem is all the greater for cultures with disparate systems of reference and expression. Wittgenstein infamously cites the difficulty in understanding the Chinese both verbally and non-verbally (cf. *CV* §1 and *Z* 219).
18 Of course, this is merely to say that objective criteria is often conflated with objective theories or conceptions of happiness (by which we mean normative in an axiological sense).
19 Frankl relates later: 'I said that someone looks down on each of us in difficult hours—a friend, a wife, somebody alive or dead, or a God—and he would not expect us to disappoint him. He would hope to find us suffering proudly—not miserably—knowing how to die' (Frankl, 2006: 74).
20 This phrase is borrowed from Ryff & Singer (2003).

21 There is an interesting homage to Camus in the *Matrix* movie (1999) where one of the main characters, Trinity, in hinting about the problem of the reason for life and the nature of reality, suggests to Neo (the protagonist) that 'It's the question that drives us'. This is a fundamental human predicament. See Irwin (2002) for a philosophical exposition of the movie.

22 In this sense, Sisyphus's lot is more like an invented primitive language-game (like Wittgenstein's language-game of the builders, see *PI* §2). The allegory serves a useful purpose but is intentionally narrow, limited, and unlike actual human existence. Yet it is useful to focus attention of the virtues of moral courage and persistence; no matter how bad things are we almost always will have something redeemable with which we can be thankful for and thus an opportunity to transcend the horrors of experience.

23 There is a risk of sounding glib. There are circumstances of incomprehensible evil and suffering which we don't need to explore here. Suffice to acknowledge that possibilities for adopting such an attitude are not without exception.

24 See Crutchfield (2020) who proposes a 'morality pill' should be considered for the population in order to ensure compliance with government guidance, i.e. as a 'way out' of the future pandemics or other global catastrophes. This is, I suggest, an abhorrent instrumentalist approach to public health ethics that is detached from any value of what it means to be human and reduces all human value to government conceptions of the 'common good'.

25 I take it that as moral agents we are able to reason about our actions and justify them against a normative framework. The fact that we also have some aspects to our natures that are more involuntary (such as passions, emotions) does not limit that fundamental fact about human nature. That said, it is worth noting that 'free will' is a contested concept and there have been a number of interesting recent debates in philosophy. In particular, see McFee (2000: vii) for a critical examination of the key determinists' arguments in light of what he calls the 'possibility of genuine agency'. Further, see Sandis (2012b) for an exploration of what he terms as the 'conflation' of reasons. He is particularly interested in drawing tighter distinctions for the variety of *explananda* for human behaviour and action, all of which is useful in light of deterministic conceptions of thought and action.

26 We could also add the religious attitude to life. For example, in James 1:2, he says: 'Consider it pure joy, my brothers and sisters, whenever you face trials of many kinds'. Similarly, this suggests a transcendent conception of happiness.

27 Leach & Tartaglia (2018) are correct in terms of use of the particular form of words and question, but we know that there is evidence of equivalent existential questions in religious texts. E.g. 'Vanity of vanities, saith the Preacher, vanity of vanities; all is vanity' (Book of Ecclesiastes 1:2).

28 There are important differences (not least in terms of coherence), but there are also some shared grammatical features between both 'the' meaning of life, as well as the

process of finding meaning *in* life, both of which rest on a notion of 'significance' or 'purpose'.

29 For insight into the role of literature in moral education see Mahon & O'Brien (2018) who argue that the philosophies of Rorty & Cavell convey the 'transformative power of literature'. Tellingly, at a conference in 2019 on "Epistemic vices' (hosted by Liverpool Philosophy Department), Cassam (2019a) stated that if he wanted to learn about what was important in life he would turn to *literature*, not philosophy. I think this was an important insight into the power of religious text or literature to provide moral education as much as to elicit understanding about difficult subject matter. Not by clearing confusions, for that is the role of philosophy, but by addressing our tendencies towards dogma and opening-up the human imagination to other possibilities and ways of thinking.

30 Hacker (2007a) makes a related point when he discusses the active force of reason-making as both backward and forward looking, specifically in the context of the concept of rationality 'Janus-faced', (see 2007a: 3). Also see Hacker (2021: 293) where he applies the term to 'most' psychological concepts in terms of justificatory reasons.

31 The ancient Greeks had a range of distinctions between kinds of 'cause'. For example, Aristotle distinguishes (*aitia*); matter (*hyle*); mover (*kinoun*); form (*eidos*); and end (*telos*); cf. Preus (2007).

32 Von Wright (1974: 49) held: 'causal relations exist between natural events, not between agents and events'.

33 Nagel (1986) famously advocated for a 'view from nowhere' as an orienting principle aim of transforming philosophy and ethics on the model of objective science: '[t]he question is how limited beings like ourselves can alter their conception of the world so that it is no longer just the view from where they are but in a sense a view from nowhere' (Nagel, 1986: 83). This seems to lead Nagel down a misconceived path. For example, Nagel (1986: 66) suggests, 'none of us occupies a metaphysically privileged position'; but instead of this insight bringing him back to the public nature of concepts, as I suggest it should, it has the unfortunate, albeit predictable, effect of compelling him towards a 'quest for objectivity'. The bearing on the notion of the meaning of life is that this impulse to objectivity, based on the possibility of 'total' knowledge is, I suggest, a mistaken and somewhat naïve response to the existential crisis following Enlightenment. See Friedman (1990) for a critique of Nagel's quest for the objective.

34 See Metz (2013) and Cottingham (2005).

35 Of course, the line is not always so clear because naturalists can also see things in cosmic, albeit impersonal, terms. For example, Hawking (1988: 193) puzzles over this kind of question in teleological terms: 'Up to now, most scientists have been too occupied with the development of new theories that describe what the universe is to ask the question why ... However, if we discover a complete [and unified] theory

[combining quantum physics with general relativity] ... we shall all ... be able to take part in the discussion of the question of why it is that we and the universe exist. If we find the answer to that, it would be the ultimate triumph of human reason' [comments added].

36 Also see, Schinkel (2017) and Mulhall (2012)
37 Anti-natalists espouse related claims in terms of the value of human life. But for similar reasons, the philosophy is incoherent (and deeply unethical). For example, 'If it were better for a person that she lives than that she should never have lived at all, then if she had never lived at all, that would have been worse for her than if she had lived. But if she had never lived at all, there would have been no her for it to be worse for, so it could not have been worse for her' (Broome 1999: 168). Also see Piller (2023) for more recent related arguments.
38 '... the fact that we act in such-and-such ways, e.g. punish certain actions, establish the state of affairs thus and so, give orders, render accounts, describe colours, take an interest in others' feelings. What has to be accepted, the given – it might be said – are facts of living' (*RRP I* §630)
39 Moyal-Sharrock, (2017: 18) has also stated: 'The nonepistemic nature of our basic certainties is ascertained by the logical absence of justification and verification as regards our assurance of them'.
40 This is to contrast with Nagel's (1986: 11) concept of a view from 'nowhere'. Nagel's primary aim was to seek 'to combine the perspective of a particular person inside the world with an objective view of that same world, the person and his viewpoint included ... to transcend its particular point of view and to conceive of the world as a whole'.
41 See Vainio (2020) for a thorough and very recent critique of religious language and some arguments against Wittgenstein's notion of distinct language-games (which he calls 'mimimalism').
42 Cf. *PI* §109.
43 Calhoun (2015) adopts a similar framework preferring the distinction between 'procedural' instead of trivial, alongside 'substantive'.
44 Hutto (2012) gives an enlightening anthropological and theoretical account for the role of story-telling in human history, primarily through helping our ancestors to develop their 'capacity to understand intentional actions in terms of reasons', which he suggests, has a 'decidedly sociocultural basis'.
45 Wolf (1997b) 'meaning arises in a person's life when subjective attraction meets objective attractiveness'. Also, see Calhoun (2015) for a critique of Wolf (1997b) and a defence of his conception of agent-centred subjectivism in regard to meaning.
46 For context, the Blob is one of three cases raised by Wolf, the other two is the pig farmer, from one of Wiggins' (1976) examples, and the other is the alienated housewife. The pig farmer 'buys more land to grow more corn to feed more pigs to

buy more land to grow more corn to feed more pigs' and so seems trapped in an endless cycle of business growth with little else in his life. The alienated housewife is very active but lives a life of relentless household duties devoid of self-expression. Wolf characterizes her life as one that is full of activity but where she is 'not actively engaged'.

47 This is contestable in light of the fact that whether he agrees with this or not, as a human being the Blob is a social creature and relations matter for social beings. In this case, if nothing else, it is a loss for the Blob and others in terms of his failure to be a good example of human 'being' to others, although he can become an example of what *not* to do or how *not* to be.

48 We can only infer that Wolf is referring to the physical beating of children whilst a teacher in rural Austria (cf. Monk, 1991: 163–195).

49 Calhoun (2015: 15) orients this tension between achievement and goodness better I think when he says: '"Meaningful" nestles among "admirable", "humanly good or excellent", and "significant". It is to be connected with accounts of distinctively valuable human capacities and their exercise, of human achievement and contribution to human progress, and of the duty of beneficence, particularly supererogatory discharges of that duty'.

50 See Cassam (2018) and Cassam (2019b). Also, Frankfurt (2005).

51 The fact that we must practice these virtues daily without much fanfare suggests to me that daily living is somewhat of a heroic experience (or can be). This is related to the Christian daily practice of taking up one's cross through self-sacrifice (thus exemplifying or expressing the fruits of the Spirit of God, so conceived). This is a profound practice that requires great discipline and effort and is impossible to achieve. Nevertheless, this impossibility is attended to through the Christian concept of grace (see Ephesians 2:8). Of course, we need not have a religious belief system in order to practice such virtues (as any Stoic will tell you) but having a framework within to operate provides a strong motivating factor, e.g. whether through fear of God, fervour for holiness or deep love and compassion for others.

52 For obvious reasons there will be other more local factors to account for within particular normative frameworks which have had favour over various periods of history, such as strength, rationality, knowledge or magnanimity etc.

53 As I suggested in Chapter 6.

54 This is not to be conflated with 'moral luck' (see Pritchard, 2005, and Williams 1982)

55 Bortolotti (2018) suggests delusions can also (at least potentially) make 'a contribution to people's sense of themselves as competent and largely coherent agents.' This is because self-delusion can (and often does) lead to improved conceptions of oneself so there are some 'epistemic benefits' that could be acknowledged. I would suggest that Bortolotti's claim is somewhat restricted to cognitively impaired individuals. Ordinarily, far better to push through delusions

bravely even if that means heading towards what might appear as an abyss (i.e. the unknown).
56 See Cassam (2014: 259)
57 Strictly speaking, Wittgenstein's focus is on philosophers philosophizing – but I take an ordinary approach to his point here because, as I suggest, the same lessons can be drawn in order to bring one to a point of personal transformation.
58 To be clear, I am not merely proposing a form of attitudinal change along the somewhat banal affirmations of psychological positivity. Nor am I suggesting that there are shortcuts to personal transformation: '[i]n philosophizing we may not terminate a disease of thought. It must run its natural course, and slow cure is all important'. (Z §382)

Concluding Remarks

1 For example, as Baker (2004: 74) suggests with regards to nonsense, '[s]ome cases may yield patent nonsense'... (such as: '[c]olorless green ideas sleep furiously', or more subtle 'logical jokes' (e.g. 'I know that I am in pain'; cf. PI §246). At their heart is misunderstanding, made all the funnier (so conceived) by the fact that it is often intellectuals within the academy that misunderstand terms that they should, perhaps, otherwise have mastered.
2 Not 'the' order (Cf. PI §132)
3 Such as 'doing well', 'faring well' or thriving.
4 I should also acknowledge, however, that for some there could be an uncomfortable feeling of open-endedness here because no final accounting has been done. But this is to miss the point. My aims are to resolve unhelpful ways of thinking about these *kinds* of problems. Once this is realized then we are better able, as masters of our concepts, to grasp and grapple with the problems that we ourselves raise.
5 This helps to identify what is important about certain generalizable claims to knowledge and ethics (e.g. with regards to notions of dignity, liberty or universal human rights) without the need for recourse to spiritualist or other premises (though they are also are in some senses strengthened by the criterial claims highlighted here). This offers us a framework for better understanding why some reasons have more justificatory (as opposed to explanatory) power than others i.e. the reasons for *good* reasons.
6 I borrow this phrase from Sandis (2012b).
7 Cf. PI §38. Also see PI §203: 'Language is a labyrinth of paths. You approach from one side and know your way about; you approach the same place from another side and no longer know your way about.'
8 E.g. consider the concept of 'good': good hammer vs good person etc. are distinct but related concepts.

9 This is the title of a paper I delivered at the ECPR annual conference 2022 where I made similar arguments for two conceptions of normative agency.
10 Cf. Fricker (2008) for an exploration of the related concern of epistemic injustice.
11 Cf. Wittgenstein suggests that such formulations produce an 'illusion of being an empirical proposition, but which is really a grammatical one' (*PI* §251).
12 Although as Hacker (2007a: 182) highlights, we need for further distinguish between the regularity that the term 'nomological' implies and the rule-governed 'descriptions' that we use to attribute nomic or 'regular' characteristics as seen in much of nature.
13 A fortiori, researchers who use interdisciplinary methods to shed light on philosophical problems. See Naor & Okon-Singer (2014) who claim, misguidedly, that whilst philosophical methods help psychology and neuroscience to gain a conceptual footing, equally, neuroscience feeds back to inform knowledge in both psychology and philosophy.
14 As Glock (2009: 660) highlights, '… in Wittgenstein's functional conception of grammatical rules: the logical status of a sentence is due not to its linguistic form, but to the way it is used, and for this reason it can change'.
15 Similarly, what is particular to an occasion, is fixed and made clearer by insight into all the multifarious reference points of a person's life; it is contextual and person-relative. See Travis (2008), Baker (2004) and Sandis (2015).
16 This happens in politics as well as within any relationship of power and abuse. Persons misapplying terms are either misguided, malevolent or simply deceived.
17 See McGinn (2021). In her exegesis of Wittgenstein's latter works, McGinn distinguishes between two forms of naturalism: one form of 'scientific' naturalism that we see in the hard sciences, and another, 'Aristotelian naturalism' that she reads into Wittgenstein's method. On my reading, I take this as an exploration of *kinds*, that is, as categorial in orientation rather than merely biological.
18 I would prefer an approach that respects, firstly, conceptual insight over claims to 'knowledge' per se. As I have suggested, the logically prior nature of normative concepts matters on ethical or moral issues. (cf. Hacker, 2021, and Korsgaard, 1996). Indeed, my approach to philosophy differs to epistemological methodologies which tend to focus on narrower analyses for the use of terms. Nevertheless, it may be useful to see the seminal work by Fricker (2007). Also, Kidd, Medina & Pohlhaus (2019) for an overview of the concept of 'epistemic injustice'. Further, more recently Byskov (2021) who explores the concept in the context of what he calls the 'conditions for epistemic injustice'.
19 As outlined in the Introduction, one aspect or connection of flourishing is similar (but distinct) to MacIntyre's communalist conception. Relatedly, it is also similar, but distinct, to the African philosophical and humanistic conceptions of *ubuntu* that places a high regard for caring, sharing, hospitality, forgiveness, compassion, empathy, honesty, humility and brotherhood (see Venter, 2004), where 'a person is a

person through other persons' (Wiredu, 2004: 157). Further, notions of social meaning and purpose in life, without which flourishing is precluded, are closely tied to family and tradition for Confucius (see Leach & Tartaglia, 2018; Ch. 1).

20 For example, see the recent 'global study' of flourishing by Gallup (2021), in collaboration with researchers at Baylor University and Harvard University. Here, the researchers use a six-point scale of measures across the world to map flourishing internationally.
21 Cf. Wittgenstein's remarks on the 'very general facts on nature' (cf. *PPF*, xii, §365).
22 I do not by any stretch romanticize our Western traditions or history which is littered with vast and wide-reaching injustices; but I do value our liberal-democratic developments because they are founded upon the accumulation of 'hard-won' cultural knowledge, understanding and normative practices.
23 As highlighted in Chapter 5, I adopt broad and ethical conception of agency that pays attention to the specific kind of being we are, but evading the enticing entrapments of parochial bias, speciesism and lingualism.
24 As limited by use, purpose, and conceptual criteria. See Chapter 2.
25 See Hughes (2016) for a challenging but balanced account of the developing role and use of technology. As he suggests, in our march toward 'progress', technology tends to reinforce and reify existing power structures, and in so doing, exacerbates social inequalities.

Bibliography

AARONOVITCH, D. (2010). *Voodoo Histories: The Role of the Conspiracy Theory in Shaping Modern History*. NYC (USA): Riverhead Books.
ABBASI, K. (2020). 'Covid-19: politicisation, "corruption," and suppression of science'. *BMJ*. Available at https://www.bmj.com/content/371/bmj.m4425 [last accessed 29.06.21].
AGENOR, C. & ARORIAN, K. (2017). 'Flourishing: An Evolutionary Concept Analysis'. *Issues Mental Health Nursing*. Vol. 38(11), pp. 915–923.
ALEXANDROVA, A. (2017). *A Philosophy for the Science of Well-being*. Oxford: Oxford University Press.
ALUCHNA, M. & IDOWU, S. O. (eds). (2017). *The Dynamics of Corporate Social Responsibility: A Critical Approach to Theory and Practice*. New York: Springer.
ALVAREZ, M. (2010). 'Reasons for Action and Practical Reasoning'. *Ratio*. Vol. 23(4).
ANSCOMBE, G. E. M. (1975). 'The first person'. In S. GUTTENPLAN (ed.), *Mind and Language*, Oxford: Oxford University Press, pp. 45–65.
ANTONOVSKY, A. (1979). *Health, Stress, and Coping*. San Francisco: Jossey-Bass Inc.
AQUINAS, T. (2023). *Summa Theologica*. Available at http://summa-theologiae.org/
ARENDT, H. (1976). *The Origins of Totalitarianism*. London: Harvest.
ARISTOTLE. (2014). *Aristotle: Nicomachean Ethics* (2nd edn, Cambridge Texts in the History of Philosophy) (R. Crisp, ed.). Cambridge: Cambridge University Press.
AUSTIN, J.L. (1962). *Sense and Sensibilia*. Oxford: Oxford University Press.
BAEHR, J (2014). 'Sophia: Theoretical Wisdom and Contemporary Epistemology'. In *Virtues and Their Vices*, KEVIN TIMPE and C. BOYD (eds), New York: Oxford University Press, pp. 303–325.
BAKER, G.P. & HACKER, P.M.S. (1990). 'Malcolm on Language and Rules'. *Philosophy*, Vol. 65(252), pp.167–179.
BAKER, G.P. & HACKER, P.M.S. (2005a). Wittgenstein: Understanding and Meaning: Volume 1 of an Analytical Commentary on the Philosophical Investigations, Part I: Essays. Oxford: Wiley-Blackwell.
BAKER, G.P. & HACKER, P.M.S. (2005b). Wittgenstein: Understanding and Meaning: Volume 1 of an Analytical Commentary on the Philosophical Investigations, Part II: Exegesis §§1–184. Oxford: Wiley-Blackwell.
BAKER, G.P. & HACKER, P.M.S. (2009). Wittgenstein: Rules, Grammar, and Necessity – Volume 2 of an analytical commentary on the Philosophical Investigations. 2nd edn. Oxford: Wiley-Blackwell.
BAKER, G.P. (2004). *Wittgenstein's method: Neglected aspects: essays on Wittgenstein*. Malden, MA: Blackwell.

BARKER, C. (2002). *Making Sense of Cultural Studies*. London: Sage.
BASELMANS, B. M. L. & BARTELS, M. (2018). 'A genetic perspective on the relationship between eudaimonic – and hedonic well-being'. *Scientific reports Journal*. Vol. 8, pp. 1–10 (2018).
BATES, A. (2021). *Moral Emotions and Human Interdependence in Character Education: Beyond the One-Dimensional Self.* Oxford: Routledge.
BBC. (2021). 'Why are people talking about Dr Anthony Fauci's emails?'. Available at https://www.bbc.co.uk/news/world-us-canada-57336280 [last accessed 2 9.06.21].
BEALE, J. (2020). 'Types of "Misleading Picture" in Wittgenstein's Later Philosophy'. Paper presented at the *University of Reading's Wittgenstein Forum*, the University of East Anglia's 'Wittgenstein's Philosophy in Times of Crisis' series.
BEALE, J. & KIDD, I.J. (2017). *Wittgenstein & Scientism*. Oxford: Routledge.
BENNETT, G. (2019). 'The politics of intrinsic worth: why bioethics needs human dignity'. In E. PARENS & J. JOHNSON. *Human Flourishing in an Age of Gene Editing*. Oxford: Oxford University Press.
BENNETT, M.R., DENNETT, D., HACKER, P.M.S., SEARLE, J. & ROBINSON, D. (2009). *Neuroscience and Philosophy: Brain, Mind, and Language*. (1st edn). New York: Columbia University Press.
BENNETT, M.R. & HACKER, P.M.S. (2003). *Philosophical Foundations of Neuroscience*, Oxford: Blackwell.
BENTHAM, J. (1776). *A Fragment on Government*. Oxford: Clarendon.
BERLIN, I. (1969). 'Two Concepts of Liberty'. In BERLIN, I. (2002). *Four Essays on Liberty*, London: Oxford University Press.
BERMÚDEZ, J. (2016). *Philosophy of Psychology – a contemporary Introduction*. London: Routledge.
BERRIDGE, K., KENT, C. & KRINGELBACH, M. (2013). 'Towards a Neuroscience of Well Being: Implications of Insights from Pleasure Research'. In *Human Happiness and the Pursuit of Maximization, Happiness Studies*; H. BROCKMANN AND J. DELHEY (eds) 2013, pp. 81–100.
BEST, D. (1978). *Philosophy and Human Movement*, London: George Allen & Unwin.
BLAKE, W. (2011). *'The Marriage of Heaven & Hell'*. M. Phillips (ed.). Chicago: Chicago University Press.
BLOOM, B. S., ENGELHART, M. D., FURST, E. J., HILL, W. H. & KRATHWOHL, D. R. (1956). 'Taxonomy of educational objectives: The classification of educational goals'. *Handbook I: Cognitive domain*. New York: David McKay Company.
BOESCH, C. & TOMASELLO, M. (1998). 'Chimpanzee and Human Cultures,' *Current Anthropology*. Vol. 39(5), pp. 591–614.
BONIWELL, I. (2008). *Positive Psychology in a Nutshell: A Balanced Introduction to the Science of Optimal Functioning*. 2nd edn. London: PWBC.
BOOK OF ECCLESIASTES, Available at https://www.biblegateway.com/passage/?search =Ecclesiastes+12%3A12&version=NIV [last accessed: 01.08.20].

BOOK OF EPHESIANS, Available at https://biblehub.com/ephesians/2-8.htm [last accessed 13.12.20].
BOOK OF JAMES. Available at https://biblehub.com/james/ [last accessed 22.10.23].
BOOK OF JOHN. Available at https://biblehub.com/john/15-13.htm [last accessed 13.12.20].
BOOK OF JUDE, Available at https://www.biblegateway.com/passage/?search=Jude+1&version=NKJV [last accessed: 01.08.20]
BOOK OF LUKE, Available at https://biblehub.com/luke/6-31.htm [last accessed 13.12.20].
BORTOLOTTI, L. (2018). 'Stranger than Fiction: Costs and Benefits of Everyday Confabulation', *Rev.Phil.Psych.* Vol. 9, pp. 227–324.
BORLOTTI, L (2023). *Why Delusions Matter.* London: Bloomsbury Publishers.
BRADBURN, N. (1969). *The Structure of Psychological Well-Being.* Chicago: Aldine Pub. Co.
BRIGHOUSE, H. (2008). 'Education for a Flourishing Life'. In *Yearbook of the National Society for the Study of Education*, Vol. 107, pp. 58–71.
BROOME, J. (1999). *Ethics out of Economics.* Cambridge: Cambridge University Press.
BROWN N.J., SOKAL A.D. & FRIEDMAN, H.L. (2013). 'The complex dynamics of wishful thinking: the critical positivity ratio'. *Am Psychol.* Vol. 68(9), pp.801–813.
BROWN, N.J., SOKAL A.D. & FRIEDMAN, H.L. (2014). 'The persistence of wishful thinking'. *Am Psychol.* Vol. 69(6), pp. 629–632.
BROWN, N., LOMAS, T. & EIROA-OROSA, F (eds). (2018). *The Routledge International Handbook of Critical Positive Psychology.* Oxford: Routledge.
BRUNWASSER, S. M., GILLHAM, J. E. & KIM, E. S. (2009). 'A meta-analytic review of the Penn Resiliency Program's effect on depressive symptoms'. *Journal of consulting and clinical psychology*, Vol. 77(6), pp. 1042–1054.
BRYMAN, A. (2015). *Social Research Methods* (5th edn). Oxford: Oxford University Press.
BYFORD, J. (2011). *Conspiracy Theories: A Critical Introduction.* London: Palgrave Macmillan.
BYNUM, W.F., BROWNE, E.J., & PORTER, R. (1981). *The Macmillan dictionary of the History of Science.* London: Macmillan.
BYSKOV, M.F. (2021). 'What Makes Epistemic Injustice an "Injustice"?'. *J Soc Philos*, Vol. 52, pp. 114–131.
CALHOUN, C. (2015). 'Geographies of Meaningful Living'. *Journal of Applied Philosophy.* Vol. 32, No. 1, p. 201.
CALL, J. & TOMASELLO, M. (2008). 'Do chimpanzees have a theory of mind: 30 years later'. *Trends in Cognitive Science*, Vol. 12, pp. 187–192.
CAMUS, A., (1955). 'Homage to an Exile'. In CAMUS, A. (1961). *Resistance, Rebellion, Death.* Justin O'Brien (trans.). New York: Alfred A. Knopf.
CAMUS, A. (2013). *The Myth of Sisyphus.* London: Penguin Modern classics.
CARLSON, L. & KITTAY, E.F. (2009). 'Introduction: Rethinking Philosophical Presumptions In Light Of Cognitive Disability'. *Metaphilosophy*, Vol. 40, pp. 307–330.

CARRUTHERS, P. (2011). *The Opacity of Mind: an integrative theory of self-knowledge*, Oxford: Oxford University Press.
CARVER, C. S. & SCHEIER, M. F. (2002). 'Optimism'. In C. R. SNYDER & S. J. LOPEZ (eds), *Handbook of positive psychology*. London: Oxford University Press, pp. 231–243.
CASSAM, Q. (2014). *Self-Knowledge for Humans*, Oxford: Oxford University Press.
CASSAM, Q. (2018). 'Epistemic Insouciance', *Journal of Philosophical Research*, Volume 43, pp. 1–20.
CASSAM, Q. (2019a). 'The vices of vice epistemology', talk given at Epistemic Vices: Individual and Collective conference. (17.12.19). Details available at https://www.eventbrite.co.uk/e/epistemic-vices-individual-and-collective-tickets-79553136573 [last accessed 13.12.20].
CASSAM, Q. (2019b). *Vices of the Mind: From the Intellectual to the Political*. Oxford: Oxford University Press.
CASSAM, Q. (2021). *Extremism: A Philosophical Analysis*. Oxford: Routledge.
CHANG, E. C., DOWNEY, C. A., HIRSCH, J. K. & LIN, N. J. 2016. *Positive psychology in racial and ethnic groups: Theory, research, and practice*. Washington, DC: American Psychological Association.
CHOMSKY, N. (1957). *Syntactic Structures*. Martino Fine Books. New York: Mouton Du Gruyter.
CICERO. (2011). *De Finibus: Bonorum Et Malorum*. London: Nabu Press.
CLARK, A. (2007). *Divine Qualities: Cult and Community in Republican Rome*. Oxford: Oxford University Press.
COADY, D. (2006). *Conspiracy Theories: The Philosophical Debate*, 1st edn. Oxford: Routledge.
COCHRANE, R. C. (1958). 'Francis Bacon and the Architect of Fortune.' *Studies in the Renaissance*. Vol. 5, pp. 176–95.
COTTINGHAM, J. (2005). *On the Meaning of Life*. Oxford: Routledge.
COTTINGHAM, J. (2008). *The Cambridge Companion to Descartes*. Cambridge: Cambridge University Press.
CRICK, F. (1995). *The Astonishing Hypothesis: The Scientific Search for the Soul*. New York: Simon & Schuster, Touchstone.
CRUTCHFIELD, P. (2020). 'Morality pills' may be the US's best shot at ending the coronavirus pandemic, according to one ethicist. *The Conversation*. Available at https://theconversation.com/morality-pills-may-be-the-uss-best-shot-at-ending-the-coronavirus-pandemic-according-to-one-ethicist-142601 [last accessed 13.12.20].
CSIKSZENTMIHALYI, M. (1990). 'Flow: The Psychology of Optimal Experience'. *Journal of Leisure Research*, 24(1), pp. 93–94.
CSIKSZENTMIHALYI, M. (2014). *Flow and the Foundations of Positive Psychology: The Collected Works of Mihaly Csikszentmihalyi*. New York: Springer.
CSIKSZENTMIHALYI, M. & HUNTER, J. (2003). 'Happiness in Everyday Life: The Uses of Experience Sampling'. *Journal of Happiness Studies*. Vol. 4, pp. 185–199.

CULBERTSON, L. (2007). '"Human-ness", "dehumanisation" and performance enhancement', *Sports, Ethics and Philosophy* Vol. 1(2), pp. 195–217.

CULBERTSON, L. (2015). 'Perception, Aspects and Explanation: Some Remarks on Moderate Partisanship'. *Sport, Ethics and Philosophy*. Vol. 9(2), pp. 182–204

CURNOW, T. (2011). 'Sophia and Phronesis: Past, Present, and Future'. *Research in Human Development*, Vol. 8:2, pp. 95–108.

DAVIES, W. (2015). *The Happiness Industry: How the government and big business sold us well-being*. London: Verso.

DE GAYNESFORD, M. D. (2006). *The Meaning of the First-Person Term*. Oxford: Oxford University Press.

DE LEEUW, R. & BUIJZEN, M. (2016). 'Introducing positive media psychology to the field of children, adolescents, and media'. *Journal of Children and Media*. Vol. 10(1), pp. 39–46.

DE RUYTER, D. J. (2004). 'Pottering in the garden? On human flourishing and education'. *British Journal of Educational Studies*. Vol. 52(4), pp. 377–389.

DIENER, E. (1984). 'Subjective well-being'. *Psychological Bulletin*, Vol. 95(3), pp. 542–575.

DONNE, J. (1636). *No Man Is an Island*. New York (US): Villard/Random House.

EAGLETON, T. (1983). *Literary Theory: an introduction*. Oxford: Basil Blackwell.

EDGAR, A. & PATTISON, S. (2016). 'Flourishing in Health Care'. *Health Care Analysis*. Vol. 24(2), pp.161–173.

EGAN, K. (2002). *Getting it wrong from the beginning: Our progressivist inheritance from Herbert Spencer, John Dewey, and Jean Piaget*. New Haven: Yale University Press.

EMILIANO, I. (2015). *Heuristic Reasoning: Studies in Applied Philosophy, Epistemology and Rational Ethics*. Switzerland: Springer International Publishing, pp. 1–2.

EVANS, J. (2019). 'The dismal fate of flourishing in public policy bioethics: a sociological explanation'. In E. PARENS & J. JOHNSON. 2019. *Human Flourishing in an Age of Gene Editing*. Oxford: Oxford University Press.

FLIEGENDE BLÄTTER (1892) "Kaninchen und Ente" ("rabbit and duck"). 23rd October, Vol. 17: No. 2465. Available from https://commons.wikimedia.org/wiki/File:Kaninchen_und_Ente.svg [last accessed 23.04.23]

FORESIGHT MENTAL CAPITAL AND WELLBEING PROJECT (2008). Final Project report – Executive summary. The Government Office for Science, London.

FORSTER, M. N. (2004). *Wittgenstein on the arbitrariness of grammar*. Princeton: Princeton University Press.

FRANKEL, P. MILLER, F. PAUL, J (eds) 1999. *Human flourishing*. Cambridge: Cambridge University Press.

FRANKFURT, H. (1998). *The Importance of What We Care About: Philosophical Essays*. Cambridge: Cambridge University Press.

FRANKFURT, H. (2005). *On Bullshit*. Princeton: Princeton University Press.

FRANKFURT, H. (2006). *Reasons for love*. Princeton: Princeton University Press.

FRANKL, V. (2006). *Man's search for meaning*. Boston: Beacon Press.

FREDRICKSON B.L, LOSADA, M.F. (2005). 'Positive Affect and the Complex Dynamics of Human Flourishing'. *Am Psychol*; 60(7):678–686.
FREDRICKSON, B.L. (2013). 'Updated thinking on positivity ratios'. *Am Psychol.* Vol. 68(9), pp. 814–22.
FRICKER, M. (2007). *Epistemic Injustice: Power & the Ethics of knowing.* Oxford: Oxford University Press.
FRIEDMAN, M. (1990). 'Going Nowhere: Nagel on Normative Objectivity'. *Philosophy*, Vol. 65(254), pp. 501–509.
FUKUYAMA, F. (2004). "The world's most dangerous ideas: Transhumanism" (reprint). *Foreign Policy.* Vol. 144, pp. 42–43.
GALLIE, W. B. (1994). 'Essentially Contested Concepts'. *Inquiry: Critical Thinking Across The Disciplines.* Vol. 14(1) pp. 167–198
GALLUP. (2021). *Global Flourishing Study Questionnaire Development Report.* Gallup & Baylor University. Available at https://hfh.fas.harvard.edu/files/pik/files/globalflourishingstudy_report.pdf?mc_cid=a2603520c6 [last accessed 05.01.21].
GARLAND-THOMSON, R. (2019). 'Welcome to the unexpected'. In E. PARENS & J. JOHNSON. 2019. *Human Flourishing in an Age of Gene Editing.* Oxford: Oxford University Press.
GARVER, E. (1978). 'Rhetoric and Essentially Contested Arguments'. *Philosophy and Rhetoric.* Vol. 11(3), pp. 156–172.
GASKING, D. A. T., JACKSON, A. C. (1967). 'Wittgenstein as a Teacher'. In K. T. FANNED, *Ludwig Wittgenstein: The Man and his Philosophy.* New Jersey: Humanities Press.
GLOCK, H.J. (1996). *A Wittgenstein Dictionary.* Oxford: Blackwell.
GLOCK, H.J. (2009). 'Concepts, Conceptual Schemes and Grammar', *Philosophia*, pp. 37: 653–68.
GLOCK, H.J. (2019). 'Agency, Intelligence and Reasons in Animals'. *Philosophy.* Vol. 94, pp. 645–71.
GLOCK, H. J. & HACKER, P.M.S. (1996). 'Reference and the First Person Pronoun.' *Language & Communication.* Vol.16(2), pp. 95–105.
GOERTZEL, T. (1994). 'Belief in conspiracy theories'. *Political psychology.* Vol. 15(4).
GOODMAN M, TAGLE D, FITCH D, BAILEY W, CZELUSNIAK J, KOOP B, BENSON P, SLIGHTOM J. (1990). 'Primate evolution at the DNA level and a classification of hominoids'. *Journal of Molecular Evolution.* Vol. 30(3), pp. 260–266.
GRASO, M., XUAN CHEN, F. & REYNOLDS, T. (2021). 'Moralization of Covid-19 health response: Asymmetry in tolerance for human costs'. *Journal of Experimental Social Psychology*, Vol. 93.
GREENE, J.D., MORRISON, I. SELIGMAN, M.E.P (eds) (2016). *Positive Neuroscience.* Oxford: Oxford University Press.
GRICE, H.P. & STRAWSON, P.F. (1956). 'In Defence of a Dogma', Philosophical Review, 65, pp. 141–58.
GRICE, H.P. (1941). 'Personal Identity', *Mind*, Vol. 50, pp. 330–350. Reprinted in: J. PERRY (ed.), 1975. *Personal Identity*, Berkeley: University of California Press, pp. 73–95.

GRIMM, S. R. (2015). 'Wisdom'. *Australasian Journal of Philosophy*. Vol. 93(1), pp. 139–154.

HACKER, P.M.S. (1986). *Insight & Illusion*. Oxford: Clarendon Press.

HACKER, P.M.S. (1999). *Wittgenstein on human nature*. London: Phoenix Press.

HACKER, P.M.S. (2001). *Wittgenstein: Connections and Controversies*. Oxford: Clarendon Press.

HACKER, P.M.S. (1995). Wittgenstein: Meaning and Mind: Volume 3 of an Analytical Commentary on the Philosophical Investigations. Oxford: Basil Blackwell.

HACKER, P.M.S. (2007a). *Human Nature: The Categorial Framework*. Oxford: Blackwell.

HACKER, P.M.S. (2007b). 'Gordon Baker's Late Interpretation of Wittgenstein'. In G. KAHANE, E. KANTERIAN & O. KUUSELA (eds) (2007). *Wittgenstein and His Interpreters: Essays in Memory of Gordon Baker*. Oxford: Wiley-Blackwell.

HACKER, P.M.S. (2010). 'Philosophy: a Contribution Not to Human Knowledge but to Human Understanding'. In ANTHONY O'HEAR (ed.), *Conceptions of Philosophy* (Royal Institute of Philosophy Lectures Suppl. 65; Cambridge: Cambridge University Press, pp. 129–54.

HACKER, P.M.S. (2012). 'The Sad and Sorry History Of Consciousness: Being, Among Other Things, A Challenge To The Consciousness-Studies Community'. In C. SANDIS & M.J. CAIN (eds, 2012) '*Human nature*'. *Royal Institute of Philosophy Supplement*: Vol: 70. Cambridge: Cambridge University Press.

HACKER, P.M.S. (2013a). *The Intellectual Powers: A Study of Human Nature*, Oxford: Wiley-Blackwell.

HACKER, P.M.S. (2013b) 'Metaphysics: from ineffability to normativity'. In H.J. GLOCK AND J. HYMAN (eds). (2015) *Blackwell Companion to Wittgenstein*. Oxford: Wiley-Blackwell.

HACKER, P.M.S. (2015). 'Forms of life'. *Nordic Wittgenstein Review Special Issue 2015* (Wittgenstein and Forms of Life).

HACKER, P.M.S. (2018). *The Passions: A Study of Human Nature*. Oxford: Wiley-Blackwell.

HACKER, P.M.S. (2021). *The Moral Powers: A Study of Human Nature*. Oxford: Wiley-Blackwell.

HAND, M. (2023) (forthcoming). 'Against flourishing as an educational aim'. In BEALE, J. & EASTON, C. 2023 (forthcoming). *The Future of Education: Reimagining its Aims and Responsibilities*. Oxford: Oxford University Press.

HARDING, S. D. (1982). 'Psychological well-being in Great Britain: An evaluation of the Bradburn Affect Balance Scale'. *Personality and Individual Differences*, Vol. 3(2), pp.167–175.

HARVARD. (2021). 'Our flourishing measure'. *The Human Flourishing Program, Institute for Quantitative Studies. University of Harvard*. Available at https://hfh.fas.harvard.edu/measuring-flourishing [last accessed 27.07.21].

HAWKING, S. (1988). *A brief history of time*. Toronto: Bantam Books.

HAYWOOD, A. 2000. *Key concepts in politics*. London: Palgrave Macmillan.

HEINZE T, JAPPE A, PITHAN D. (2019). 'From North American hegemony to global competition for scientific leadership? Insights from the Nobel population'. *PLOS ONE*, Vol. 14(4).

HM TREASURY. (2021). *Wellbeing Guidance for Appraisal: Supplementary Green Book Guidance*. London: The Stationery Office (Crown Copyright).

HODGES, T. D. & CLIFTON, D. O. (2004). 'Strengths-based development in practice'. In A. LINLEY & S. JOSEPH (eds) (2004). *Handbook of Positive psychology in practice*. Hoboken, New Jersey: John Wiley and Sons, Inc., pp. 256–268.

HOSSEINI, R. (2015). *Wittgenstein and Meaning in life: in search of the human voice*. Hants: Palgrave Macmillan.

HOULDERS, J.W., BORTOLOTTI, L. & BROOME, M.R. (2021). 'Threats to epistemic agency in young people with unusual experiences and beliefs'. *Synthese*.

HOUSE, R., KALISCH, D. & MAIDMAN, J. (eds) (2017). *Humanistic Psychology: Current Trends and Future Prospects*. London: Routledge.

HUBBERT, F. (2009). 'Psychological Well-being: Evidence Regarding its Causes and Consequences'. *Applied Psychology, Health & Well-being*, Vol. 1(2), pp. 137–164.

HUGHES, B. (2016). *The Bleeding Edge: Why Technology Turns Toxic in an Unequal World*. Oxford: New Internationalist.

HULL, G., PASQUALE, F. (2013). 'Toward a critical theory of corporate wellness'. *BioSocieties*. Vol(13), pp. 190–212.

HUPPERT, F. A. & SO, T. (2009). *What percentage of people in Europe are flourishing and what characterises them?* Briefing document for the OECD/ISQOLS meeting 'Measuring subjective well-being: an opportunity for NSOs?' 23–24 July, 2009, Florence, Italy.

HUPPERT, F. A. & SO, T. (2013). 'Flourishing Across Europe: Application of a New Conceptual Framework for Defining Well-Being'. *Social Indicators Research*. Vol. 110(3), pp. 837–861.

HURKA, T. (1996). *Perfectionism*. Oxford: Oxford University Press.

HURSTHOUSE, R. (2010). 'Virtuous Action'. In T. O'CONNOR & C. SANDIS (eds). 2010. *Blackwell Companion to the Philosophy of Action*. Oxford: Blackwell

HUTTO, D. (2012). *Folk Psychological Narratives*. Mass. USA: MIT Press.

HYMAN, J. (2012). 'Action, Knowledge, and Will'. In O. KUUSELA & M. MCGINN (eds). 2012. *The Oxford Handbook of Wittgenstein*. Oxford: Oxford University Press.

HYSLOP-MARGISON, EMERY J. & NASEEM, M. AYAZ (2007). *Scientism and Education Empirical Research as Neo-Liberal Ideology*. London: Springer.

IRWIN, W. (2002). *The Matrix and Philosophy: Welcome to the Desert of the Real*. Chicago: Open Court.

JOPLIN, D. (2000). *Self-Knowledge and The Self*. Oxford: Routledge.

JOSEPH, S. (2015). (ed.) *Positive Psychology in Practice: Promoting Human Flourishing in Work, Health, Education, and Everyday Life*. (2nd edn). New Jersey: John Wiley & Sons.

JUBILEE CENTRE. (2017). 'A Framework for Character Education in Schools'. University of Birmingham. URL Available at https://www.jubileecentre.ac.uk/userfiles/jubileecentre/pdf/character-education/Framework%20for%20Character%20Education.pdf [last accessed 27.07.21].

KANT, I. (1996). *The Metaphysics of Morals*. Cambridge: Cambridge University Press.

KEYES, C. L. M. & WESTERHOF, G. J. (2010). 'Mental Illness and Mental Health: The Two Continua Model Across the Lifespan'. *Journal of Adult Development*, Vol. 17(2), pp.110–119.

KEYES, C. L. M. (2002). 'The mental health continuum: From languishing to flourishing in life'. *Journal of Health and Social Behavior*, Vol. 43(2), pp. 207–222.

KIDD, I.J., MEDINA, J. & POHLHAUS, G. Jnr (eds). 2019. *The Routledge Handbook of Epistemic Injustice*. Oxford: Routledge.

KOK, N, VAN GURP, J., VAN DER HOEVEN, J.G., et al. (2023). 'Complex interplay between moral distress and other risk factors of burnout in ICU professionals: findings from a cross-sectional survey study.' *BMJ Quality & Safety*, Vol. 32, pp. 225–234.

KORKONTZELOS, Y. (2023). *Inaugural lecture: Can machines understand human language?*. Law Department. Edge Hill University. Details available from URL: https://www.edgehill.ac.uk/event/professor-yannis-korkontzelos-inaugural-lecture-can-machines-understand-human-language/ [last accessed 30.04.23].

KORSGAARD, C. M. (1996). *The Sources of Normativity*. Cambridge: Cambridge University Press.

KORSGAARD, C. M. (2008). The Constitution of Agency: essays on practical reason and moral psychology. Oxford: Oxford University Press.

KRINGELBACH, M.L. & BERRIDGE, K.C. (2009). 'Towards a functional neuroanatomy of pleasure and happiness', *Trends in Cognitive Sciences*, Vol. 13(11), pp. 479–487.

KRINGELBACH, M.L, & BERRIDGE, K.C. (2010). 'The Neuroscience of Happiness and Pleasure'. *NIH*; Vol. 77(2), pp. 659–678.

KRINGELBACH, M.L, & BERRIDGE, K.C. (2011). 'The Neurobiology of Pleasure and Happiness'. In JUDY ILLES & BARBARA J. SAHAKIAN (eds). *Oxford Handbook of Neuroethics*. Oxford: Oxford University Press, pp. 15–33.

KRISTJÁNSSON, K. (2021). *Flourishing as the Aim of Education: A Neo-Aristotelian View*. Oxford: Routledge.

KUO, P., CARP, J., LIGHT, K.C. & GREWEN, K.M. (2012). 'Neural responses to infants linked with behavioral interactions and testosterone in fathers'. *Biological Psychology*. Vol. 91(2), pp. 302–306.

KUNZLER, A.M., HELMREICH, I., KÖNIG, J., CHMITORZ, A., WESSA, M., BINDER, H. & LIEB, K. (2020). 'Psychological interventions to foster resilience in healthcare students.' *Cochrane Database Syst Rev*. Vol. 20:7(7).

KUSTERS, W. 2020. *A Philosophy of Madness*. London: MIT Press.

LARSON, K.E., CHATURVEDI, M. LEE, M. (2020). 'Education for flourishing standards'. Available at https://www.educationforflourishing.org/resources [last accessed 27.07.21].

LEACH, S. & TARTAGLIA, J. (2018). *The Meaning of Life and the Great Philosophers.* London: Routledge.

LEE, M.T., VANDERWEELE, T.J. & KUBZANKSY, L.D. (2021). (eds) *Measuring Well-Being: Interdisciplinary Perspectives from the Social Sciences and the Humanities.* Oxford: Oxford University Press.

LIU, W., ZHANG, W., VAN DER LINDEN, D. et al. (2023) 'Flow and Flourishing During the Pandemic: The Roles of Strengths Use and Playful Design.' *J Happiness Stud.*

LOCKE, J. (1979). *An Essay concerning Human Understanding.* P. H. Nidditch (ed.). Oxford: Clarendon Press.

LONGWORTH, G. (2020). 'Ruin a work of philosophy by inserting "normativity".' Available at https://twitter.com/GuyLongworth/status/1255377502543007746 [Last accessed 02.03.21].

LYUBOMIRSKY, S. & LEPPER, H.S. (1999). 'A Measure of Subjective Happiness: Preliminary Reliability and Construct Validation'. *Social Indicators Research* Vol. 46(2), pp.137–155.

MACINTYRE, A. (1981). *After virtue: a study in moral theory.* Paris (France): University of Notre Dame Press.

MACINTYRE, A. (1998). *A Short History of Ethics.* First Edition: New York: University of Notre Dame Press.

MACINTYRE, A. (1999). *Dependent Rational Animals: Why Human Beings Need the Virtues.* Chicago: Open Court.

MAHON, Á. & O'BRIEN, E. (2018). Resonance, Response, Renewal: Literary Education in Rorty and Cavell. *Journal of Philosophy of Education*, Vol. 52, pp. 695–708.

MALCOLM, N. (1989). 'Wittgenstein on Language and Rules, *Philosophy* Vol. 64, pp. 5–28.

MARTIN, E. (2003). *Oxford Dictionary of Law* (7th edn). Oxford: Oxford University Press.

MASLOW, A. (2013). *A Theory of Human Motivation.* Radford: Wilder Publications.

MEERLOO, J. (2021). (originally print: 1956). *Rape of the Mind: The psychology of Thought Control, Menticide & Brainwashing.* CT (USA): Martino Fine Books.

MCFEE, G. (2000). *Free Will.* London: Routledge

MCFEE, G. (2015). *How to do Philosophy: A Wittgensteinian Reading of Wittgenstein.* (Unabridged edn). Newcastle-Upon-Tyne: Cambridge Scholars Publishing.

MCGINN, M. (2021). *Wittgenstein, Scepticism and Naturalism Essays on the Later Philosophy* (Anthem Studies in Wittgenstein). Oxford: Blackwell.

MCKITTERICK, R. (2008). *Charlemagne: The Formation of a European Identity.* Cambridge: Cambridge University Press.

METZ, T. (2013). *Meaning in Life.* Oxford: Oxford University Press.

MICHALOS, A. C. & ROBINSON, S. R. (2012). 'The Good Life: Eighth century to third century BCE'. In K. C. LAND, A. C. MICHALOS & M. J. SIRGY (eds),

Handbook of social indicators and quality of life research (pp. 23–61). Dordrecht, The Netherlands: Springer.

MILL, J.S. (1863). *Utilitarianism* (1st edn). London: Parker, Son & Bourn.

MONAGHAN, J. & JUST, P. 2000. *Social and Cultural Anthropology: A Very Short Introduction.* Oxford: Oxford University Press.

MONK, R. (1991). *Ludwig Wittgenstein: The Duty of Genius.* London: Vintage Publishers.

MOORE, G.E. (1903). *Principia Ethica.* London: Hardpress.

MORE, M. 2013. 'The Philosophy of Transhumanism'. In *The Transhumanist Reader.* M. MORE & N. VITA-MORE. (2013). Oxford: Wiley-Blackwell.

MORE, M. & VITA-MORE, N. (2013). *The Transhumanist Reader.* Oxford: Wiley-Blackwell.

MORGAN, A., ZIGLIO, E. (2007). 'Revitalising the evidence base for public health: an assets model'. *Global Health Promotion.* Vol. 14(2). Suppl., pp. 17–22.

MORIARTY, M. (trans.) (2008). In DESCARTES, R. 2008. *Meditations on First Philosophy with Selections from the Objections and Replies.* Oxford: Oxford University Press.

MORRIS, K. (2004). (ed.) In BAKER, G. P. (2004). *Wittgenstein's method: Neglected aspects: essays on Wittgenstein.* Malden, MA: Blackwell.

MOYAL-SHARROCK, D. (2015). 'Wittgenstein on Forms of Life, Patterns of Life, and Ways of Living'. *Nordic Wittgenstein Review Special (Wittgenstein and Forms of Life).*

MOYAL-SHARROCK, D. (2017). 'Knowledge and Certainty'. In *A Companion to Wittgenstein.* HANS-JOHANN GLOCK, JOHN HYMAN (eds). Oxford: Blackwell.

MOYAL-SHARROCK, D. & SANDIS, C. (2019). 'Lived gender' project – Available at https://researchprofiles.herts.ac.uk/portal/en/projects/lived-gender(41c9a3f8-bf5a-4436-91ab-88319b1dc9b7).html [last accessed 02.03.21].

MOUNTBATTEN-O'MALLEY, E. (2021). 'Taking the 'human' in conceptions of human flourishing in education seriously.' Online. 26.4.21. (University of Winchester Philosophy of Education, Philosophy of Education Society of Great Britain seminar series). Abstract Available at https://www.winchester.ac.uk/news-and-events/events/event-items/taking-the-human-in-conceptions-of-human-flourishing-in-education-seriously-.php

MOUNTBATTEN-O'MALLEY, E. (2023). FlourishCafé: 'Problematizing flourishing as "the" aim of education'. In-person workshop. *Philosophy of Education Society of Great Britain Annual conference 2023.*

MOUNTBATTEN-O'MALLEY, E. (2024). 'Lost in Wonder: a response to Schinkel's concept of "deep wonder"'. *Journal of Philosophy of Education.* Oxford: Oxford University Press.

MULHALL, S. (2012). 'Wonder, Perplexity, Sublimity: Philosophy as the Self-Overcoming of Self-Exile in Heidegger and Wittgenstein'. In *Practices of Wonder: Cross-Disciplinary Perspectives*, VASALOU, S. (ed). (2012), Eugene, Oregon: Wipf & Stock Pub.

NAGEL, T. (1986). *The View from Nowhere*. Oxford: Oxford University Press.
NAOR, N., BEN-ZE'EV, A., OKON-SINGER, H. (2014). 'The modern search for the Holy Grail: is neuroscience a solution?' *Front Hum Neurosci*. Jun 4; Vol. 8, p. 388.
NATIONAL RESEARCH COUNCIL (US). (2001). 'Panel on a Research Agenda and New Data for an Aging World. Preparing for an Aging World: The Case for Cross-National Research'. In *Well-Being: Concepts and Measures*. Washington (DC): National Academies Press.
NEILL, E. & NEVIN, A (2021). 'Flourishing in Canada: How to Get the Good Life'. Canada: Institute for Flourishing in Canada.
NIDA-RÜMELIN, J. & ÖZMEN, E. (eds). (2012). '19. Kolloquium'. Welt der Gründe XXII. Deutscher Kongress für Philosophie. 11–15 September 2011 an der Ludwig-Maximilians-Universität München. Kolloquienbeiträge. Felix Meiner Verlag Publishers.
NIXON, S. & FORMAN, L. (2008). 'Exploring synergies between human rights and public health ethics: A whole greater than the sum of its parts'. *BMC International Health & Human Rights*, Vol. 8(2).
NOWELL, A. (2010). 'Defining Behavioral Modernity in the Context of Neandertal and Anatomically Modern Human Populations'. *Annual Review of Anthropology*. Vol. 39, pp. 437–452.
NOZICK, R. (1989). 'What is Wisdom and Why do Philosophers Love it So'. *The Examined Life*. New York: Touchstone Press, pp. 267–278.
NUSSBAUM, M. (1986). *The Fragility of Goodness: Luck and Ethics in Greek Tragedy and Philosophy*. New York: Cambridge University Press.
OLIVER, M. (1990). *The politics of disablement*. London: Macmillan Education.
ONS (Office for National Statistics). (2021). 'Well-being'. Available at https://www.ons.gov.uk/peoplepopulationandcommunity/wellbeing [last accessed 27.07.21].
PARFIT, D. (1951). *The Social System*. Glencoe, IL: The Free Press.
PARFIT, D. (1971), 'Personal Identity', *Philosophical Review*, Vol. 80, pp. 3–27.
PARFIT, D. (1984). *Reasons and Persons*. Oxford: Oxford University Press.
PARFIT, D. (1995). 'The unimportance of identity'. In H. HARRIS (ed.), *Identity*. Oxford: Oxford University Press, pp. 13–45.
PARFIT, D. (2012). 'We Are Not Human Beings'. *Philosophy* 87 (1), pp. 5–28.
PARSONS, T. (1951). *The Social System*. Glencoe, IL: The Free Press.
PAUL, L.A. (2014). *Transformative experience*. Oxford: Oxford University Press.
PEARSALL, J. (1998). *The New Oxford Dictionary of English*. Oxford: Oxford University Press.
PETERSON, C. & SELIGMAN, M. (2004). *Character Strengths and Virtues: A Handbook and Classification*. Oxford: Oxford University Press.
PETERSON, M. (2007). 'Should the precautionary principle guide our actions or our beliefs?' *Medical Ethics*, Vol. 33, pp. 5–10.
PHELPS, W.L. (2018). *Robert Browning, how to Know him*, (Franklin Classics). USA. Good Press.

PILLER, C. (2013). 'Benatar's Anti-Natalism: Philosophically Flawed, Morally Dubious.' *Philosophia*, Vol. 51, pp. 897–917.

POPE, A. (2007). Gurr Elizabeth (ed.) Oxford Student Texts: Alexander Pope: *The Rape of the Lock*. Oxford: Oxford University Press.

PORTERFIELD, C. (2021). 'Dr. Fauci On GOP Criticism: "Attacks On Me, Quite Frankly, Are Attacks On Science"'. *Forbes*. Available at https://www.forbes.com/sites/carlieporterfield/2021/06/09/fauci-on-gop-criticism-attacks-on-me-quite-frankly-are-attacks-on-science/?sh=44a15d8a4542 [last accessed 29.06.21).

PREUS, A. (2007). Historical Dictionary of Ancient Greek Philosophy: Historical Dictionaries of Religions, Philosophies, and Movements, No. 78. Plymouth (UK): The Scarecrow Press Inc.

PRITCHARD, D. (2005). 'Moral and Epistemic Luck'. *Metaphilosophy*, Vol. 37, pp. 1–25.

PUTNAM, H. (2002). 'The Collapse of the Fact/Value Dichotomy and Other Essays'. *Science and Society*. Vol. 68(4), pp. 483–493.

PUTNAM, H. (2012). 'Was Wittgenstein Really and Antirealist about Mathematics?'. In H. PUTNAM, *Philosophy in an Age of Science: Physics, Mathematics and Skepticism*, Harvard: Harvard University Press, pp. 355–403.

RACHELS, J. & RACHELS, S. (2014). *The Elements of Moral Philosophy*. New York: McGraw-Hill Education.

READ, R. (2005). 'Throwing away the bedrock'. *Proceedings of the Aristotelian Society*. New Series, Vol. 105, pp. 81–98. Published by: Oxford University Press.

READ, R. (2020). *Wittgenstein's Liberatory Philosophy: Thinking Through His Philosophical Investigations*. Oxford: Routledge.

REID, T. (2010). 'Essays on the Active Powers of Man—A Critical Edition'. In KNUD HAAKONSSEN AND JAMES A. HARRIS (eds). *The Edinburgh Edition of Thomas Reid* (Vol. 7). Edinburgh, UK: Edinburgh University Press. (Original work published in 1788.)

Rich, G. J. (2001). 'Positive Psychology: An Introduction'. *Journal of Humanistic Psychology*, 41(1), pp. 8–12.

ROBINSON, D.N. (1999). *Aristotle's Psychology*. Published by Daniel N. Robinson.

ROGERS, C. (1961). *On Becoming a Person*. London: Constable; (1st edn).

ROTHSTEIN, M. A. (2004). 'Are traditional public health strategies consistent with contemporary American values?' *Temple Law Review*, Vol. 77(2), pp. 175–192.

ROWLANDS, M. (2016). 'Animal Personhood'. *Animal Sentience*. Vol. 101.

ROYO-BORDONADA, M. Á. & Román-Maeestre, B. (2015). 'Towards public health ethics'. *Public Health Reviews*, Vol. 36(1), pp. 1–15.

RUBIN, A., SHEINTUCH, L., BRANDE-EILAT, N. et al. (2019). 'Revealing neural correlates of behavior without behavioral measurements'. *Nature Communications*. Vol. 10. 4745.

RYAN, S. (2012). 'Wisdom, Knowledge and Rationality'. *Acta Analytica* 27 (2), pp. 99–112.

RYAN, R. M. & DECI, E. L. (2000). 'Self-determination theory and the facilitation of intrinsic motivation, social development, and well-being'. *American Psychologist*, Vol. 55(1), pp. 68–78.

RYFF, C. D. (1989). 'Happiness is everything, or is it? Explorations on the meaning of psychological well-being'. *Journal of Personality and Social Psychology*, Vol. 57(6), pp. 1069–1081.

RYFF, C. D. & SINGER, B. (2003). 'Flourishing under fire: Resilience as a prototype of challenged thriving'. In C. L. M. KEYES & J. HAIDT (eds), *Flourishing: Positive psychology and the life well-lived* (pp. 15–36). American Psychological Association.

RYFF, C.D., BOYLAN, J.M., KIRSCH, J.A. (2020). 'Disagreement about recommendations for measurement of well-being'. *Preventive Medicine: An International Journal Devoted to Practice and Theory*, Vol. 139, Article 106049.

RYLE, G. (1946). "I.—Knowing How and Knowing That: The Presidential Address." *Proceedings of the Aristotelian Society*. Vol. 46(1) (1945), pp. 1–16.

RYLE, G. (2009). *Concept of Mind* (60th Anniversary Edition). Oxford: Routledge.

SANDIS, C. (2012a). 'Understanding the Lion For Real'. In A. MARQUES & N. VENTURINHA, (eds) *Knowledge, Language and Mind: Wittgenstein's Thought in Progress*. Berlin: de Gruyter.

SANDIS, C. (2012b). *The Things we do, and Why we do them*. New York: Palgrave Macmillan.

SANDIS, C. (2015). '"If Some People Looked Like Elephants and Others Like Cats": Wittgenstein on Understanding Others and Forms of Life'. *Nordic Wittgenstein Review Special Issue 2015* (Wittgenstein and Forms of Life).

SANDIS, C. (2019). 'Are reasons like shampoo?'. In G. SCHUMANN (ed.), (2019). *Explanation in Action Theory and Historiography: Causal and Teleological Approaches*. Oxford: Routledge.

SANDIS, C. (2021). 'Virtue Ethics and Particularism', *Aristotelian Society* Supplementary Volume, Vol. 95(1), pp. 205–232.

SASS, L. A. (1994). *The Paradoxes of Delusion: Wittgenstein, Schreber and the Schizophrenic Mind*. Ithaca, NY: Cornell University Press.

SCHINKEL, A. (2016). 'Education and Life's Meaning'. *Journal of Philosophy of Education*. Vol. 50(3).

SCHINKEL, A. (2017). 'The Educational Importance of Deep Wonder', *Journal of Philosophy of Education*, Vol. 51(2).

SCHOTANUS-DIJKSTRA, M., PIETERSE, M. E., DROSSAERT, C. H. C., WESTERHOF, G. J., DE GRAAF, M. & BOHLMEIJER, E. T. (2016). 'What factors are associated with flourishing? Results from a large representative national sample'. *Journal of Happiness Studies*, Vol. 17(4), pp. 1351–1370.

SELIGMAN M. & CSIKSZENTMIHALYI, M. (2000). 'Positive psychology. An introduction'. *American Psychologist*. Vol. 55(1), pp. 5–14.

SELIGMAN, M. (2011). *Flourish: A New Understanding of Happiness and Well-Being*. Boston, MA. Nicholas Brealey Publishing.

SEN, A. (1999). *Development as freedom*. Oxford: Oxford University Press.

SHAKESPEARE, W. (1992). *Macbeth*. Oxford: Wordsworth Classics.
SHARROCK W. & DENNIS A. (2008). 'That We Obey Rules Blindly Does Not Mean that We Are Blindly Subservient to Rules'. *Theory, Culture & Society*, Vol. 25(2), pp. 33–50.
SHELLEY, M. W. (1994). *Frankenstein; or, The Modern Prometheus*. In D.L. MACDONALD & K. SCHERF. (eds). Peterborough: Broadview Press.
SHOEMAKER, S. (1963). *Self-Knowledge and Self-Identity*. Ithaca: Cornell University Press.
SHOEMAKER, S. (1984). *Personal identity*. Edited by Richard Swinburne. Oxford: Blackwell.
SHOEMAKER, S. (1979). 'Identity, Properties, and Causality', *Midwest Studies in Philosophy*, Vol. 4, pp. 321–342.
SINGER, P. (1993). *Practical Ethics*, Cambridge: Cambridge University Press.
SINGER, P. 2009. *Animal Liberation: A New Ethics for our Treatment of Animals*, New York: Harper Perennial Modern Classics.
STANDISH, P. (2017). 'Something Animal? Wittgenstein, Language, and Instinct'. In PETERS, M. & STICKNEY, J. (eds) *A Companion to Wittgenstein on Education*. Singapore: Springer.
STANLEY, J. & WILLIAMSON, T. (2001). 'Knowing How', *The Journal of Philosophy*, Vol. 98(8), pp. 411–444.
STANLEY, J. & WILLIAMSON, T. (2017). 'Skill'. *Noûs*. Vol. 31(4), pp. 713–726.
STEPHENS, C. (2014). 'What children need to be happy, confident and successful: step by step positive psychology to help children flourish', *Educational Psychology in Practice*, pp. 109–110.
STRAWSON, P. F. (1992). *Analysis and Metaphysics*, Oxford: Oxford University Press.
STRAWSON, G. (1999). 'Self, Body, and Experience', *Aristotelian Society Supplementary Volume*. Vol. 73(1), pp. 307–332.
STRUHL, K. (2016). 'Marx and Human Nature: The Historical, the Trans-Historical, and Human Flourishing'. *Science & Society*. Vol. 80, pp. 78–104.
TATARKIEWICZ, W. (1976). *Analysis of Happiness*. Warsaw: Polish Scientific Publishers.
THE HAPPINESS INDEX. (2021). Available at https://thehappinessindex.com/ [last accessed 27.07.21].
THE SUPREME COURT (2020). 'Begum (Respondent) v Secretary of State for the Home Department (Appellant). Case ID: UKSC 2020/0158'. Available at https://www.supremecourt.uk/cases/uksc-2020-0158.html [last accessed 05.08.21].
THOMSON, J.J. (2008). *Normativity*. Chicago: Open Court.
TOMASELLO, M. & HERRMANN, E. (2010). 'Ape and Human Cognition: What's the Difference?' *Current Directions in Psychological Science*, Vol. 19(1), pp. 3–8.
TOYNBEE, A. (1987). *A Study of History*. Oxford: Oxford University Press.
TRAVIS, C. (1989). *The Uses of Sense: Wittgenstein's Philosophy of Language*. Oxford: Oxford University Press.

TRAVIS, C. 2008. *Occasion-Sensitivity: Selected Essays*. Oxford: Oxford University Press.
UNIVERSITY OF BUCKINGHAM. (2016). 'University of Buckingham to become Europe's first Positive University'. Available at https://www.buckingham.ac.uk/news/university-of-buckingham-to-become-europes-first-positive-university/ [last accessed 27.07.21].
UUSIAUTTI, S. (2013). 'On the Positive Connection between Success and Happiness'. *International Journal of Research Studies in Psychology*, Vol. 3(1), pp. 1–11.
VAINIO, O. (2020). *Religious Language*. Yujin Nagasawa (ed.). Cambridge Elements. Cambridge: Cambridge University Press.
VANDERWEELE T. J. (2017). 'On the promotion of human flourishing'. *Proceedings of the National Academy of Sciences*. Vol. 114(31), pp. 8148–8156.
VANDERWEELE T. J. (2019). 'Measures of Community Well-Being: a Template'. *Int. Journal of Com.*, Vol. 2, pp. 253–275.
VANDERWEELE T. J. (2021). 'How to Measure Well-Being'. *Psychology Today*. Available at https://www.psychologytoday.com/us/node/1163412/preview [last accessed 27.07.21].
VASALOU, S. (2013). *Practices of wonder: Cross disciplinary perspectives*. Cambridge: James Clarke & Co.
VENTER, E. (2004). 'The Notion of Ubuntu and Communalism in African Educational Discourse'. *Studies in Philosophy and Education*, Vol. 23, pp. 149–160.
VITTERSØ, J (ed). (2016). Handbook of Eudaimonic Well-Being. International Handbooks of Quality-of-Life. Switzerland: Springer.
VON WRIGHT, G.H. (1968). *Varieties of Goodness*. New York: Routledge & Kegan Paul.
VON WRIGHT, G.H. (1974). *Causality and Determinism*. New York: Columbia University Press.
WADE, D. & HALLIGAN, P. (2004). 'Do biomedical models of illness make for good healthcare systems?' *BMJ*, Vol. 11(329), pp. 398–401.
WAHID, A.N.M. (2002). *Frontiers of economics: Nobel laureates of the twentieth century*. Westport, Conn.: Greenwood Press.
WARD, A (2019). 'The Survival of Persons: A Reply to Parfit's Psychological Reductionism', *Argumenta* Vol. 5(1), pp. 113–124.
WATERMAN, A. S. (2013). 'The humanistic psychology–positive psychology divide: Contrasts in philosophical foundations'. *American Psychologist*, Vol. 68(3), pp. 124–133.
WATSON, L. (2018). 'Educating for Good Questioning: a Tool for Intellectual Virtues Education'. *Acta Analytica*, Vol. 33(3), pp. 353–370.
WATTS, A. (1977). *The Essential Alan Watts*. California: Creative arts.
WEDGWOOD, Ralph (2007). *The Nature of Normativity*. Oxford: Oxford University Press.
WEINBERG, J. (2021). 'Interview with Peter Hacker' (16.7.21). *Daily Nous*. Available at https://dailynous.com/2021/07/16/interview-with-peter-hacker/ [last accessed 27.01.21].

WEIS, A., BATES, T. C. & LUCIANO, M. (2008). 'Happiness Is a Personal(ity) Thing: The Genetics of Personality and Well-Being in a Representative Sample'. *Psychological Science*, Vol. 19(3), pp. 205–210.

WEISBERG, J. (2021). 'Formal Epistemology'. *Stanford Encyclopaedia of philosophy*. Available at https://plato.stanford.edu/entries/formal-epistemology/#Bib [last accessed 13.08.21].

WHITCOMB, D. (2011). 'Wisdom'. In *The Routledge Companion to Epistemology*. Sven Berneker and Duncan Pritchard (eds), (2011). New York: Routledge, pp. 95–106.

WHITE, J. (2011). *Exploring Well-Being in Schools: A Guide to Making Children's Lives More Fulfilling*. London: Routledge.

WHITFIELD, S.J. (2004). *A companion to 20th century America*. Oxford: Blackwell.

WIGGINS, D. (1967). *Identity and Spatio-temporal Continuity*. Oxford: Blackwell.

WIGGINS, D. (1976). 'Truth, Invention, and the Meaning of Life'. In *Proceedings of the British Academy*, LXII.

WILD, M. & BRANDT, R. (2012). 'Einführung'. In '19. Kolloquium'. J. NIDA-RÜMELIN, E. ÖZMEN, AND ELIF ÖZMEN (eds). Welt der Gründe XXII. Deutscher Kongress für Philosophie. 11–15 September 2011 an der Ludwig-Maximilians-Universität München. Kolloquienbeiträge. Felix Meiner Verlag Publishers.

WILLIAMS, B. (1982). *Moral Luck Philosophical Papers 1973–1980*. Cambridge: Cambridge University Press.

WINCH, P. (1990). *The Idea of a Social Science – and it's relation to Philosophy*. (2nd edn). London: Routledge.

WINCH, C. (2006). *Education, Autonomy and Critical Thinking*. Oxford: Routledge.

WIREDU, K (ed.) (2004). *A Companion to African Philosophy*. Oxford: Blackwell.

WITTGENSTEIN, L. (1949). 'Letter to P. Sraffa', 23 August 1949; cited in C. SANDIS (2015) '"If Some People Looked Like Elephants and Others Like Cats": Wittgenstein on Understanding Others and Forms of Life'. *Nordic Wittgenstein Review Special Issue* (Wittgenstein and Forms of Life).

WITTGENSTEIN, L. (1967). *Lectures and Conversations on Aesthetics, Psychology and Religious Belief*. C. Barrett (ed.), Berkeley: University of California Press.

WITTGENSTEIN, L. (1969). *On Certainty*, G. E. M. Anscombe and G. H. von Wright (Eds.), G. E. M. Anscombe and D. Paul (Trans.). Oxford: Basil Blackwell.

WITTGENSTEIN, L. (1974). *Tractatus Logico-Philosophicus*. D. F. Pears & B. F. Mcguinness (trans.). Revised edn, London: Routledge & Kegan Paul.

WITTGENSTEIN, L. (1975). *Wittgenstein's Lectures on the Foundations of Mathematics, Cambridge, 1939: From the Notes of R.G. Bosanquet, Norman Malcolm, Rush Rhees, and Yorick Smythies*. Ithaca, N.Y.: University of Chicago Press. R. G. Bosanquet & Cora Diamond (eds).

WITTGENSTEIN, L. (1979). *Remarks on colour*. Oxford: Blackwell.

WITTGENSTEIN, L. (1980). *Remarks on the Philosophy of Psychology* (Vol. I) ed. G.E.M. Anscombe and G.H. von Wright, tr. G.E.M. Anscombe, Oxford: Blackwell.

WITTGENSTEIN, L. (1991). *The Blue and Brown Books: Preliminary Studies for the 'Philosophical Investigation'*, Peter Doherty (ed.), 2nd edn, Oxford: Wiley-Blackwell.

WITTGENSTEIN, L. (1991). *Zettel*. Oxford. Oxford University Press.

WITTGENSTEIN, L. (1998). *Culture and Value*. (revised edn). Oxford: Blackwell.

WITTGENSTEIN, L. (2005). *The Big Typescript*. Oxford: Blackwell.

WITTGENSTEIN, L. (2009). *Philosophical Investigations*, P. M. S. Hacker and J. Schulte (eds). G. E. M. Anscombe, P. M. S. Hacker and J. Schulte (trans.), 4th edn, Oxford: Wiley-Blackwell.

WITTGENSTEIN, L. (2009). '*Philosophy of Psychology – A Fragment*'. In *Philosophical Investigations*, P. M. S. Hacker and J. Schulte, (eds) G. E. M. Anscombe, P. M. S. Hacker and J. Schulte, (trans.), 4th edn, Oxford: Wiley-Blackwell.

WOLBERT, L.S., DE RUYTER, D.J. & SCHINKLE, A. (2015). 'Formal criteria for the concept of human flourishing: the first step in defending flourishing as an ideal aim of education'. *Ethics and Education*, Vol. 10(1), pp. 23–35.

WOLF, S. (1997a). 'Meaning and Morality,' *Proceedings of the Aristotelian Society*, Vol. 97: 1, pp. 299–316.

WOLF, S. (1997b). 'Happiness and Meaning: Two Aspects of the Good Life', *Social Philosophy & Policy*. Vol. 14(1), p. 207.

WOLF, S. (2007). 'The Meanings of Lives'. In J. PERRY, M. BRATMAN & J. FIRSCHER, (eds), (2007). *Introduction to Philosophy: Classical and Contemporary Readings*. Oxford: Oxford University Press.

WOLF, S. (2010). *Meaning in Life and Why It Matters*. Princeton: Princeton University Press.

WOLF, S. (2015). *The Variety of Values: Essays on Morality, Meaning & Love*. Oxford: Oxford University Press.

WONG, J. K. (2004). 'Are the learning styles of Asian international students culturally or contextually based?' *International Education Journal*, Vol. 4, pp. 154–166.

WORLD HEALTH ORGANISATION (2020). 'Basic Documents, 49th Edn: Constitution'. Available at: https://apps.who.int/gb/bd/ [last accessed 15.10.23].

Index

ability/abilities (human)
concept-possession 55
context of use 4
degrees of ability 189, 207 n.16.
deluded about 143
goals 110
imaginative, 129–130
judgement, skill, competence, 39, 44–45
know-how 10, 27
language-games, 175
learning, 83
linguistic, reflective, 75–79
moral failure, 174
moral powers, 69
moral responsibility, 173
resilience, 159
skills for life, 85
social structures, 81
spontaneity, as a power, 115–117
to reason, 112
understanding, 36
vs animals, 50 & 119–121
vs capability, 70
wisdom, 96 & 148–149,
See also capacity
absurd/ity/ies/ism
'Bad Blob' 174
Camus 160–161
Chomsky 56–57
of the Self 134–139
'The Kindness Pill' 162
'The Meaning of Life' 163
agency/agent
'acting' vs mere doing 113
animal agency 112, 115
Artificial Intelligence 115
automaticity – animal vs human 114, 120
autonomy 107
behaviour 114
biological reductionism 123–128
biological vs social agency 117–118
blinded to flourishing 113
COVID-19 78, 117
complex emotional repertoire 120
complex language 113
conditions for flourishing 119–122
contributing to the good 59, 94, 109
dehumanization 120
exercise of agency 118
form of life 47, 110, 117
freedom to act 117
harms of authoritarianism/
    totalitarianism 119
human abilities 70
human dignity 78
human power 115, 117
human rights 70, 117
injustice 122
moral agency 109, 112
new beginnings (ARENDT, H) 119
normativity A vs normativity B 118–119
paternalism 122
performance 120
personhood 115–117
political language 123
political power 11, 109, 112, 117–119
positive neuroscience 123
psychological vs behavioural 119–123
purpose 114
rationality 75
reasons for acting/action 110, 112
reordering of the world 120
rights and responsibilities 115
reflexive capacity 112
Self, the 77, 109
scientism 125
'scale' of agency, (FRANKFURT, H) 111
space for action and innovation 119
technical concept 109
teleology 114
unhealthy habits 120
victimized groups/persecution 122

ALVAREZ, M 109, 205 n.1.
animal kingdom 22, 47, 112, 129, 202 n.4.
ANSCOMBE, G.E.M 135, 210 n.10.
Antinatalist/ism 217 n.37.
aporia 59, 60, 167
   See also wonder
ARENDT, H 119
ARISTOTLE
   Ancient Greek culture (CRISP, R) 204 n.14
   eudaimonia 9–11, 94–97
   neo-Aristotelianism 6, 11, 91, 156, 194 n.12.
   on conceptual analysis 49
   on forms of causality 216 n.31
   on *phronesis* 211 n.26
   on virtues 134
   on the soul or mind 205 n.16
   practical wisdom (RYLE, G) 144
aspect seeing 25, 55, 60–62, 175.
attitude/attitudinal
   adopting an attitude of hope 119
   adversity 101
   animal ethics 111, 206 n.2
   attitude to life 99, 162, 166, 168
   behavioural criteria 81
   dogmatic attitude 186
   epistemic pluralism 141
   flexibility of attitude/happiness 159
   gratitude 161
   folly 198 n.19
   negative attitude (FRANKL, V) 161
   moods, temporality, time-scales 103
   limited nature of animal attitudes 120
   objective attitudes to value 213 n.5
   positive attitude 100, 219 n.58
   philosophical vs psychological 200 n.7
   religious attitude to life 215 n.26
   totalitarian attitude (MEERLOO, J) 189
   will, new ways of seeing 175
   See also will
AUSTIN, J.L 105, 198 n.28,
autonomy
   agency, freedom to act 111
   dehumanization 189
   education, learning and development 145, 188
   fundamental to flourishing 129–130
   health ethics 195 n.15
   human rights 70
   linguistic 34
   pictures of mind (BERMÚDEZ, J.L) 127
   on freedom rationality, autonomous thinking 52, 75
   transhumanism 8
   See also agency
axiology/axiological
   axiological concepts 5
   axiological conception of 'health' (HACKER, P.M.S) 118
   criteria for meaning 151
   complex duality 202 n.8
   fickle notions of happiness (HACKER, P.M.S) 156
   materialism 213 n.6
   normative 28, 59, 97
   normative 'A' and normative 'B' 129, 181, 207 n.15
   relationship with 'pleasure' 121
   social contexts 23
   See also normativity

BAKER, G
   concepts vs conceptions 91
   dispute with P.M.S HACKER 48, 199 n.2, 200 n.7
   human understanding 37
   identifying new patterns, aspect-blindness 62
   liberatory philosophy 5, 25
   knowing *how* 31
   metaphysics 201 n.11
   misleading pictures 210 n.13
   personal histories, therapy, person-relativity 60, 180, 220 n.15
   philosophical disquiet 104
   pluralism 28
   problematic terms 84
   rules and ways of seeing 39
   voluntariness of philosophical therapy 53
behaviour/behaving/behavioural
   amoral 93
   animal behaviour 120
   animal understanding 71

automaticity, instinct in humans 121
action first, then reflection 206 n.10
biological reductionism 123–128
categories 73
criteria and evidence 158
cultural grammar 187
criteria for happiness 99–101
development of rationality 75–76
etiquette 117
explanation for behaviour 51
explanations for behaviour in terms of goals 165, 215 n.25
flourishing behaviours 14
forms of behaviour and purpose 114
human error 69
intelligence (RYLE, G) learning how to act 142–144
inner/outer 17–18, 81
linguistic behaviour, normative 'A' 196 n.3
limited living 173
language-games 35
mimicry 37
normative vs nomological 129
performance 116
personhood 138–139
reasons for action 16
reasons for moral behaviour 161–162
responsibility 78
unethical, instrumental behaviour 204 n.10
Utilitarian 8
vicious behaviours 174
belief/s
belief system 8, 147
concept of Self 77–78
conceptual relations 113
deluded about 143
infinite regress 51
hold in high esteem 120
political beliefs 147
religious belief 117, 166, 218 n.51
spooky beliefs 17
self-limiting 140
rational beliefs 146
relationship with meaning 170
theories vs beliefs 204 n.5

BENTHAM, J 6
BERMÚDEZ, J.L
'bottom-up' 111, 124
'bridging principles' 127
See also agency
BERLIN, I 188, 207 n.14.
BEST, D 44, 201 n.12.
Bible, The 147.
See also Christianity
blind/blind spots/blinkers
aspect-blindness 60–62
blind 25, 55
blinded 113, 197 n.15
blind habits 142
blind-spots/blinkers 140, 170, 175, 180, 183
limits of language 136
Blob, The (WOLF, S) 25, 171–176.

CAMUS, A 152, 159, 160–62, 167, 188, 215 n.21.
capacity/capability/capacity
abstract thought 70
agency 133
capacity to act 109
inner life/capacity to think 121
for mind 120
mental capacity 118, 207 n.18
new beginnings 119
leadership 149, 190
legal capacity 75, 77, 92
physical capacity 69
reasoning 75, 206 n.1
reflexive 112
sense-making 7
story-telling 217 n.44
See also abilities
capitalist/capitalism 6, 90, 131,
See also Neoliberalism
See also Materialism
See also Consumerism
Cartesian 8, 139, 194 n.11.
See also DESCARTES, R
CASSAM, Q 142–149, 184–185, 194 n.9, 216 n.29, 218 n.50, 219 n.56.
causes/causal/causality
biological 109, 123–129
conspiratorial 203 n.5

of misery 7
reasons vs causes 16, 23, 109, 111, 167, 208 n.29, 216 n.32
scientific 1–5
telos 164–167
vs correlation 126
See also agency
certainty 62, 206 n.1.
See also knowledge
character/characterological
characterological hallmark 173
character and wisdom 212 n.34
'circumstantial luck' 174
educating for good questioning' (WATSON, L)
flaws 70
meaning in life 204 n.11
moral orienteering 25
personal growth 131, 140
poor role models 173
positive education 14
problems of life 150, 159–160
relation to flourishing/self-knowledge 84–85, 90, 98, 106, 122, 129, 131, 143
relation to well-being 102
self-deception 157
transcendence vices 170
See also virtue
See also vice
See also moral
See also personal growth
See also maturity
See also wisdom
virtue (ARISTOTLE) 10–11
CHOMSKY, N 42, 56–57.
CHRIST, JESUS 166, 170.
Christianity/Christian 88, 91, 166–167, 188, 208 n.25, 209 n.2, 213 n.9, 218 n.51.
See also Bible
See also AQUINAS. T
CICERO 156, 213 n.9.
citizen/citizenship 11, 15, 78, 122, 156, 188, 190.
civic duty 10, 92, 156, 190.
See also duty
See also ethics

civilisation /civilizational 71, 82, 112, 117, 161, 188, 203 n.4, 206 n.6.
See also democracy
See also common good
coach 187
Cognitivism 38,
coherence/coherent/incoherent 8, 15–16, 21, 39, 51, 140–141, 187, 189, 218 n.55, 217 n.38, 218 n.55
See also concepts
See also methods
Common Good, The 6, 92, 94, 186, 188, 215 n.24.
See also Good life, The
See also justice
consciousness
agency 116
animal 120
dualism 9
experience 167
functionalism 8
'hard problem', the 128
human powers, the mind 70, 75, 77
Identity 132
inner-outer 168, 176
meaninglessness 171
mental states 147
multi-focal concept 203 n.1
self-consciousness 140
See also *mind*
concepts/conceptual
biological concepts 123–128
'blurry', 'woolly', 'technicalized' concept 3, 51–52, 74, 109, 190
categorial error 73, 203 n.1, n.3
concept of agency, self-efficacy 109–130, 136, 139, 175–177
conceptual boundaries, logical parameters 74–75
concept-deploying creature 81, 131
conceptual elucidation, connective analysis 55–60, 185
concept of good/goodness 88–90, 180
concept of happiness 99–102, 151–177
concept of human 67, 72, 111
concept of knowing-*how* vs knowing-*that* 141–150
concept of language, emancipatory concepts 123

conceptual leap 125
concept of life 89
concept of love 10, 31, 69–71, 79–81,
    119–120, 143, 157, 170, 203 n.12,
    218 n.51
conceptual mastery 44, 46, 141, 149,
    181
concept of personal growth &
    development 85, 88–89, 106,
    131–133
concept of personhood 79, 92, 110,
    115–117, 137
concept of pleasure, neurobiology of
    pleasure 8, 13, 18, 71, 111,
    120–121, 125–128, 154–158,
    161, 170–171
conceptual problems, confusions 4,
    65
concepts in public policy 179
concept of a legal person/corporation
    93
concept-possession 29, 41, 44, 50, 55,
    84, 90, 121, 139,
concept of success 97–99, 155–158
conceptual tools/toolkit 183, 191
conceptual truisms, truth 77, 85
concept of the 'Self' 77–79, 134–141
concept of the unconscious
    (FREUD, S) 60–61
concept of wisdom 146–149
concept of well-being 102–105
distinctions on grammar 40–45
exclusion of animals to the grasping of
    concepts 214 n.13, 120–121
family resemblance concept 73, 75,
    81
flourishing, as a 'catch-all' concept 1
flourishing as a 'contested' concept 2
grasping a concept, nature of concepts
    44–46
history of the method (conceptual
    analysis) 49, 186
human-ness 71
infinite regress, normative nature,
    logical geography, terrain,
    schema 5, 51, 83
key conceptualizations of flourishing
    6–20
legal concepts 78

logico-grammatical space/interlocking
    language-games/conceptual
    grammar/interconnections/
    conceptual landscape/complicated
    network/relations 29–30 &
    32–31–35, 53, 73, 84, 181, 183
normative concepts 70–71
occasion-sensitivity (TRAVIS) 41, 66
perspicuity 63
philosophical anthropology 47, 49, 186,
    199 n.3, 201 n.18
pluralism, flexibility 52
problematic concepts, research,
    logically prior to empirical
    investigations 51, 62, 65, 125,
    172, 184
rules 36–39
surveyability/*übersicht* 54–55, 84
sense & nonsense, obvious nonsense
    36, 121
therapeutic role of the philosopher
    53–54
temporal concepts 69
'trouser-word' concept (AUSTIN, J.L)
    105–106
community/communities
    animal communities 116–120
    community activists 190
    community flourishing 12, 88, 129
    community/ies of inquiry 60
    community of language speakers,
        linguistic community 36, 52, 75,
        81, 113
    community of thinkers 3, 54
    community norms, rules of a
        community 23, 78–79
    moral community 116, 173, 186–188
    stable community 11
    problem of context 16, 185
    religious communities 78
    social relations/standing 112, 135
consumerism/consumerist 155, 171.
    See also Capitalism
    See also Materialism
COTTINGHAM, J 151, 206 n.2, 216 n.34.
courage
    moral courage 111, 122, 188, 190, 215 n.22
    as a general virtue 148, 161, 172, 174
    See also virtue

CSIKSZENTMIHÁLYI, M 13, 18, 194 n.14.
   See also flow
creativity 112, 182.
   See also agency
   See also imagination
   See also education
CRICK, F 125
   See also reductionism
   See also behaviourism
   See also scientism
culture/enculturation
   animal cultures 116
   ancient Greek culture 95, 204 n.14
   Christian culture 88–92
   communication issues 44, 113, 202 n.4
   cultural differences 113, 214 n.17
   customs 37
   enculturation 198 n.24
   forms of life 80–81, 202 n.4
   human culture/form of life 187
   modern culture 206 n.6, 211 n.25
   notions of value 146
   perfectionist cultures 11
   Polish culture 95, 100
   positive psychology 7
   sub-cultures, other cultures 117–118, 157–158
   Viking culture 91
   Western culture 155, 212 n.28
      See also education

dehumanization/dehumanizing 7, 15, 70, 78, 111, 121, 189–190.
   See also human
democracy/democracies/democratic 2, 186, 188, 190.
   See also politics
   See also citizen
   See also community
   See also duty
   See also West
DESCARTES, R 8, 111, 120, 136, 195 n.21, 206 n.2.
development
   abilities/powers 27, 29, 55, 75, 83, 92, 94, 129, 189
   civilizational development 188–189, 221 n.22

developmental beings/creatures 107, 118, 174
developmental problems 123
growth and education 195 n.17
'Human development Index' 6
human rights 82, 122
theories of human development 62, 67, 69
   of character 84–85, 98–99, 204 n.11
   of corporations 204 n.9
   of ideas, things 90–91
   of linguistic norms 36
   of understanding/know-how/praxis 41, 50, 98, 130, 166, 177, 181
personal growth & spiritual development/person-relative/moral development 112, 119, 131–150, 175, 180, 187, 198 n.19, 200 n.7, 212 n.34
   See also personal growth & development
   See also maturation
dignity human 20, 65, 70, 78, 82, 159, 188, 202 n.8, 207 n.18, 219 n.5.
disquiet/disquietude philosophical 48, 53, 60, 104.
   See also aporia
dogma/dogmatic/dogmatism/dogmatically 2, 24, 52, 56, 62, 85, 119, 120, 142, 175, 186, 189, 198 n.19, 207 n.19, n.20, 209, 216 n.29, 209 n.30, 12 n.28.
   See also scientism
   See also totalitarianism
doubt 2, 45, 167–169, 174.
   See also certainty
   See also knowledge
dualism/dualist 8–9, 49, 194 n.11.
   See also Descartes
   See also metaphysics
duty/duties (moral/ethical) 122, 130, 132, 150, 156, 174, 184, 187–190, 218 n.46, n.49,
   See also responsibility
   See also ethics

ecosystem/ecological/environment/ environmental 11, 44, 90–92, 113, 118, 168, 188, 204 n.9, 208 n.24.
  See also flourishing
  See also ethics
  See also duty
education/educational/educative
  artificial intelligence & education 211 n.23
  education systems 119, 188
  enculturation 198 n.24
  development of abilities 45–46, 130, 135, 148
  higher education 7
  implications for change 187, 189–191
  philosophy of education/educational aims/flourishing as the aim of education/moral education 9, 14–15, 131, 195 n.17, 216 n.29
  positive education 11–14, 179, 184
  well-being as flourishing 51, 125, 182
  wonder as *inquiry* 201 n.15
  See also learning
ego/egoism
  individualistic egoism 131, 136, 148, 156
  ethical egoism 209 n.2
empirical
  categorial ambiguity 57, 62, 220 n.11
  confusion in methods 83, 194 n.9
  contrasted with conceptual analysis 34, 49, 51, 181, 184–186
  contrasted with conceptual truism 99, 122, 159
  education research not generalizable 15–19
  empirical evidence 89
  conceptual analysis of 'use' not to be confused with corpus linguistic surveys 197 n.10
  hybrid models 182, 194 n.9
  infinite regress 5, 51, 184
  knowledge vs understanding 179
  'measuring the unmeasurable' 3, 194 n.9.
  over-inflated importance 7
  reductionism, conceptual leaps 4, 123–128

epistemic/epistemological/ epistemology
  angst 60
  blinkers/blind-spots 140, 170
  epistemic abandon/scepticism 2, 168–169
  epistemic agency 186–187
  epistemic authority 17, 19, 101, 158
  epistemic bias 175–177
  epistemic harms/injustice 189, 203 n.10, 220 n.10, n.18
  epistemic insouciance 174
  epistemic pragmatism 42
  epistemological tyranny 187
  epistemic virtues/confusions 134
  discovery, mining (metaphor) 4, 34, 197 n.10
  dogmatism 198 n.20
  goods 24
  identity 136
  insecurity 141
  private language, privatism/solipsism 38, 132, 136
  reference points 117
  personal/psychological vs philosophical 166
  self-delusion as an 'epistemic benefit' 218
  weaknesses 25
  wisdom, Grimm's epistemic focus 147–149
  See also self-knowledge
  See also ignorance
  See also FRICKER, M.
essences
  essentialism 4, 33, 39, 65, 72, 181
  conceptual truths 22, 27, 32, 65–73, 75, 85
  linguistic 31–36, 45 49, 52, 74
  metaphysics 81, 180, 197 n.11
  of human nature 202 n.8
  of flourishing 92
  of the Self 17
  See also metaphysics
  See also research
ethics 9–12, 95, 111–112, 130, 152, 155–157
  See also responsibility
  See also morals

evil 90, 170, 173, 203 n.4, 205 n.1, 206 n.1, 215 n.23.
experience
  animal experience 120–121
  empiricism 198 n.19
  flow 13
  maturation 60, 85, 103, 106, 113, 119, 141, 143–144, 149, 173, 196 n.25, 199 n.5, 206 n.10, 215 n.22
  mental ill health/madness 98, 209 n.6
  subjective/mental experience 12–13, 17, 58, 79, 96, 116, 139–140, 155, 158, 161, 163, 167–168, 201 n.15, 210 n.16
    See also phenomena
    See also metaphysics
    See also subjectivism
    See also public vs private
exists/existence human/non-existence/whole of existence/existential crisis
  absurdity 152
  agency 162
  animal purpose 168
  eudaimonic 96
  lacking meaning 171–174
  not the same existence/experience 151
  Otherness 176
  primitive language-game 215 n.22
  problematic 159
  reasons for living/purpose in life 160–168
  worthy human experience 114

first-person authority 104, 158, 210 n.9.
  See also happiness
flourish/flourishing
  Aristotelian 9–11
  biological reductionism/positive neuroscience 123–128, 182
  cluster of relations 110
  complexity 63, 83
  competing models, contested concept 2
  conditions for flourishing 175
  conditions for life 89–91
  essentialism 62
  ethical duties of decision-makers 188–189
  humanistic psychology 16–20
  key features philosophical insight 83–84
  knowing-*how* to live the 'Good Life' 146–150
  knowing-*how* to play the language-game of flourishing/knowing 'how to go on' 176–177, 180
  methodological problems 4
  moral dimension/imperative 88, 131, 187
  normative nature 5, 29–34, 183–185
  performative uses 88
  persons vs things 91–93
  philosophical concept 180
  positive psychology 12–16
  problematic concept 51, 55, 60, 181
  object of comparison *eudaimonia* 94–97
  object of comparison happiness 99–102
  object of comparison success 97–99
  object of comparison well-being 102–104
  relation with agency 105–119
  relation to happiness 151–156
  relation to growth 71, 81–82, 85, 131–134, 186, 122–123, 129–130
  relation to humanness, human nature 65, 83
  relation to success 157–158
  role of attitude 159–161
  sketch of uses 87
  species vs persons 93–94
  success of things 88–89
  technicalization 3
  transformative/liberatory power 2, 25, 52, 63–64, 94, 121, 132, 149–150, 175, 189–191, 212 n.35, n.36, 219 n.57, n.58
  ultimate value, the problem of *telos* 165–166
  Utilitarianism/Transhumanism 6–9
  what flourishing is not 105–106
    See also success
    See also happiness
    See also well-being
    See also personal growth and development
    See also agency

flow (states) 13.
    See also CSIKSZENTMIHÁLYI, M.
form/s of life
    human form of life 29, 34, 44, 46–47,
        113, 120–121, 133, 190
    other forms of life/sub-cultures 53, 110,
        117, 129–130, 158, 187–188,
        202 n.4, 208 n.21
    useful distinctions 197 n.12, 199 n.30
FRANKFURT, H 111–113, 206 n.3,
    218 n.50.
FRANKL, V 7, 159–162, 176, 214 n.19.
free will 159, 162, 216 n.25.
    See also *will*
    See also *agency*
FREDRICKSON, B 1, 12–14, 102, 202 n.1.
FREUD, S 60, 200 n.7, 201 n.19
    See also *unconscious*
FRICKER, M 220 n.10, n.18.
    See also *epistemic injustice*

GLOCK, H.J. 34, 40, 50, 116, 197 n.11,
    n.13, 198 n.27, 206 n.13, 210 n.9,
    220 n.14.
goals/goal-setting
    differences in human goals 44
    frustrated goals 161
    goal of understanding 38, 54, 64, 149
    goal of wisdom 147
    instrumental goals 93
    language-games of goal-setting 141
    logical nature of *eudaimonia* vs
        flourishing 71, 97–99, 165–166
        telos
    procedural goals vs agential goals
        109–110, 114, 117, 119–120,
        131, 135–136, 139–140, 143,
        146, 158
    therapeutic goals 151, 154, 157
        satisfaction/success, 200 n.7
    See also *telos*
    See also ARISTOTLE
good/goodness
    assessments of the goodness of life
        168–169
    absurd uses 126
    being a good guide 54
    common good /good society 6, 188,
        215 n.24

distinct *uses* of good 28–30, 32, 59,
    88–97, 183, 213 3, 219 n.8
goods 10
'Good Blob' 153, 174, 176
goodness 13, 25, 32, 88, 90, 109, 129,
    154, 157, 159, 168, 174, 176, 186,
    203 n.1, 205, n.1, 218 n.49
goodness begins with oneself 132
good philosophy 55
good questioning 196 n.2
good reasons 125, 129
good reason for living 160
good thinking 3
'Highest Good', The/*summum* bonum
    9, 155–158, 165
knowing-*how* to live the 'Good Life' 85,
    131–132, 146–150
moral attributes 32
practical wisdom 144–145, 206 n.10
reasons for good reasons 183, 219 n.5
relation to flourishing/moral living/
    social responsibility 107, 109,
    115, 129, 152, 180, 185–186, 190,
    195, 203 n.1, 218 n.47, n.49
traits of a good person 12, 205 n.1
what good is *not* 105
Good Life, The/a 9, 24, 85, 95, 98, 144, 146,
    149, 156.
GRIMM, S.R 24, 134, 146–148, 205 n.1,
    212 n.31, n.32.
    See also wisdom
grip/gripped 55, 60–61, 175, 183.
    See also misleading pictures

habits 39, 63, 100, 121, 142, 176, 186.
HACKER, P.M.S
    aims of conceptual analysis/concept
        possession/dissolution of
        misconceptions 50, 54
    axiological changes 118, 156
    Cartesian dualism 8
    colour concepts 36
    explanations in terms of reasons 16
    focal vs multi-focal concepts 203 n.1
    quality research 2, 51
    human abilities/understanding/
        self-consciousness 75, 128, 140
    interlocking language-games 34
    linguistic vs conceptual mode 59

masters of techniques 4
mental states 147
methods/like a map/web of words 55, 58, 84, 198 n.26, 200 n.1
nature of concepts 30, 45, 49, 201 n.14
nomic vs normative 39, 185, 220 n.12
on flourishing 158
on forms of life 197 n.12, 202 n.4
on happiness 213 n.8, 214 n.13
on know-how 145
on Sisyphus 161
on the cultural relativity of conceptual problems 198 n.21
on the dispute with G. BAKER about 'therapeutic' methods 199 n.2, 200 n.7
on the distinction between knowledge and understanding 180
on the preclusion of animal meaning in life/morals 168, 205 n.1
one vs two-way powers 115–117
particularism 85
'philosophical anthropology' 47, 49
rules 38
the 'Good Life' 152
the 'mereological fallacy' 127
useful distinctions on *meaning* 169–170
See also BAKER, G.
HAND, M 195 n.17.
See also flourishing
happiness
as a by-product of success 214 n.15
contested concept 2
eudaimonia 9–11, 94–97
hedonic happiness, lotus-eaters 51
instrumentalism/Brave New World 194 n.1, 204 n.8
language-game of happiness 25
meaningful happiness 94, 151–177, 181, 213
measurability 33
neuroscience of happiness 125–130
normative nature 5
positive psychology 12–16
reductionism/conflation with flourishing 1, 4, 182, 193 n.1, 204 n.13
relation to well-being 102–104

subjective happiness 153
transcendent happiness 215 n.26
Utilitarianism 6–9
web of relations to flourishing 47, 71, 99–102, 181, 190 n.8
See also well-being
See also success
See also good
health/healthy/healthcare
as a focal concept 203 n.1
axiological conceptions of health 118
biological/physical health 85, 102, 112, 154, 173, 175–176, 194 n.15, 205 n.18
healthcare 101
insight into 144
mental health/mental health continuum/well-being /positive psychology/resilience 6–7, 10, 12–14, 51, 69, 98, 102, 160–161, 182
of plants 90
See also public health.
Homo faber 134, 210 n.8.
Homo loquens 81, 134, 186, 191.
See also human
Homo sapiens 67, 73, 81, 116, 186.
Homo philosophicus 134.
See also perfectionism.
human/humankind/humanity/ humanness/mankind
abilities 10, 28–29, 41, 85, 149, 173–174
dehumanization 78, 189–190
form of life 46–47
human activities/practices 34, 170, 180, 189
human agency 109–130, 188
human behaviour 165, 168, 215 n.25
human consciousness 9
human culture 90
human expression 45
human good 94
human goodness 25
human nature/humanness/beings 8, 23, 49, 59, 62, 65–77, 81–82, 91–94, 140, 162, 167, 181, 183, 186
human soul 159

human species 44
human understanding 3, 37, 39, 54
humanistic ethic 134, 188, 189, 220 n.19
Humanistic psychology 16–20, 77
moral development 132, 151, 177
moral status 207 n.16
pluralistic ways of being 197 n.12
social creature/being 171, 187
Transhumanism 8
    See also civilization
    See also Homo loquens
    See also Homo sapiens
    See also Homo faber
humility 52, 172, 174, 176, 220 n.19
    See also virtue
humour 43–44, 138
    See also jokes
HUPPERT, F. A; 1, 12–13
HURKA, T 134
    See also perfectionism.

ignorance
    human condition 140, 211 n.19
    is bliss 170
    meaninglessness 166
    'predicament of ignorance'/a logical space for hope 25, 174
    self-knowledge for flourishing 149, 175, 177
    'unknown unknowns' 141
    See also vice
    See also knowledge
    See also character
intention
    animal intentions 71, 120
    action/agency 109
    human understanding/mastery of language/rules/points of reference 37, 79, 104, 217 n.44
    private intentions 43
    relation to evil 206 n.1
    relation to success/goals 98, 110
    self-deception 170
    See also agency
individualism 11, 131, 155
    See also egoism
intelligence
    animal agency 111
    artificial intelligence 211 n.23
    complex human intelligence 113
    contrasted with stupidity 76
    emotional 79
    qualitative differences with animal intelligence 208 n.21
    'Intellectualism' 141
    knowing-how/direct exercise 142–145
    See also wisdom.

jokes
    knowing-how 142
    logical jokes 219 n.1
    shared facts of life 196 n.4
    understanding /language-games 29, 33, 37, 43
    See also humour
judgement
    discernment/criteria 37–38, 43, 63, 59, 98, 101, 113, 126, 129, 202 n.6, 212 n.30
    good /practical judgements 59, 134, 144–145, 148, 205 n.22
    judging others 76
    moral/value/normative judgements 89, 90, 122, 196 n.2, 213 n.5
    poor judgement 70, 115
    skill 43, 148–149
justice
    contested concept 2, 47
    social justice 10, 23, 71, 109
    system 78
    See also Common Good, The
    See also agency

KEYES, C.L.M 12–13, 99.
knowing-how
    ability/practical knowledge 85, 141–149, 175, 211 n.23, 212 n.34
    'how to go on' 4, 46, 50, 64, 129, 141, 180
    See also wisdom
    See also flourishing
    See also abilities
    See also concepts
    See also knowledge
    See also aspects
    See also RYLE, G.
    See also WITTGENSTEIN, L.

knowledge
   about others 101
   change in conception vs new knowledge 39
   community of thinkers vs elite knowledge or experts, knowledge vs understanding/normativity of knowledge 3, 50, 52, 132, 142, 179–186, 189, 194 n.9, 195 n.19, 212 n.30, 220 n.18
   deference to future knowledge 128
   epistemic pluralism 186
   evaluating claims about flourishing 181
   fact vs value 28
   'hard-won' knowledge 175, 221 n.22
   scepticism 2
   spooky knowledge 17
   knowing how to live well/the 'Good Life' 146–149
   knowing that vs knowing how 141–146
   language-game 18, 168
   limits of knowledge 52
   nature of knowledge 34
   relation to Self/self-knowledge 77, 131–133, 140–141, 146, 166, 170, 174–176, 209 n.6
   research 19
   scientism 128
   tacit knowledge 90, 206 n.10
   traditional conceptual analysis 49
      See also wisdom
      See also ways of seeing
      See also aspects
      See also certainty
      See also epistemic
      See also research
KORSGAARD, C 95, 183, 220 n.18,
   See also normativity
KRISTJÁNSSON, K 14–15.
   See also flourishing
KRINGELBACH, M 23, 125–128

languishing 13, 98, 103, 105, 113.
   See also suffering
leadership 92, 188, 190.
   See also ethics
   See also duty

learning
   compare with mimicry/understanding rules 37, 75
   human abilities 83
   intellectualized 142
   learning how to flourish 149
   problematic relation to flourishing 195 n.17
   relation to agency 145
   relation to education 15
   relation to rationality 74
   self-knowledge/iterative development 139, 140, 175
   skills/practical wisdom 143–144
      See also mind
      See also education
liberation/liberatory/liberating from philosophical anxieties 25, 48, 52, 54–55, 63–64, 110–111, 121, 149, 150, 153, 180, 212 n.36.
   See also transcendence
   See also redemption
   See also aporia
liberty/libertarian 70, 78, 115, 122, 129, 188–189, 207 n.14, 219 n.5.
   See also BERLIN, I.
   See also agency.
   See also politics.
logic (conceptual) 5, 22, 25, 30, 34–36, 39–45, 50, 52–53, 55–59, 75, 83–85, 89–95, 106, 110, 112–113, 129, 132, 134–135, 141, 153, 158, 162, 168, 174, 181, 183, 185, 189, 197 n.10, n.13, 198 n.24, 201 n.11, 203 n.12, 217 n.39, 219 n.1, 220 n.14.
   See also concepts
   See also jokes
   See also method
love 10, 31, 69–70, 79, 80–81, 119, 120, 138, 143, 157, 169–170, 203 n.12, 218 n.51.

MACINTYRE, A 11, 91–93, 193 n.1, 205 n.22, 213 n.9, 214 n.11, 220 n.19.
madness 132, 209 n.6.
   See also health.

materialism/materialist 7, 128, 155–157, 213 n.6.
   See also egoism
   See also consumerism
   See also capitalism
   See also individualism
mature language users/maturity/ maturation of character 4, 75, 85, 118, 133–134, 141, 146, 146, 208 n.28.
   See also self-knowledge
   See also wisdom
   See also character
MASLOW, A 1, 213 n.2.
MCFEE, G 64, 109, 123, 200 n.7, 209 n.5, 215 n.25.
   See also BAKER, G
meaning, meaningfulness, meaninglessness, meaning of life
   contested concept 2
   meaningfulness of words/terms 2, 4–7, 14, 16, 19, 30–36, 38, 41–45, 49–50, 53, 57, 63, 67, 73–75, 106, 113–114, 132, 143, 147, 183–186, 197 n.10, n.11, 198 n.22, 199 n.5, 200 n.9, 201 n.11, 208 n.22, 213 n.5
   meaningful use of flourishing/growth/ agency/happiness 82, 85, 91, 100, 105–106, 119, 129, 131, 145, 149, 154, 181, 187–188, 190–191, 221 n.19
   meaninglessness 159–162, 171–174, 198 n.19
   meaning of life meaning in life/ meaningful life 1, 11–13, 18, 25, 71, 102, 112, 125–126, 151–152, 158, 160, 174, 176, 181, 163–171, 197 n.12, 215 n.28, 216 n.28, 216 n.23, 217 n.45, 218 n.49
   See also telos
   See also meaning in life
   See also teleology
measurement (of flourishing, normative concepts) 1, 7, 16, 39, 54
   See also method
MEERLOO, J 188.
   See also tyranny

memory 15–16, 24, 136, 138, 206 n.2
   See also learning
mental states 102, 212 n.31.
   metaphysics/metaphysical 4, 8–9, 13, 24, 49–52, 57–60, 70, 72–73, 77, 128–129, 133–139, 169, 201 n.11, 210 n.11, n.15.
   See also essence.
mereological fallacy 127.
   See also HACKER, P.M.S
method
   Aristotelian naturalism 220 n.17
   conceptual analysis 47–64
   conceptual analysis for self-knowledge/ personal liberation 131–132, 150
   conceptual vs empirical investigation 5
   empirical/measurable/scientific 12, 29, 38, 101
   further reading 199 n.1, 208 n.23
   infinite regress 5
   methodological concepts 3
   methodological dispute between G. BAKER and P.M.S HACKER 200 n.7
   philosophical anthropology 47, 49, 109, 186, 199 n.3, 201 n.18
   political nature of language 123
   problems with methods 14–20, 51, 101–104, 127, 179–187, 195 n.25, 220 n.13
   recognising the limits of methods 194 n.8
   reductive methods 4
   techniques 4, 45–46, 132
   See also concepts
   See also understanding
   See also research
MILL, J.S 6, 49.
   See also liberty
mind 3, 8–18, 30, 32–33, 50, 57–64, 70, 75, 77, 81, 96, 99, 103, 120, 124–128, 132, 136–142, 160, 162, 189, 194 n.11, 196 n.7, n.8, 205 n.16, 208 n.21, 210 n.12, n.16, 212 n.30, n.31.
   See also consciousness
   See also abilities
   See also rationality
   See also human

misleading picture/s 63–64, 128, 184, 210 n.13, 212, n.28.
moral/morality
   healthy scepticism towards the moral claims of those in power 188, 202 n.8
   moral agent/agency/choice 109, 112, 121, 134, 141, 162, 186–187, 204 n.11, 205 n.1, 209 n.2, 215 n.25
   moral approach to philosophy/moral insight for flourishing 132, 149–150
   moral categories/system of concepts 24, 116, 131
   moral civilizations 203 n.4
   moral development/duty of understanding 177, 184, 187–188, 198 n.19, 206 n.5
   moral dilemma 69
   moral dimension of corporations 204 n.9
   moral dimension of flourishing 88–92
   moral distress 7
   'moral ecosystem' 208 n.24moral courage 122, 174, 190, 215 n.22
   moral education 14–15, 216 n.29
   moral/ethical imperative/duty 23, 122, 131, 150–151, 171, 173
   moral exemplars 172
   moral expression 129
   morality and meaning 171–177
   moral norms 196 n.3, 213 n.1
   moral orienteering/moral compass 25, 153, 171, 172, 174, 181, 200 n.7
   moral powers/moral being/creature 23, 69, 81, 118, 171, 173, 190
   moral rights and responsibilities/moral community/moral and legal person/moral status 115–116, 119, 122, 205 n.16
   moral rules/norms, 32 moral attributes 29, 220 n.18
   See also good
   See also ethics
Myth of Sisyphus, The 160–161.
   See also CAMUS, A
   See also absurd

NAGEL, T 176, 216 n.33,
Naturalism/naturalist 91, 94, 137, 166, 186, 220 n.17,
   See also McGINN, M.
   See also philosophical anthropology
   See also HACKER, P.M.S.
Nazi/Nazism 78, 122, 159.
Neoliberal/Neoliberalism 6–7, 131, 204 n.8
   See also capitalism
   See also instrumentalism
   See also Utilitarianism
neuroscience/neurobiology/neurology of pleasure/well-being/happiness 14, 23, 111, 123–128, 179, 194 n.11, 220 n.13.
normative/normativity
   agency 117–118
   cultural/social norms 71, 97, 109, 118, 152–153, 183, 196 n.1, n.2, 202 n.8, 208 n.30, 213 n.1, 214 n.18, 215 n.25
   flourishing 5, 29, 71, 184
   human rights 70
   linguistic/conceptual/rule-governed/rules for use 38, 43, 47, 59, 65–66, 71, 95, 126, 151, 156, 158, 174, 179, 186, 197 n.18, 203 n.12, 213 n.1, 220 n.18
   normative concepts 3, 5, 16, 27–46, 79–81, 132, 176, 189, 196 n.19
   normative questions 4
   normativity A – rule-governed - vs normativity B – social norms/axiological 118–122, 147, 181, 183, 187, 189, 193 n.6, 196 n.2, n.3, 207 n.15
   normativity of the 'Self' 202 n.7
   vs empirical/vs 'nomic' 39, 182, 184–185

paradox, paradoxical/paradoxes 38, 157, 210 n.9.
PARFIT, D 137, 139, 210 n.14, n.15.
pathology/pathological 12, 14.
perception 58, 71, 77, 84, 113, 131, 201 n.11, n.12.
   See also aspects

perfectionism 97, 137.
　　See also *Homo philosophicus*
　　See also HURKA, T.
persons 23, 32, 35, 59, 78, 86,88, 91–94,
　　111, 117, 119, 129, 134, 177, 183,
　　186, 203 n.1, 204 n.10, 209 n.2,
　　n.6, 210 n.9, 210 n.14, n.16,
　　212 n.34, 217 n.37, n.40, n.45,
　　219 n.8, 220 n.15–16, n.19.
personal growth/personal development
　　88, 94, 112, 119, 131–150, 181,
　　195 n.17, 198 n.19, 200 n.7,
　　See also maturation
personhood 4, 57, 77–79, 92, 110,
　　115–117, 137.
personal pronoun, The 'I' 135–140.
　　See also *Self*, The
phenomenal/phenomenological 17, 57,
　　136.
　　See also experience
play/playful 16, 28–29,30, 37, 44, 104, 141,
　　176, 180.
　　See also imagination
　　See also powers
　　See also abilities
　　See also pluralism
pleasure/pleasurable 6, 8, 13, 25, 71, 111,
　　120–128, 153–158, 161, 170,
　　214 n.14.
　　See also happiness
philosophical anthropology (method)
　　47, 49, 109, 186, 199 n.3,
　　201 n.18.
　　See also HACKER, P.M.S.
　　See also method
　　See also research
pluralism/pluralistic/plurality 16, 28, 40,
　　44, 52, 123, 141, 163, 166–167,
　　175, 189, 197 n.12.
policy/policy-makers/policy
　　　framework
　　education policy 15
　　instrumentalism 194 n.10
　　policy framework/agenda 7
　　policymakers 93, 184, 188, 190
　　policy structures 15
　　public policy 6, 8, 106, 179, 182,
　　　186–187, 193 n.4
　　well-being policy 9

politics 10–11, 70, 78, 114, 118, 123, 130,
　　145, 189–190, 220 n.16,
positive education 6, 12–16, 179.
　　See also education
　　See also research
positive psychology 7–20, 51, 102, 131,
　　179, 184, 213 n.4.
　　See also psychology
　　See also research
powers (human)
　　agential/two-way powers 83, 103,
　　　114–117, 121, 129–130, 140, 183,
　　　206 n.9
　　analytic powers 145–146
　　complex linguistic powers 118, 121
　　failure to use innate powers
　　　205 n.23
　　general capabilities 71, 77, 85, 94, 110,
　　　122–123, 174
　　imaginative powers 120
　　intelligent powers 142
　　moral and rational 11, 69, 81, 85,
　　　91–92, 112, 173, 190
　　of expression 45
prospering/prosperity 97–99, 158, 190.
　　See also success
psychology
　　humanistic psychology 16–20
　　positive psychology 1, 7, 9–16, 20,
　　　33–34, 51, 102, 131, 179, 184,
　　　213 n.4
　　problems with the general enterprise
　　　125, 128–129, 182, 220 n.13
public health (incl. ethics) 78, 178–179,
　　195 n.15, 215 n.24.
　　See also health.
public vs private language 18, 38–39, 43,
　　136, 195 n.19, n.22.
PUTNAM, H 29, 185, 208 n.30, 209 n.30.

READ, R 123, 193 n.7, 212 n.36.
redemption 160–161 via absurdity.
　　See also Camus, A.
　　See also transcendence.
reductionism
　　biological 111, 127, 139
　　linguistic 4 9, 14, 65, 106, 181
　　metaphysical 122–123
　　psychological 136, 139

relativism/relativist 34, 38.
research
  conceptual confusions, esp. in empirical research 1–5, 19–20, 27, 29, 51–52, 55, 57, 63, 106, 154, 179, 181–182, 184–185, 194 n.9
  dehumanizing research 190
  developments in positive psychology 14
  moral education/positive education 14–15
  originality 180
  problems and prospects with qualitative methods/self-report 18–19, 104
  problems with 'hybrid' or 'interdisciplinary' research and philosophy 194 n.9, 208 n.29
  research design 51, 57, 184, 186–187, 189, 196 n.25
  See also method
  scientism 125, 128
resilience/resilient 1, 7, 13–14, 51, 99, 101, 131, 159, 160–161.
  See also suffering
responsibility 14, 15, 92, 116, 132, 173–176, 190, 204 n.7, n.9, 206 n.1.
  See also duty
ROGERS, C 1, 17, 195 n.19.
  See also psychology
RYLE, G 5, 113, 114, 142, 144–150.

SANDIS, C 16, 45, 95, 101, 123, 183, 197 n.12, 199 n.30, 208 n.29, 214, n.17, 215, n.25, 220 n.15.
scientism 4, 65, 109, 155, 181, 207 n.19, 210 n.13, 211 n.25.
  See also dogma
scepticism/skepticism 2, 24, 38, 153, 168, 189.
  See also knowledge
  See also epistemology
SCHINKEL, H 167, 201 n.15, 217 n.36.
  See also wonder
  See also metaphysics
SEN, A 109, 122–123.

Self-concept/concept of Self 8, 17–18, 24, 77–79, 133–141, 195 n.20,
  See also self-knowledge
  See also personal identity
  See also delusions
self-deception 135, 157–158, 174, 180.
self-knowledge 131, 133–134, 140–143, 146, 149–150, 166, 170, 175, 186, 195 n.19, 209 n.6, 212, 29.
  See also personal growth and development
SHOEMAKER, S 137, 139, 210 n.14.
skill 44–45, 79, 81, 85, 95, 113–114, 117, 134, 142, 145–149, 157, 176, 188, 211 n.24, 212 n.34.
  See also abilities
social creature/being 81, 150, 161, 187, 218 n.47.
  See also human
solipsism 132 209 n.6, 210 n.12.
  See also private vs public
subjectivism 4, 18, 65, 106, 181, 217 n.45.
  See also research
success 62, 83, 85, 88–91, 94, 97–99, 101, 105, 106, 148, 151, 155–158, 173, 182, 214 n.13, n.14, n.15.
  See also prospering
  See also flourishing
STRAWSON, P 58, 139, 198 n.28, 200 n.10.
suffering 5, 7, 29, 100, 105–106, 159, 161, 170–171, 206 n.2, 213 n.7, 214 n.19, 215 n.23,
  See also languishing
suicide 95, 98, 160, 164, 167.
  See also suffering
summum bonum 156–158, 165, 177, 213 n.9,
  See also good

TATARKIEWICZ, W 155–157, 213 n.8, 214 n.14.
teaching 15, 50, 54, 142, 144–145.
  See also education
  See also learning
***telos*/teleology/teleological** 97–98, 109, 113–114, 120, 135, 156, 165–166, 216 n.35.
  See also causes
  See also goals

totalitarianism 78, 119, 189.
See also ARENDT, H.
transcendence/transcend/transcendent
10, 148, 153, 161–162, 170–171,
212 n.32, 215 n.22, 215 n.26,
217 n.40.
See also redemption
See also liberation
**transformation/transformative/
transformational (power of
flourishing)** 2, 8, 25, 64, 103,
132, 149–150, 172, 189–190,
210 n.17, 216 n.29.
**transhuman/transhumanism/
transhumanist** 8, 51, 71, 179.
TRAVIS, C 28, 41–43, 64, 85, 198 n.28,
220 n.15,
tyranny/tyrant 187–188, 202 n.8.
See also totalitarianism

übersichten (German concept) 58, 132.
ubuntu (African concept) 220 n.19.
understanding
addressing social problems 187
being human 47, 65–82, 119
concepts/language-games/rules/
contexts 27, 35–46, 181–182,
186–187, 189, 195 n.22,
210 n.13
human flourishing 83–107, 180–181,
184, 191
interpersonal understanding/cultural
context/form of life 32, 199 n.30,
214 n.17
methods 49–64
on certainty 206 n.10
self-knowledge 132, 136, 146, 170, 175,
195 n.19, 198 n.19
the power of religion or literature
216 n.29
vs knowledge in research 2–4, 7, 19,
128–130, 142, 179–180, 184
what it means to live the 'Good Life'
131
See also know-how
See also concepts
See also knowledge
Utilitarianism 5–9, 15, 51.
See also BENTHAM, J.

vice/s 70, 119, 129, 162, 170, 174–175,
207 n.19, 216 n.29.
See also virtue
See also character
virtue/virtue/virtuous 1, 9–12, 52, 70, 76,
95–96, 100, 102, 119, 129, 134,
145, 148, 162, 172–174, 182, 190,
203 n.2, 211 n.26, 212 n.34,
215 n.22, 218 n.51.
See also vice
See also character

WATTS, A 201 n.13.
way/s of seeing 14, 39, 44, 56, 59–64, 85, 122,
153, 160, 166, 162, 167, 175, 185,
189, 198 n.20, 200 n.11, 210 n.7.
See also aspects
well-being
Aristotelianism/Eudaimonianism
9–12, 94–97, 106
biological reductionism 123–130
financial well-being 92
Humanistic psychology/well-being
18
measurability 194 n.9
policy/instrumentalism 193 n.4, n.10,
204 n.9
well-being and wisdom 146–150
well-being of corporations 93
well-being/subjective well-being 1, 4–6,
12–16, 29–33, 47, 51 81, 85, 99,
102–104, 154, 158–159, 182, 188
welfare economics (SEN, A) 109, 122,
and NEILL & NEVIN (2021)
202 n.8
Utilitarianism 6–9
West the/Western 6, 11, 78, 82, 89, 100,
122, 155, 186–188, 212 n.28,
221 n.22.
WIGGINS, D 137–139, 210 n.14, 217 n.46,
will (human) 53, 70, 115, 153, 159–162,
170, 175, 191, 215 n.25.
See also agency
WINCH, C 145, 188
WINCH, P 57–58
wisdom/practical wisdom/*phronesis* 24,
96, 99, 112, 131, 144, 146–149,
186, 205 n.1, 211 n.26, n.27,
212 n.34.

WITTGENSTEIN, L
    context and occasion 41–45
    description 52
    grammar 40–41
    hinge propositions 168
    knowledge as a social practice 142, 144, 149–150
    language-games 32–35
    meaning 49–50
    meaning and use 30–31
    on religious belief 166
    on will and motivation to see clearly 175
    rules 36–39
    self-development 132
    styles of thinking 163
    technicalization/measurability of concepts 3, 51
    therapeutic philosophy 53–55, 57, 63
    wonder 57, 58, 69–70, 157, 161, 167, 201 n.15
        See also aporia

www.ingramcontent.com/pod-product-compliance
Lightning Source LLC
Chambersburg PA
CBHW071814300426
44116CB00009B/1304